NEW YORK to HOLLYWOOD

New York to Hollywood

THE PHOTOGRAPHY OF KARL STRUSS

Barbara McCandless

Bonnie Yochelson

Richard Koszarski

Introduction by William I. Homer

Afterword by John and Susan Edwards Harvith

Amon Carter Museum   Fort Worth, Texas

University of New Mexico Press   Albuquerque, New Mexico

Printed in Canada

Library of Congress Cataloging-in-Publication Data

McCandless, Barbara, 1949–
      New York to Hollywood: the photography of Karl Struss / Barbara
   McCandless, Bonnie Yochelson, Richard Koszarski; introduction by
   William I. Homer; afterword by John and Susan Edwards Harvith.
         p.   cm.
      Includes index.
      Filmography: p.
      ISBN 0-8263-1637-9. – ISBN 0-8263-1638-7 (pbk.)
      1. Photography, Artistic. 2. Struss, Karl, 1886–1981
   3. Cinematographers--United States--Biography.   I. Yochelson,
   Bonnie. II. Koszarski, Richard. III. Title.
   TR653.M39 1995
   778.5'3'092--dc20
      [B]   95-4977
                                                   CIP

Frontispiece:

Edward Weston, *Karl Struss*, c. 1922-23, toned platinum print,
Amon Carter Museum

CONTENTS

FOREWORD AND ACKNOWLEDGMENTS

In 1983, the Amon Carter Museum acquired the photographic estate of Karl Struss (1886-1981), one of the key artists who championed the pictorial style in New York City before World War I. The collection of over five thousand original negatives, more than two hundred vintage exhibition prints, fifty-five Lumière autochrome plates, and approximately two thousand vintage film stills from motion pictures of the 1920s is the most complete single resource for Struss' work. As such, it not only offers insights into his career but also has broadened our understanding of this period in photographic history. Furthermore, since Struss eventually had a more extended career in film, this collection also demonstrates how early pictorial photography eventually influenced the developing cinematic aesthetic.

Although Struss was an important contributor to the pictorialist movement in photography, his work was largely forgotten after photographic fashion changed to "straight" photography. His rediscovery began late in his lifetime, when John and Susan Edwards Harvith began their groundbreaking work on Struss' photography in the mid-1970s. Working side by side with the artist himself, the Harviths produced *Man with a Camera* (1976), a catalogue and retrospective touring exhibition of Struss' early photographic work. Their efforts helped bring Struss' work to the attention of scholars and attracted more admirers. The Harviths have most generously shared information for both the book and the exhibition, drawing on their extensive personal knowledge of Struss and their interviews with him in the 1970s, as well as their own collection of his photographs and papers. Their Afterword to this volume recounts some of their experiences with the elderly but still energetic Struss.

The Museum is also indebted to Stephen White, who served as Struss' agent from 1976 to 1981 and continued to represent his heirs until 1991, helping to distribute his work to interested museums and collectors. White not only assisted the Museum in acquiring the collection of prints and negatives from the Struss Estate, but also allowed the Museum library to copy all papers and catalogues in his possession and the interviews he had conducted with the Strusses in 1976. These materials were invaluable as research on the Struss collection progressed.

Struss' grandchildren, particularly Craig Struss Rhea and Richard Rhea, have provided the Museum with biographical information and graciously offered their collections for our research. Craig Rhea looked through unsorted material in his house, which had been Karl Struss' home for most of his life, and discovered previously unknown letters between Struss and his family during World War I. This fortuitous discovery has unraveled the true story concerning Struss' decision to leave a promising career in New York and begin a new career in Hollywood after the war.

As plans for this exhibition and publication were being developed, other scholars were invited to add their evaluation of Struss' two careers. Bonnie Yochelson's extensive knowledge of the imagery of New York City and her understanding of Clarence White's influence as a teacher and photographer have provided much greater appreciation for Struss' New York photographs and his importance to pictorial photography. Richard Koszarski's expertise in early film production provided the perfect background to analyze Struss' career in cinematography. We are also grateful to William Innes Homer, the H. Rodney Sharp Professor of Art History, University of Delaware, who read the essays and contributed the introduction, and to independent film scholar Kristin Thompson, Madison, Wisconsin, and Sarah Greenough, Curator of Photographs, National Gallery of Art, who served as readers.

Numerous institutions and private collectors have generously agreed to lend their photographs to the exhibition that accompanies this volume. Our sincere gratitude is extended to the Warren and Margot Coville Photograph Collection, Bloomfield Hills, Michigan; the J. Paul Getty Museum; the Photographic Collection at Hallmark Cards, Inc., Kansas City; John and Susan Edwards Harvith, Syracuse; the Herbert F. Johnson Museum of Art, Cornell University; the Los Angeles County Museum of Art; the Metropolitan Museum of Art, New York; the Museum of Fine Arts, Boston; the New Orleans Museum of Art; Princeton Art Museum; Craig Struss Rhea, West Hollywood; and Marjorie and Leonard Vernon, Los Angeles.

Other individuals and institutions who assisted our staff and authors during research on Struss are the Margaret Herrick Library, Academy of Motion Picture Arts and Sciences; Albright-Knox Art Gallery, Buffalo; Baltimore Museum of Art; Beinecke Library Rare Books and Manuscript Collection, Yale University; Bowdoin College Museum of Art; Harold B. Lee Library, Brigham Young University; California Museum of Photography; Canadien Centre for Architecture; Center for Creative Photography, Tucson; Colorado Historical Society; Cranbrook Academy of Art Museum, Bloomfield Hills, Michigan; The Detroit Institute of Arts; International Museum of Photography, George Eastman House, Rochester; The Minneapolis Institute of Arts; The Museum of Fine Arts, Houston; the Museum of Modern Art, New York; Lawrence Miller Gallery, New York; National Archives, Washington, D.C.; The Oakland Museum; Philadephia Museum of Art; Saint Louis Museum of Art; The Toledo Museum of Art; Oral History Program, UCLA Library; The University of Michigan Museum of Art; Harry Ransom Humanities Research Center, The University of Texas at Austin; American Heritage Center, University of Wyoming; Visual Studies Workshop, Rochester; Joy Weber, Santa Fe; Maynard P. White Jr., Queenstown, Maryland; Pam Wilson, Madison, Wisconsin; and Yale University Art Gallery. Special appreciation is also extended to our colleagues at the University of New Mexico Press for their participation in this publication.

Many Amon Carter Museum staff members have supported this project from its inception. I particularly wish to acknowledge Barbara McCandless, Assistant Curator of Photographs, who has overseen every phase of the exhibition and publication with impeccable care and enthusiasm. She drew upon the expertise and assistance of photography curators Thomas Southall and John Rohrbach, archivist Paula Stewart, secretary Carol Griffin, and former collection assistant Helen Plummer. Former curator Martha Sandweiss was instrumental in securing the collection for the Museum in 1983, and Carol Roark provided important organizational groundwork. Finally, as with all the Museum's publications, other staff have contributed their talents during the preparation of this catalogue, including Jane Myers, Rick Stewart, and former curator Doreen Bolger, who served as readers; librarians Milan Hughston and Sherman Clarke; photographers Rynda Lemke, Steven Watson, and Dorothy Tuma; and editors Nancy Stevens and Jane Posey.

The National Endowment for the Arts, a federal agency, and the Texas Commission on the Arts, a state agency, have provided critical funding for this project. With their support this publication and accompanying exhibition and education programs can be enjoyed by the Museum's many local, regional, and national audiences.

Jan Keene Muhlert
Director, Amon Carter Museum

COLOR

In 1917, when he published an article on color photography in the journal *American Photography*, Karl Struss wrote: "Newness of vision is very rare and one looks to new workers not only for inspiration but for new methods of expression." Color photography, which had only been practical for ten years (with the introduction of the Lumière brothers' autochrome process), offered photographers the challenge to reevaluate and revise their artistic vision. Struss was always attracted to new methodologies, and he quickly became an advocate for the potential of color photography.

In the fall of 1907, when autochrome plates became available in New York City for the first time, stores were unable to keep up with the demand. Struss was then a young amateur photographer who had yet to discover the artistic potential of photography and was still a year away from his first class with Clarence White. But like all photographers, amateur and professional alike, who were excited about the possibility of color, Struss purchased some plates and began to experiment with the process, making straightforward self-portraits, portraits of his family and friends, and studies of flowers. By 1910, after learning the principles of pictorial composition, he was producing some of the most advanced images made with this early color technology. His mastery of the process allowed him to capitalize on its slow speed, producing a blurred flash of brilliant color and creating a stunning dance of movement and design in *Boardwalk, Long Island*. On the other hand, in the bright sunlight of Bermuda, he was able to freeze a moment of action in *Tennis Match, Hamilton, Bermuda*, stopping the flight of a ball.

Because autochromes were transparent glass plates, they were difficult to display publicly, and Struss apparently never exhibited any of his. However, he became convinced of the commercial potential of using color work in illustrations and sold several of his autochromes to magazines and newspapers. As early as 1913 his images were published in four-color reproductions on the cover of the *Saturday Magazine* of the *New York Evening Post*. A variant of *Ethel Prague with Umbrella* (opposite) became a color cover for *The Independent*.

By the time he published the article in *American Photography* in 1917, Struss had realized that the autochrome was impractical because of its long exposure time and the inability to print it on paper for multiple reproductions. In the article, he described and championed the experimental Hess-Ives paper process, which produced a color print from three color separation negatives. He even included an example of the process in a portfolio titled *The Female Figure*, and although Hess-Ives prints proved unstable, their delicate tones and accurate colors are evident in the four-color reproduction on p. 8.

Struss' experimentation with color photography illustrates the freshness of his vision. It is also a fitting introduction to his imagery, symbolic of his love for photographic technology, which also led him to manufacture soft-focus pictorial lenses, master alternative printing processes like gum and platinum printing, and create his own method of multiple platinum printing to perfect the pictorial aesthetic. This same technological impulse would lead him to apply the pictorial aesthetic to motion photography, to master the complexities of making color motion pictures, and eventually to pioneer in 3-D motion photography. As he wrote in 1917, "I have always been interested in the technical as well as the pictorial side of photography (the two are really inseparable)."

Ethel Prague with Umbrella,
Long Island, New York,
c. 1910, Lumière autochrome,
Amon Carter Museum

Tennis Match, Hamilton,
Bermuda, c. 1913,
Lumière autochrome,
Amon Carter Museum

Boardwalk, Long Island,
New York, c. 1910,
Lumière autochrome,
Amon Carter Museum

Autumn, Long Island,
New York, c. 1910,
Lumière autochrome,
Amon Carter Museum

Ward House, Living Room,
Queens, Long Island,
New York, c. 1910,
Lumière autochrome,
Amon Carter Museum

*Dancers, Queens, Long
Island, New York*, c. 1913-14,
Lumière autochrome,
Amon Carter Museum

Steel Workers, New York,
1916, Lumière autochrome,
Collection of John and
Susan Edwards Harvith

TOP
*Adolph Bolm, Ballets Russes
Dancer, in Sadko*, 1916,
Lumière autochrome,
Amon Carter Museum

BOTTOM
Nude Draped in Gauze, 1917,
four-color reproduction from
Hess-Ives color print,
Amon Carter Museum

UNHERALDED GENIUS: KARL STRUSS, PHOTOGRAPHER

William Innes Homer

Karl Struss is one of the treasures of American photography. Known and respected as a pioneering Hollywood cinematographer, he was also a still photographer of the first rank. But in this latter capacity he has remained little known to the public at large, and the influence of his earlier work in still photography on his later cinematographic career has not been fully addressed by film historians. Although he was "discovered" by John and Susan Harvith in 1974 and through them became the subject of a 1976-77 traveling exhibition and an informative catalogue, he has not received sustained and focused attention since then.

The reasons for the neglect of Struss' photography are hard to fathom. He possessed enormous talent and enjoyed a great deal of attention and respect in the heyday of pictorialism. The period of his finest photographic achievement—1909-17—was relatively brief, however, and he turned principally to cinematography after a stint in the army during World War I. Although he did not give up still photography entirely while making motion pictures, that earlier phase of his photographic legacy became secondary to his reputation for the Hollywood films he made. Once he turned to cinematography, Struss did not promote his pictorial photography until the Harviths began to work with him in preparation for the traveling exhibition. At that point, they encouraged him to rediscover his own photographic past, and he consciously celebrated it, especially during public events linked with the exhibition. The Harviths were very much a part of this project and deserve a great deal of credit for the Struss revival. Their personal reminiscences of their work with Struss, in the Afterword, make fascinating reading.

At the same time, a Los Angeles photography dealer, Stephen White, began to promote and market Struss' work, and the photographer's prints thus became available to collectors, museums, and other dealers. Prominent auction houses, too, began to sell his photographs, though in relatively small numbers. In the meantime, the Amon Carter Museum acquired the Struss estate; a year later, the Getty Museum purchased the collection of the eminent photography collector and dealer Daniel Wolf, including a substantial collection of Struss photographs.

Karl Struss' youthful experiments with the camera, described in detail by Barbara McCandless, prepared him to join the circle of the distinguished photographer Alfred Stieglitz, who championed the efforts of the best American pictorial photographers and who, in 1905, opened a gallery for the Photo-Secession at 291 Fifth Avenue, New York. Struss, in turn, often visited the gallery, absorbing the new photographic language of pictorialism, both European and American. In 1908, Struss decided to ally himself with this movement by enrolling in Clarence White's evening classes at Columbia University. As Bonnie Yochelson points out in her essay, White heavily influenced Struss, especially in the art of space filling, and soon the two became close friends. Struss was to take over White's studio in 1914 and also taught at Columbia at the recommendation of the older photographer.

As Yochelson observes, White was not the only photographer who influenced Struss' work. Stieglitz and Alvin Langdon Coburn provided models for his photographic interpretation of New York City. Stieglitz, in turn, valued Struss' exceptional skill in platinum printing and, because he so respected the younger man's images, brought him into the Photo-Secession, showing his photographs in the important 1910 Albright Art Gallery exhibition in Buffalo and publishing a selection of his prints in *Camera Work*.

Although Struss was highly sensitive to abstract design (as Yochelson points out, he may have anticipated Paul Strand in this regard), he also had a conservative side and did not embrace all of the tenets of modernism. Some of his prints, perhaps under the influence of Coburn's painterly photographic style, have a soft-focus "pictorial" look. This latter trait endeared him to a group of older photographers, including some former members of the Photo-Secession, who initiated a break from Stieglitz. In 1916, in association with White, Coburn, and Gertrude Käsebier, Struss formed the Pictorial Photographers of America to give much wider exposure to the traditional veins of pictorial photography. Stieglitz, now much enamored of the "straight" approach to the medium and deeply involved with the promotion of ultramodern art, seemed to have no time for his former colleagues.

Struss' photographic career was interrupted by a term in the United States Army. The chapter by McCandless tells in fascinatingly fresh detail how the United States government doubted Struss' patriotism, in the wake of the anti-German fervor of World War I, and how he concealed this embarrassing episode in his young life. In any case, upon his release, rather than returning to New York and the disagreement between the more traditional pictorial photographers and those changing to a modernist style, he immediately made his way to Hollywood to be a cameraman, an ambition he must have quietly nurtured in the service. As Richard Koszarski observes in his comprehensive account, Struss felt that his skill in the photographic art of space filling could be profitably employed in motion pictures. Thanks to Cecil B. De Mille, he was hired by the Famous Players-Lasky Studios.

For the next two decades and more, Struss sought to place his art at the service of cinematography. He was one of the few who brought a profound awareness of still photography's artistic potential to the film industry. Thus, as Koszarski points out, he was able to move away from both factual, high-key camera imagery and exaggerated, Rembrandt-like lighting toward a new realm: the expression of dramatic content through subtle effects of lighting, tone, and spatial composition. Struss believed in—and wrote about—a new kind of picture play, one in which the (silent) film's ideas would be conveyed visually, rather than merely depending upon titles.

Thanks to his profound understanding of pictorial tone and composition, he became one of the few truly artistic cinematographers in the motion picture industry's formative years. Rebelling against old-school "crank turners" who "know nothing of photography," Struss substituted a finely developed aesthetic sensibility, honed during his New York years, which he skillfully adapted to the medium of the film. His innovative way of visualizing things photographically, with rich tonal gradations and pictorial effects, brought him respect and acclaim from his professional colleagues—including the first Oscar ever awarded for cinematography—and the public at large.

All things considered, Struss must be recognized as one of the finest pictorial photographers of the early twentieth century. He often equalled White in his feeling for spatial composition and Coburn in sensitively capturing the mood of the city. Struss' sense of design often paralleled that of Stieglitz, though the younger man tended toward less brittle and planar imagery. When he was exercising his abstract sensibilities to the fullest, Struss anticipated Paul Strand's most radical photographic designs.

The essays in this book reveal much about Struss that is worth knowing. Each author has made a distinctive contribution: McCandless in shaping Struss' biography during his New York years and his transition to Hollywood; Yochelson in critically appraising his city photographs; Koszarski in providing the most complete account to date of Struss' cinematic accomplish-

ments. Finally, the Harviths provide a rich and touching account of their contacts with Struss in his last years. The picture is fuller and more detailed than any before and pays well-deserved homage to one of the most talented Americans working in the medium of photography. Whether making still images or a motion picture film, Struss was always an artist.

Figure 1. Clarence White, *Portrait of Karl Struss*, N.Y., 1912, platinum print, Amon Carter Museum

A COMMITMENT TO BEAUTY

Barbara McCandless

Karl Struss had not one but two careers with a camera. From 1907 to 1917, he was a rising star in New York's photography circles, producing work that was innovative and unique and earning the approval of such photography greats as Alfred Stieglitz and Clarence White. He dropped from view, however, while serving in the army during World War I, and following his discharge from the service in early 1919, he headed west, to Hollywood, to establish himself all over again as one of the most innovative cinematographers of his day. Instead of becoming one of the century's best-known photographers, however, the effect of these dual careers has been to somewhat obscure Struss' accomplishments. Photohistorians have recognized his role in the world of photography but have been unfamiliar with—even unaware of—his work in cinematography. Likewise, film historians, while applauding his innovative film work during the 1920s, have not paid any attention to his career in still photography prior to World War I. Considered as a whole, however, Struss' half-century of work with a camera, from his youthful days photographing New York to his filming of television series when he was in his early seventies, reveals a surprisingly unified set of aesthetic principles—a commitment to beauty.

When questioned about his reasons for leaving New York and switching careers, Struss always attributed his decision to both his desire to live in a warmer climate and his belief that he could do better work than the cinematographers who were then making movies. While these were no doubt factors in his decision to move across the country and change occupations, the real story is much more complex, illustrating the tenuous nature of building a successful career as an artist. While developing his artistic voice, he had to deal with many distractions, including conflicts between various artistic factions and personalities, unsuccessful commercial ventures, and a political atmosphere that hampered his professional activities. Although some of his choices got him into trouble, Struss' perseverance eventually triumphed. Through all of his struggle to find a niche for his artistic talents, he remained committed to the idea of pictorial beauty. Applying much of what he had learned about artistic photography to cinematography, he helped to instill a needed sense of beauty into a young industry just discovering its own far-reaching power.

THE EXAMPLE
OF HIS FATHER

His family's German immigrant background had a strong influence on Struss' life, and the example set by his grandfather, father, and siblings inspired the artist to strive for success and believe in his own natural talents. His grandfather, Henry Struss, had come from a modest rural background in Swearingen, Germany, a small village south of Hannover. Emigrating to the United States in 1851, probably to escape the serious economic problems that plagued Germany, he soon prospered with a retail grocery business in lower Manhattan. He died while serving in the Civil War, leaving two children, both American-born: Karl's father Henry Jr. and his aunt Wilhelmina. As these first-generation Americans assimilated into the middle-class lifestyle of New York City, they left behind most of their German roots but maintained a strong pride in their heritage.[1]

Henry Jr. became a strong role model for his children. He attended city public schools only until the age of twelve but later completed studies at the Packard Business College in New York. He also found early success in his chosen field of clothing manufacturing, becoming a junior partner in a dress trimming manufacturing firm, then building two silk mills in New York

Figure 2. Henry Struss designed the family residence at 126 73rd St. in New York; it was completed in 1886, shortly before Karl's birth. Modern print from original acetate negative, Struss Family Collection

and New Jersey. By the age of twenty-two, his business had prospered sufficiently for him to travel to Germany, where he met and proposed to Marie Fischer, of Cologne. She emigrated to the United States the following year to marry him, and they raised six children—three daughters and three sons. All but Karl, the youngest, were born in the house where their father had been born, adjacent to the grocery store their grandfather had managed. Eventually Henry moved the family uptown, to a house that he designed and built himself on the Upper West Side (fig. 2). Karl was born there on November 30, 1886, and throughout his life he felt a distinction in stating that he had been born in the house his father designed and built.[2]

recover his financial stability, and in 1896, he bought back his personally designed house near the Riding Club's stables.[4]

Henry Struss was also an accomplished mechanical engineer, and when automobiles were introduced to the United States in the 1890s, he wasted no time experimenting with the new technology. He built and patented the first gasoline-powered automobile in New York City, completing all of the machine work himself at the Dakota Stables near their home and finishing the car in 1896.[5] He also helped edit the first automobile magazine, *Horseless Age*.[6]

Karl Struss, who had seen his father lose his business but build it back through hard work and dedication, greatly admired his parent for being a self-made man. The fact that the elder Struss was a multi-talented writer, artist, architect, mechanical engineer, and expert rider also may have intimidated his son. As the youngest of the family, Karl was spoiled by his mother and three older sisters, none of whom married, but his father, who expected a lot from all of his children, was strict with him, and their relationship was strained.

Having recovered its financial stability, the Struss family began a tradition of renting a summer cottage away from the city, frequently on the south shore of Long Island. In 1898, Karl, his mother, and his sister Elsa spent a month with his aunt Wilhelmina. Her husband, Charles Willis Ward, ran a one-hundred-acre nursery in Queens and was the oldest son of David Ward, whom Karl called the "lumber king of Michigan." Karl spent much time with the Wards during his childhood and through them learned some of privileged society's ways of leisure. While at his aunt's, Karl enjoyed hurdling, pole-vaulting, and sailing and many of the popular new pastimes of the leisure class, including pool, tennis, and golf. An intense need for physical recreation would stay with him his entire life.

Figure 3. Karl Struss, *Henry and Marie Fischer Struss*, c. 1910, modern print from original glass plate negative, Amon Carter Museum

Although Marie Struss was German-born, her husband and their children were thoroughly assimilated into American middle-class culture.[3] An expert horse-rider, Henry Struss served as president of the New York Riding Club, which quartered at the Eighth Avenue stables down the block from their house. Endowed with literary and artistic talents, he also wrote a book on ring riding and added some of his own watercolors for cover illustrations. Unfortunately, his success was not immune to economic cycles, and during an economic depression in 1892, when Karl was six years old, Henry Struss' silk mill business went bankrupt. Forced to sell the house he had built, he moved his family farther north, to a more rural area of New York. Far from being crushed by the experience, however, he worked hard to

Figure 4. Karl (on the right) greatly admired his brother
Will (on the left); on family vacations at Arverne,
Long Island, they spent a lot of time together. Modern
print from original glass plate negative, c. 1903,
Amon Carter Museum

During these summers, Karl also first
developed an interest in photography. In 1896,
for their summer vacation in Babylon, Long
Island, his thirteen-year old brother William purchased a Pony Premo camera, easily portable and
designed for "Wheelmen and Tourists."[7] Karl,
who idolized Will and "was interested in anything he was doing,"[8] watched while Will took
photographs with his new camera. In the fall,
after they returned to the city, the boys developed
the negatives together in a darkroom illuminated
by a candlelamp covered with red glass. Karl
didn't take any photographs of his own that year

and only helped with the processing, but Will
eventually let him use his camera during another
summer vacation five years later.

Growing up in an atmosphere of physical
activity, intellectual and creative stimulation, and
mechanical ingenuity, Karl developed a passion
for variety and excitement in his own life. However, his strained relationship with his father
would frustrate his desires for stimulation during
much of his young adulthood. As the youngest
of the Struss children, he saw all of his siblings
develop their own talents: his brother Harry went
into an electrical business, two sisters became
schoolteachers, and another attended the New
York Architecture League. His brother Will (fig.
4) was the star of the family; good-looking, popular, and bright, he was president of his high
school class for four years. Henry Struss was still
struggling with his business and could not afford
college tuition, but Will received a scholarship to
study mechanical engineering at Columbia
University.[9] Karl may have been intimidated by
the talents of his father and his older brothers
and sisters, and he may have had some difficulty
finding his own strengths.

Although Karl was a robust youth who enjoyed a variety of physical exercise, he also had frequent bouts with colds and flus. In 1903, during
his third year at DeWitt Clinton High School,
Karl got pneumonia and was out of school for
two months. A family photograph made at this
time illustrates a very sickly looking Karl sur-
rounded by the rest of his very healthy family
(fig. 5). This juvenile sickliness may have been
more than his father could stand; Henry Struss
removed his son from school and sent him out of
the city to stay with the Wards on Long Island.
By the time Karl recovered, it was May, near the
end of the school year, and for some reason—
perhaps a lack of faith or patience in his youngest
son, or disappointment in Karl for becoming ill
and not having better physical health, or simply a

Figure 5. The entire Struss family posed for this group portrait around the time that Karl (first row on the right) was recuperating from pneumonia, c. 1903. Modern print from original glass plate negative, Amon Carter Museum

work, and Karl hated it. He knew he would never be happy or successful in the manufacturing business, but he remained with his father's company for eleven years, all the while yearning for something more stimulating.

THE CAMERA AS SALVATION

In 1906, three years after Karl started at Seybel & Struss, he found the stimulation he needed following a family tragedy. Will Struss died suddenly of spinal meningitis, at the age of twenty-two. The shock of his death devastated the entire family but especially Karl, who worshipped his brother and believed that Will was the true technical and creative genius of the family. The following summer, when the family vacationed in New Hampshire, Karl got his first camera, perhaps his brother's Pony Premo. Photography reminded Karl of his brother, and he may have wanted to hold onto those memories or carry on something his brother had started. Oddly, Will's death may have liberated him enough to discover his own aesthetic talents and interests, and he began to photograph in earnest.

desire to have one of his children to follow him into his business without spending more time on education—Henry Struss removed Karl from school permanently after that illness.

In an act that hurt Karl deeply and caused him lifelong bitterness, his father put the young man to work at the Seybel & Struss bonnet wire factory, not in the office, but as a laborer operating the machines that covered wire with colored threads of various fabrics. Such work required both hands and feet, and machine operators remained on their feet the entire day. Karl worked from seven in the morning until five-thirty, five days a week and a half-day Saturday mornings, and earned from four to fifteen dollars a week. Although he did what he could to improve the efficiency of the machines and invented a spring to take up the slack in thread, it was still tedious

One day in New Hampshire, riding in the back of a buckboard wagon as they returned to their cottage, Karl photographed a seemingly banal country landscape that somehow caught his imagination (see figs. 12 and 13). "I just happened to turn around and there was a vision and I reached down and got the camera and turned

Figure 6. Karl Struss, *Self-portrait*, c. 1907, modern print from original glass plate negative, Amon Carter Museum

Figure 7. Karl Struss, *Self-portrait in Michigan Campsite*, *1908*, modern print from original glass plate negative, Amon Carter Museum

around and snapped."[10] This experience helped him realize that photography could reveal the latent beauty in the ordinary world. When he returned to New York, he began tentatively to photograph around the city and at the Ward house in Queens.

The following summer, Karl's Uncle Charlie asked him to come to Michigan to photograph forest fires threatening David Ward's lumber business. Someone supplied him with an 8x10 camera, hoping that he would be able to operate it. The family camp, on a lake, consisted of one large building and a boathouse. The primitive conditions challenged Karl to use his wits. He developed the plates at night in the boathouse, laboring until the early hours of the morning and using a safelight made from a pocket flashlight covered with dull green paper.

Contending with cold weather and no running water, he raised the developer to the proper temperature by resting a large washbasin of it in another basin of hot water obtained from the camp cook.

When Karl returned to New York at the end of the summer, he started to read about photography. Only then did he realize that it could be more than just a hobby. He discovered that the Photo-Secession, an organization devoted to the promotion of photography as a fine art, was centered in New York and that photographs by its members were exhibited regularly at the 291 Gallery on Fifth Avenue. The Photo-Secession, formed in 1902 by Alfred Stieglitz and other leading photographers, had become the primary American proponent of the photographic style known as pictorialism. These photographers argued against the habits of the snapshooting amateur and instead believed that photography could be as valuable a medium of artistic expression as the other fine arts.

Struss also discovered that Clarence White, a founding member of the Photo-Secession and one of the most prominent pictorial photographers, recently had begun to teach a photography course at Teachers College, Columbia University, very close to the Struss home. Extension courses were offered in the evening to accommodate people like Struss, who wanted to study after a full day's work. Classes met two evenings a week, for two hours each, in the studios and labs of the college's School of Industrial Arts, then reconvened on Saturday afternoons for practice in the field.[11] Offered through the Teachers College art department—whose chairman, Arthur Wesley Dow, was a progressive art teacher and early champion of photography—White's classes were a mixture of art and technique that perfectly suited Struss' personality. In addition to providing basic instruction in the use of the camera and in methods of developing, printing, and presenting the final print, White emphasized the application of art principles to photography. Students also could take courses in art history and design taught by the painter Max Weber.[12]

Struss enrolled in White's class in 1908 and studied with him in the evenings for the next four years. The classes were informal and involved training the eye by looking at art in museums and galleries and making photographic excursions into the field. On Saturday afternoons, the class frequently took photography walks along Riverside Drive, on the edge of the Hudson River. Only about twelve students were in these classes, and although men dominated the commercial photography field and jumped into it with a minimum of training, more of White's students were women. White himself hypothesized that women might be more willing to take the time

for training their eyes, because they possibly were greater idealists than men.[13]

Struss was charming and handsome and easily developed strong friendships with women. On his Saturday photographic excursions, he was frequently in the company of Amy Whittemore, Eleanor Pitman Smith, or Francesca Bostwick, all students in White's class. These don't appear to have been romantic relationships; Bostwick and Smith were both married, and Whittemore was eleven years his senior. They were, however, good friends and respected colleagues who shared the same passion for photography. He was very fond of these women and frequently gave them gifts of his photographs. He also included them in his photographs, using them as models to experiment with artistic techniques of portraiture, and collaborated with them on special projects (figs. 8 and 9).[14]

In February 1909, in the middle of his first year studying with Clarence White, Struss went to see the International Exhibition of Pictorial Photography at the National Arts Club. The hanging committee, chaired by Alfred Stieglitz and including White and other members of the Photo-Secession, selected works by pictorial photographers in the Photo-Secession, the British pictorial association the Linked Ring, and the German association Kleebatt.[15] This may have been the first major photographic exhibition that Struss saw, and he would not have taken its examples lightly. It also had a separate section on "natural color photography," featuring the new technology of autochromes by several photographers, amateurs as well as professionals. As early as 1907, when autochrome plates were first available in New York, Struss had made some family portraits and self-portraits using the technique, but now he also saw its aesthetic possibilities.

During his long workdays at his father's factory, Struss' mind was on photography. Whenever he got the chance, he made studies of other

Figure 8. Karl Struss, *The Camera Class, Tarrytown, N.Y., 1911* [Amy Whittemore and Eleanor Pittman], modern print from original glass plate negative, Amon Carter Museum

Figure 9. Karl Struss, *Kodak Advertising Contest, 1916* [Amy Whittemore photographing interior of Pennsylvania Station], modern print from original glass plate negative, Amon Carter Museum

workers (fig. 10) or photographed scenes from the factory window (see figs. 52 and 53). In the evenings and on weekends, he traveled throughout New York City, taking photographs that reflected its excitement, as Bonnie Yochelson discusses thoroughly in her essay, "Karl Struss' New York." He also photographed at home, using family members to experiment with portrait techniques, and during the summers at the resort areas where his family vacationed (fig. 11).

In keeping with Clarence White's admonitions to simplify compositions and fill the space of the picture frame, Struss used lenses twice the length of a normal camera lens—basically telephoto lenses. The normal lens for his four-by-five-inch camera had a six-inch focal length and gave a wider-angle view than he wanted, so Struss instead used a twelve-inch focal length lens. Likewise, he used a seven-inch lens on the smaller camera. In addition to allowing him to crop his images in the camera and concentrate on the tight compositions that he favored, these longer lenses tended to flatten the depth of field. He also experimented with a special camera lens of his own design, which he adapted from a projection lens and attached to the cameras with a brass mount. This crudely fashioned lens, which had only a single element and was therefore "uncorrected," produced an effect similar to that of a pinhole camera—all planes of the image, from foreground to far distance, were in focus simultaneously, but without being sharp. The resulting images thus combined an overall softness with tight compositions, leading the viewer to concentrate on the composition rather than detail. This lens was the first of many technological innovations Struss would make in the field of photography. He eventually applied for a patent and successfully marketed it to pictorial photographers as the Struss Pictorial Lens.

Struss experimented minimally with his homemade lens during his first year of study with

White, but he had his first chance to use it extensively when he took a ten-week trip to Europe with two of his sisters, Hilda and Lilian, in the summer of 1909.[16] He was then twenty-three years old, the same age his father had been when he met Marie Fischer in Germany. His father may have hoped that Karl would find a good German wife, as he had, and settle down into his job rather than fooling around with photography. Karl, however, saw the trip as a perfect opportunity to apply what he had learned from White's class and to assemble a large body of photographs. He took two Century view cameras to Europe: a 4x5-inch camera for making straight platinum prints and another that made 3 ¼ x 4 ¼-inch negatives, which he planned to enlarge and print at four times their original size. To ensure a wide range of exposures to work with, he also took along ninety Eastman orthochromatic film packs, with twelve negatives per pack.

The Strusses arrived in southern Italy, then traveled up the coast to Milan, turned north to Lake Como, crossed the Alps, and took a train to Lucerne. They concluded their trip in Germany, stopping in Dresden and Berlin, then visiting with their mother's relatives in Cologne for a week. In all, Karl produced about a thousand exposures, which he developed, four packs a night, after returning home from the trip. It took him about a month to complete the processing, then he enlarged some negatives of his favorite images and experimented with them.[17] Following the example of other pictorial photographers like Edward Steichen, Gertrude Käsebier, and F. Holland Day, who used alternative printing processes to achieve different pictorial effects, Struss made straight platinum prints, gum prints which incorporated pigments and brush strokes into the image, and also combined the two processes, layering the pigment-carrying gum solution onto a paper previously coated with platinum.

Figure 10. Karl Struss, *Tony in Factory*, 1911, platinum print, Amon Carter Museum

One of his negatives was a very simple composition of a cloud in front of a mountaintop, taken while they were crossing Simplon Pass in the Alps. The negative, made at sunset under low light, had received insufficient exposure and thus was very contrasty, with good blacks but little detail in the highlights or the shadows. Instead of discarding this negative as a failure, Struss decided to experiment. When he printed the enlarged negative, he coated the paper with the platinum solution and, not knowing what to expect as a result, turned the paper over and coated the other side as well. After exposing one side

Figure 11. Karl Struss, *Boardwalk, Long Island*, 1910, platinum print, Amon Carter Museum

ever, hand-stippling the gum solution onto paper resulted in a non-photographic effect that looks surreal, almost nightmarish.

Struss' trip to Europe had been such a successful photographic excursion that he continued to photograph extensively during his summer vacations, primarily in Arverne, the community on the south shore of Long Island where his family rented a summer house. During the summers of 1910 and 1911, he vacationed with his sister Hilda and some of her friends in Chester, Nova Scotia, a small tourist and artists' community.[18] On the way to Nova Scotia in 1910, they stopped off in Maine to visit Clarence White's first session of the Seguinland School of Photography, and there Struss met several students who later would develop into good friends.

REPUTATION AND DISCORD

From 1908, when he first began to study photography, through mid-1914, Struss continued to work all day at the Seybel & Struss factory, then to photograph and print in the evenings and on weekends. Although he had originally considered photography a hobby, he now worked steadily to develop the skills necessary to photograph professionally. Success as a pictorial photographer depended not only on talent but also on the ability to exhibit and publish one's work. Struss' first chance came in 1910, with an important but troubled exhibition that was the first of many factionalized photographic activities.

Organized by Alfred Stieglitz, the International Exhibition of Pictorial Photography at the Albright Art Gallery in Buffalo, New York, was the last exhibition of the Photo-Secession. Other photographers considered the Photo-Secession's artistic beliefs to be controversial, and under Stieglitz's direction, the organization and its activities antagonized critics and photog-

of the print, he turned the paper over and exposed the other side, carefully keeping the image in register. He then continued this process for a total of thirteen separate times. The result was a rich print with intense blacks (see p. 70). Struss realized he had developed a new procedure for multiple platinum printing and experimented enthusiastically with it throughout the next year. Suddenly entranced with the magic and artistic control offered by the printing stage, he went back to some of his old negatives to make new prints. He even took the negative he had shot from the back of the wagon in New Hampshire in 1907 and made many variations in different processes (figs. 12 and 13). A straight platinum print produced an image that was very soft in focus but was still easy to comprehend. How-

raphers alike. For the Albright exhibition, Stieglitz invited foreign photographers and some Photo-Secessionists to exhibit in an Invitational Section and planned an Open Section for all other photographers, whose submissions would be judged by Stieglitz, photographer and critic Charles Caffin, the painter Max Weber, and Clarence White. Stieglitz' control deeply offended a very active photographic organization who perceived the Open Section as merely a conciliatory gesture to allay criticism, and all of their members except Augustus Thibaudeau boycotted the exhibition.[19]

Although Struss previously may have exhibited a few of his images in the Teachers College student gallery, he had never been included in a major exhibition like this. The prospect of submitting some of his prints may have been daunting, but he probably was encouraged by the fact that Clarence White and Max Weber were among the judges, and they may have urged their

most promising students to submit work. Since White's studio was right across the street from Stieglitz's 291 Gallery, White may even have taken Struss over to show Stieglitz some of the young man's multiple platinum prints. Struss remembered Stieglitz's reaction: surprised at the richness of the prints, he wet his finger to touch a print, then shook his head, saying he had never seen such blacks.[20] In selecting works for the exhibition, the judges were so impressed by Struss' multiple platinum and gum prints that they chose twelve of his photographs, including both European and New York views. Only one other photographer in the Open Section, William Mullins of Franklin, Pennsylvania, had as many photographs, and many better-known photographers, including members of the Photo-Secession, had fewer works accepted.

Struss must have been immensely flattered by such measures of esteem, especially for a newcomer. He took the train to Buffalo to visit the

Figure 12. Karl Struss, *New Hampshire Landscape, 1907*, platinum print, 1909-10, Amon Carter Museum

Figure 13. Karl Struss, *New Hampshire Landscape, 1907*, hand-stippled gum print, 1910, Amon Carter Museum

Figure 14. Karl Struss, *Albright Art Gallery, Buffalo, New York*
[gallery interior showing "International Exhibition of Pictorial
Photography"], 1910, platinum print, Amon Carter Museum

and Mullins." Thibaudeau would later prove to be one of Karl Struss' best supporters, admirably coming to his defense when others abandoned him, again taking an unpopular cause.[22]

Reviewers generally praised the exhibition and agreed that it was a historically significant event in proving photography's aesthetic value. The exhibition also made Struss' reputation, as critics mentioned and reproduced his work among the day's leading photographers. Record crowds attended the show, and many prints were sold, including thirteen to the Albright Art Gallery to begin a permanent collection of photography. Although the Albright did not purchase any of Struss' work, two of his photographs did find buyers—no doubt the first prints he had sold.[23]

A few months after the Albright exhibition closed, Struss found his second opportunity to exhibit. In April 1911, the Newark Art Museum organized an exhibition that in many ways followed the Albright Art Gallery's example. The Newark photographer Edward R. Dickson worked with the Museum to organize the exhibition, titled "What the Camera Does in the Hands of the Artist," and Max Weber, who had hung the Albright exhibition, also laid out this one. Since the Albright exhibition had already brought recognition to several photographic students from the area, Dickson, working with Clarence White, invited some of the latter's students from both Columbia University and the Brooklyn Institute

Albright gallery and stayed for two days, photographing the building's exterior and the gallery installation while there (fig. 14). He did not meet any of the Buffalo photographers,[21] but his prints in the show made such an impression on one photographer that they became lasting friends. Augustus Thibaudeau, the only member of the Photo-Pictorialists of Buffalo who submitted photographs to the Open Section, had written Stieglitz about the Buffalo group's animosity but had given Stieglitz his own complete support. A lawyer by profession, Thibaudeau may have been accustomed to taking unpopular causes, and he did not back down in the face of opposition from his Photo-Pictorialist colleagues. After the exhibition opened, he wrote Stieglitz: "I had my first opportunity to study the work in the open section. It is strong. I am proud of being in the company of Haviland, Genthe, Struss, Anderson,

of Arts and Letters to exhibit along with leading photographers. Not only Struss, but his good friends Amy Whittemore, Francesca Bostwick (both of whom had been included in the Albright exhibition), and Eleanor Pitman Smith were among White's students whose work was included.

By the end of 1911, Struss' status as a photographer had vastly changed. In November the Dean of the Teachers College asked him to teach the photographic course the following summer, while White was away teaching in Maine. The Teachers College also gave Struss his first solo exhibition of forty views of New York, in which he included a wide variety of street, park, and harbor views and many night and twilight scenes. Although many of these were picturesque, even symbolist, views of the river and bridges, Struss also included some of his more daring compositions, including perspectives from above and below, such as his *110th St. El Station* (see fig. 49) and *Queensboro Bridge* (also called *Blackwell's Island Bridge*, see fig. 51). Alvin Langdon Coburn, whom he had probably met through White's class, corresponded with him from the West Coast, expressing regret at missing Struss' exhibition of New York views and describing his excitement over photographing the Grand Canyon and other areas of the West. (Struss would remember this seven years later when he made a special sidetrip to photograph the Grand Canyon on his way to California.)

For Christmas, Struss celebrated his "graduation" by giving photographs to family members and associates. He gave individual prints to Coburn and to Gertrude Käsebier, whom he also had probably met through Clarence White's class, perhaps in Maine the previous summer, and who continued to be a valued friend and colleague. He also gave individual and personal images to family and friends—images made in Europe to his two sisters who had accompanied

him, images of himself and his mother to her, and ones of his friends Amy Whittemore and Eleanor Pitman Smith to each of them. For his best friends, he assembled presentation albums, selecting photographs that he felt would appeal to them: views taken in Nova Scotia for a young woman he had met while there; views from Europe, New York, and Maine (made while visiting Clarence White's Seguinland school) in one for White; and views of New York and Metuchen (where he had photographed with Amy Whittemore) in her album. He also kept several albums for himself, including one that documented the Albright Art Gallery exterior and exhibition installation.[24]

While many photographers, including Clarence White and Max Weber, broke off relations with Stieglitz following the Albright exhibition (see Bonnie Yochelson's essay for a complete discussion), Struss maintained ties with Stieglitz and appreciated his approval. The ultimate accolade from Stieglitz came in 1912, when he invited Struss to join the Photo-Secession—to become the final member, as it turned out—and included a selection of Struss' images in the April issue of *Camera Work*. Later that year, White, Struss, and Coburn arranged for an exhibition at New York City's Montross Gallery, with themselves as the selection committee. They claimed to be motivated by the "public desire to see the progress of photography in America, as a medium of personal expression," but their move also acknowledged that Stieglitz, who was becoming increasingly interested in promoting modern art and had stopped showing photographs at 291, would no longer satisfy either the public's wish to see photography or the photographers' need to exhibit their work. Although they hoped to fill Stieglitz's place in arranging photography exhibitions, they did not want to alienate him. In inviting him to participate, the selection committee may have been thankful that Struss was still on good terms with Stieglitz. When Stieglitz declined to Struss, the younger artist attempted, unsuccessfully, to get him to reconsider: "I would regret very much not being able to show any of your prints, for, in an exhibition of this character, there is no reason for the sake of good photography why you should not be represented, especially when one considers what you have done for photography."[25]

After such an impressive start to his exhibition career, Struss in 1913 focused his efforts on getting his photographs published. One had been printed in a 1911 Teachers College course schedule, and in May 1912, in the first issue of *Art and Industry in Education*, the annual publication of the Arts and Crafts Club of the Teachers College, a Struss photograph was in a portfolio of student work that accompanied White's essay on "The Educational Value of Photography as an Art." In 1913, Struss experimented with his own writing, publishing a brief essay on "The Field of Modern Photography" in *Art and Industry in Education*. In the essay, he extolled the virtues of photography in modern society, saying that "an understanding of the fundamentals of photography is an essential requirement toward successfully solving the problems which are continually before us." He even foreshadowed the direction of his own career with an assertion that the fundamentals of photography also included "the use and application of color motion photography"—several years before he began working in that field himself.[26] Struss' main emphasis in the essay was the educational benefit of photography. Asserting that fields such as manufacturing, astronomy, and medicine could be taught much more efficiently with the aid of photography, he concluded with a discussion of photography in the fine arts, explaining that the camera, as a medium of aesthetic expression, was a tool to be mastered, just like a chisel or brush.

The Edison Monthly

Figure 15. *The Edison Monthly* [The New York/Edison Company], June 1913, Amon Carter Museum

Although all of these early instances of seeing his photographs published related to White's classes and to the educational value of photography, Struss intended to follow White's encouragement to use photography in illustrations and for other commercial uses in order to make a living from it. In the summer of 1913, Struss also had some of his photographs published independently of any connection to Clarence White. *Edison Monthly*, the trade journal for the New

photographer who had organized the Newark Art Museum exhibition in 1911 and who served as editor—Clarence White, Alvin Langdon Coburn, Karl Struss, and Paul Anderson.[28] Promising "to place before readers examples of photography as a medium of expression, and to publish as well, the written, personal word on subjects possessing contemporary interest in varied fields," the editors hoped to attract readers who felt abandoned or slighted by the new editorial focus of *Camera Work*, which concentrated more on modernist painting and sculpture and less on "camera" art.

The first issue of *Platinum Print*, in October 1913, was fairly mundane, with technical articles by Coburn on the photogravure, Struss on multiple platinum printing, and Anderson on the photographic representation of motion. The second issue, in December 1913, included a pull-out photogravure insert of Struss' photograph of Columbia University at night (fig. 16)—a clear homage to White and a recognition that photography students would respond to the image. Subscribers were even invited to send for a copy of the photogravure, without the printed caption and "suitably mounted and ready for framing," for twenty-five cents each.

Struss was still working six days a week in the Seybel & Struss factory, but his increased involvement in the photographic world must have made him consider various ways to change careers. In March the leader of an expedition to the arctic contacted him about their search for a photographer to accompany them for two years.[29] Considering Struss' previous bouts with influenza and his love of summer sports, the prospect of being in an arctic climate for so long must not have been too enticing, despite the offer of a full-time photographic assignment. Moreover, his increased involvement with the publishing ventures and exhibitions of New York's photography circle made it much too exciting to leave the city at that time.

Figure 16. Karl Struss, *Earl Hall, Columbia University, Night*, 1910, gum-platinum print, Amon Carter Museum

York Edison Company, published a portfolio of his night views around the Brooklyn Bridge (figs. 15 and 32). He also sold some of his autochromes to the *Saturday Magazine* of New York's *Evening Post* newspaper, which published them as color cover images.[27]

His principal publishing effort in 1913 was to initiate a new photographic magazine, *Platinum Print*, which was subtitled "A Journal of Personal Expression." The key players in this publishing venture were Edward Dickson—the

In November 1913 he took a vacation to Bermuda, a much preferable climate to the arctic. A previous vacation in Bermuda had impressed him with both the climate and the island's colors; he reported to Alfred Stieglitz in June 1912 that it was "probably the most beautiful, charming and quaint place I have ever visited, and as for color—there is nothing like it anywhere in Europe. I hope to go again someday and will not forget to take along a few autochromes."[30] Stieglitz, who had heard about Bermuda from other people as well, in his response to Struss agreed that the color must be wonderful for autochromes[31]—the latest development in the long search for viable color photography. In the earliest days of the medium, photographers had applied paint on top of black and white images, and later they experimented with three-color printing processes. With the development of the autochrome plate—a glass plate manufactured with minute dyed starch particles that filtered the various colors in the light spectrum—color photography finally became simple and practical for all photographers. Since the finished work was a glass transparency, applications were unfortunately limited, but many pictorial photographers like Struss, who closely followed each new technological achievement, enthusiastically adopted it and tested its appropriateness for various subjects and applications. As soon as the Lumière brothers had demonstrated the process in the summer of 1907, Edward Steichen had purchased plates for himself and for Alfred Stieglitz. Within a month, these two, Frank Eugene, and Heinrich Kuehn were enthusiastically experimenting with it. Stieglitz presented several exhibitions of autochromes at his New York Little Galleries, beginning in 1907, and Steichen wrote an article on the new color photography for the April 1908 *Camera Work*.

Struss himself followed his earliest color experiments in family portraits with interior views, landscapes, and street scenes in the city (see pp. 1 and 3-5).[32] As he had planned, he took autochrome plates to Bermuda in 1913 and made many color views of the landscape, architecture, and people. Although he had visited Europe, from southern Italy to Germany, and Nova Scotia, it was in Bermuda that he first discovered the excitement and emotional quality that the vivid colors of an exotic landscape and people could bring. The brilliant tropical flowers, vivid blues of the ocean, and colorfully painted houses provided wonderful opportunities to experiment with color composition.

He had returned to New York by January 19, 1914, when the second major exhibition organized by Clarence White opened. The International Exhibition of Pictorial Photography at the Ehrich Galleries in New York included prints by European photographers Frederick Evans, J. Craig Annan, and Robert DeMachy; works by such leading American photographers as Käsebier, White, Coburn, and Struss; and examples by other White-influenced photographers like Paul Anderson and Amy Whittemore. The third issue of *Platinum Print*, published that March, stated that Struss would take over the associate editorship of the magazine, and the next issue, published in May, listed him as associate editor. However, it is doubtful that he contributed much, for he had returned to Bermuda for four months, as an official photographer for the Bermuda government—apparently a good enough offer to tempt him away from his photographic colleagues in New York.

Immediately after returning from his trip to Bermuda the previous fall, Struss had contacted Richard Butler Slawzer, who did Bermuda's tourism advertising. Slawzer already knew of Struss, having seen his print *Hamilton, Bermuda, Moonlight* (see p. 73) exhibited at the Montross Gallery in 1912. Slawzer wrote: "Is it not you who are the author of the moonlight scene exhib-

Figure 17. Karl Struss, *Bermuda, Nature's Fairyland*, 1914 [layout advertising tourist guidebook], modern print from original nitrate negative, Amon Carter Museum

Figure 18. Karl Struss, *Street—St. George, Bermuda*, 1912, platinum print, Collection of the Grandchildren of Karl Struss

ited not long ago at a West Side Photo Exhibition? Have been longing to meet some one who could catch the real spirit of Bermuda."[33] Struss was hired by the Bermuda Trade Development Board to make photographs for *Bermuda: Nature's Fairyland*, the official tourists' guidebook for 1915-16.

On this trip, he experimented with a multiple tourist camera, which used motion picture film—35mm film in fifty-foot rolls. Fully loaded, the camera took 750 still exposures without reloading, and Struss would have found it much more convenient than his view cameras for this commercial assignment. However, while enthusiastically experimenting with the increased ease of this camera, he used up the entire fifty-foot roll in the first week. It would take a week or more to have more film shipped to him from New York, so Struss decided to see if any might

be available locally. Discovering that a motion picture company was filming on the island, he went to the south shore hotel that served as the company's headquarters to meet with Charles Rosher, the film's cameraman. Rosher, who had been a portrait photographer in London before arriving in the U.S. in 1908, had been working in the motion picture industry in Hollywood only since 1911. After talking with Rosher, Struss procured some "short ends"—pieces of motion picture film that had been left over from shooting—and returned to his commercial assignment documenting the island.[34]

The guidebook (fig. 17) included a variety of images showing tourist activities, boating, swimming, fishing, and playing tennis. The images also showcase the village houses and streets (fig. 18) and illustrate many of the ships that carried tourists to the island. The editors of the book were wise to also include several of Struss' pictorial views that captured the flavor of the peaceful beauty that awaited tourists—harbor scenes framed by foliage or night views with the lights of Hamilton reflected in the harbor waters.

1914-17 - THE STRUSS STUDIO AND THE EUROPEAN WAR

The trip to Bermuda proved a turning point in Karl Struss' life, marking the beginning of his career as a professional photographer. At the age of twenty-seven, after eleven years with Seybel & Struss, Karl was finally able to resign from his job at his father's factory, and in the process release himself from his father's authority. Throughout the previous six years, his photography had increasingly come under Clarence White's influence, and in June 1914, Struss published an announcement that he was taking over White's studio after the elder photographer moved to another site. But larger events in the world were destined to affect his photographic activities. In August 1914, World War I began in Europe, and the ensuing changes in international politics and economics brought new opportunities for business and photographic assignments—and an unexpected set of problems for Struss.

As he settled into White's old studio in the summer of 1914, Struss was able to offer a variety of services that would increase his chance of success in a full-time photographic business. He advertised his ability to produce portraits made in the studio or in the home, to photograph interiors and exteriors of residences, and to make photographs for advertisements and illustrations. Because of his background in manufacturing and his penchant for technology, he also offered a manufacturing component: the pictorial lens he had constructed for his own work. This lens had received much attention and interest, and he had already made a few for friends. In early 1914 he

hired a legal firm to conduct a patent search for similar innovations to lens design, but began manufacturing the lenses even without a patent. (The application procedure proved so complicated that in 1916, he dropped his attempt to patent his invention.[35]) He also formed a partnership with fellow photographer Paul Anderson to manufacture a photographic developer. For years, Struss and many of his colleagues had favored a German developer called Rodinal, which was excellent for producing a soft negative with a broad tonal range and which came in a concentrated solution that only had to be diluted with water, making it very convenient. Once the World War started, Rodinal was no longer available. Anderson, a technical expert on photographic processes, reconstructed the chemical formula, and he and Struss marketed the new product, Kalogen, from Struss' studio.[36]

The advent of the war also influenced another of Struss' commercial ventures. After his assignment with the Bermuda Trade Development Board, his next big commercial job was to produce architectural photographs (both exteriors and interiors) for the Mergenthaler Linotype Company of New York. In 1884, Ottmar Mergenthaler, a German-born inventor who had emigrated to the United States, invented the Linotype machine, which subsequently revolutionized typesetting. Struss photographed the sites that held Mergenthaler Linotype machines in New York (fig. 19), Pittsburgh, Boston, and Washington, D.C., and his completed photographs were exhibited at the United Typothetae Convention, held at the Waldorf-Astoria in October 1914. They were also reproduced in a brochure for the Mergenthaler Company, which proclaimed, "In war as in peace, the hand that keeps the world informed."[37]

News about the war began to have a negative effect on German-Americans. Once the German transatlantic cable was cut, soon after

Figure 19. Karl Struss, *New York*, c. 1912-13 [featured
in Mergenthaler Linotype Company brochure with
caption "Bright, Sleepless Newspaper Row — Where
day and night, the world's adventure is cast into type for
New York by two hundred Linotypes"], modern print
from original glass plate negative, Amon Carter Museum

the declaration of war, all subsequent news reports displayed a pro-Allies bias, and reports of
German atrocities and arrogance began to foster
new stereotypes about the German people. A
New York Times editorial on June 1, 1915, clearly
demonstrated the changed attitude towards Germans and the common failure to distinguish the
German government from the German people.
It described how in the past forty years the German people had been "transformed from a
nation worthy of the world's esteem and admira-

tion into a people who stand apart from other
nations, distrusted and feared, disturbers of the
peace, a menace to the general security, and now
pursuing their ends by the hideous atrocities per-
petrated in Belgium and France, by deeds of
monstrous inhumanity . . . Their ideals have
been abased and their intellectual development
stifled, they have been bred away from the high
and noble things of life."[38]

Anti-German feelings soon extended to
German-Americans, the largest immigrant ethnic
group in the United States. Although German-
Americans were not the only ones who questioned the American government's pro-Allies
leanings, other Americans frequently interpreted
such disagreements as betraying divided loyalties
and cowardice. When German-Americans suggested that the United States government remain
truly neutral by imposing an embargo against
arms trading with either side, or questioned the
need for a draft and for German-Americans possibly to serve abroad, they frequently came under
suspicion for holding pro-German sympathies
that conflicted with American interests. This was
especially true after Germany sank the American
ship *Lusitania*; while many German-Americans
deplored the action, some felt that Germany was
justified.[39]

As these points of contention escalated,
newly formed patriotic organizations, such as
the American Defense Society and the National
Security League, attacked German-American
institutions as subversive. The American Protective League, formed in March 1917, took an
even more radical approach. A semi-official aux-
iliary of the Bureau of Investigation, with over
300,000 volunteer detectives eager to serve the
country, the League conducted surveillance and
investigations not only of enemy aliens but also
of American citizens who had dissenting views on
the war. Founded on fears of German conspira-
cies, the organization considered all German-

Americans suspect, alleging that the German government "counted upon two million German-Americans to help her win this war; that she knew every nook and cranny of the United States and had them mapped; that for years she had maintained a tremendous organization of spies who had learned every vulnerable point of the American defenses, who were better acquainted with our Army than we ourselves were."[40]

Several of Struss' associates were connected in some capacity with these anti-German organizations. Alice Muller Choate, a socialite whom Struss had befriended and photographed when she was a student of Clarence White's, was married to the nephew of Joseph H. Choate, whom *Vanity Fair* described as the most popular public figure in New York. Choate supported American entry into the war and was honorary president of both the National Defense Society and the American Security League. Melvin Palmer, a photographer who briefly shared Struss' studio from late 1914 through the spring of 1915, was also a staunch supporter of the Allies.

Struss was a natural target for the prevailing anti-German sentiment. Although he and his family considered themselves patriotic Americans, both his mother and his father's parents had come from Germany and his family still had relatives in that country. Some of the first photographs to bring Struss to the public's attention, both at the Albright Art Gallery exhibition in 1910 and in the 1912 *Camera Work*, were ones he had taken on his trip to Germany in 1909. Like many German-Americans at the beginning of the war, Struss, who was proud of his own and his family's accomplishments and successes, may have felt a need to defend the social status of German-Americans by defending Germany herself. Additionally, the fact that he had just opened his own studio may have encouraged him to be more assertive with his opinions. At a dinner in 1914 attended by several of his pho-

tographic associates, Struss apparently took Germany's side in an argument, asserting Germany's right to defend herself and saying that Belgium was "getting what she deserved." Several guests who were decidedly pro-Allies became concerned that since Struss appeared to be pro-German, he might also be anti-American.[41]

In addition, many of Struss' early commissions, like the one for the Mergenthaler Linotype Company, brought him into contact with Germans and German-Americans. Whether he was given these commissions, or perhaps even sought them out, because of their common German heritage is unknown, but these associations could have led to discussions about the war in the presence of Melvin Palmer and any of the studio assistants that Struss hired. Palmer apparently left the studio in 1915 because of disagreements with Struss concerning the war. Although he had no way of knowing it at the time, such seemingly minor events would have major repercussions for Struss as anti-German feelings grew to near-hysteria later in the war.

The war also impinged on one of the studio's main sources of business, making photographic illustrations for magazines such as *Vogue*, *Harper's Bazaar*, and *Vanity Fair*. Struss' working relationship with *Vanity Fair* may eventually have been affected by the magazine's editorial slant, which became distinctly pro-Allies by 1917. In addition to frequent articles about the war, criticizing Germany and "slackers" (those who resisted military service), the magazine also printed ads enlisting members for the National Defense Society and the American Security League. Another client affected by international events was the Metropolitan Opera, which in 1917 removed all German operas from the program and also canceled the contracts of five German artists, including Melanie Kurt and Johannes Sembach, whom Struss had photographed for the Opera Company in 1916.[42]

Despite the war, and his own need to secure commercial assignments for his studio,
Struss continued his close ties to pictorial photography circles. He enrolled as a special student in
Clarence White's new School of Photography in
1915-16—perhaps to have continued contact
with students and White himself, and access to
equipment he may not have had at his studio—
and he taught photography at the Brooklyn
Institute of Arts and Sciences with White and
Anderson in 1916-17. He also increased his submissions to photographic exhibitions. In August
1914, just as he took over White's studio, he contributed his first work to an exhibition abroad
when Alvin Langdon Coburn invited him to
submit five prints to the American Invitational
Section of the 59th Annual Exhibition at the
Royal Photographic Society of Great Britain.
Coburn, who also requested five prints each from
White, Stieglitz, and Frank Eugene, four from
Anderson and seven from George Seeley, would
continue to organize these London exhibitions
for many years, with Struss as a virtually annual
contributor throughout the 1910s and 1920s.

His involvement with the magazine
Platinum Print helped Struss make connections
with pictorial photographers on the West Coast,
and he began exhibiting in San Francisco and
Los Angeles as well. The officers of the magazine also organized a collection of prints to circu-
late among museums and galleries; the Platinum
Print Loan Collection (sometimes including
work by only White, Struss, and Dickson) was
exhibited in eastern cities such as Pittsburgh,
Syracuse, and Elmira, New York. From 1915
through 1917, Struss appeared in twenty-three
exhibitions throughout the United States and in
England and frequently won awards for his photographs [see Appendix].

The collaboration that began with *Platinum Print* continued when Struss, White, and
Dickson started a new society, the Pictorial Pho-

tographers of America, in the fall of 1915. In
their first formal meeting, on January 15, 1916,
at the office of White's friend and student, Dr.
Charles Jaeger, a committee consisting of Jaeger,
White, Dickson, Struss, and Mary White, another White student, drew up a constitution for the
association. Designed to give pictorial photographers an alternative to Stieglitz's Photo-Secession, the new organization was also more highly
organized and provided increased activities.
The founders listed a number of ambitious goals
for the Pictorial Photographers of America, including publication of newsletters and annuals,
lectures and workshops by prominent photographers, and regular traveling exhibitions by
members. They also encouraged museums and
libraries around the country to purchase pictorial
photographs. *Platinum Print* became the organization's primary publication; in 1917 the title was
changed to *Photo=Graphic Art* to reflect a shift in
emphasis from the fine print to photographs for
illustration.[43]

Struss was elected to a two-year term on the
executive committee for 1917-18, and at a second
meeting was reelected to the executive committee, to serve through 1921. However, though he
was instrumental in the organization's founding
and planned on extended service with the association, his name mysteriously disappeared from
the roster of the PPA in its 1918 annual report.[44]
Although he never knew exactly why—he by that
time was serving with the U.S. Army in Kansas—
the war had begun to influence organizations like
the PPA, and Struss' earlier views on the war had
disturbed a number of its members.

MILITARY SERVICE

By 1917, the photographic community in New
York had changed significantly from only a few
years before. The last photography exhibit at 291
had been shown in early 1916, the last issue of

Camera Work was published in June 1917, and the Photo-Secession ceased to exist. The Pictorial Photographers of America filled the void in many ways, holding exhibitions and publishing *Photo=Graphic*, but they had not received the support of all photographers working in the field. Further aggravating the schism within the community were the economic changes caused by the war. As early as 1914, *American Photography*, the leading journal for amateur photographers, had predicted in "The Effect of the War on Photography" that, because Germany was the largest source of photographic supplies, photographers would find it difficult to get certain necessary products. In 1917, another journal, *Photo-Era*, reported that even the Army was unable to procure appropriate lenses for their needs and asked photographers to "enlist" or sell their lenses to the Photographic Division of the Signal Corps. Clearly, a greater mission was at hand, and art photography began to seem not only more difficult but less important as many photographers began to concentrate more on the wartime needs of the country.[45]

After the United States entered the war in April 1917, those who had criticized American policy or actions in regard to the war (especially German-Americans) had to prove their undivided loyalty to the United States. Although Struss had initially supported Germany and had hoped that the U.S. would remain neutral, his greatest loyalty was always to the United States. By the time the Selective Service became law, on May 18, 1917, he and most other German-Americans believed that an unwillingness to serve their country would be cowardice. Some pacifists, including German-American Mennonites, delayed their registration until they could find noncombatant ways to serve their country, but Struss did not delay at all. He registered for the draft on June 5, the day that registration commenced nationally, and received certificate #39 in the New York City precinct.[46] He still did not want to serve abroad and be forced to fight against Germans, but he felt he could serve his country through his photography.

Since Struss had always been most interested in the technical side of photography, he hoped that the U.S. Army would use his technical knowledge and talent for experimentation. The British and French had developed excellent techniques in aerial photography in the early years of the war, and now the U.S. needed accomplished photographers and technicians for these purposes. In 1917 the Pictorial Photographers of America invited Major Kendall Banning of the Signal Corps to speak about the government's need for photographers who, "being the eye of the army, would be instrumental in winning the war."[47] Banning handed out "experience blanks," which would give the government a census of photographers who might be contacted if their services were needed. In August, perhaps inspired by Banning's description of the Aerial Division of the Signal Corps, Struss traveled to Washington, D.C., to speak to Major James Barnes, the head of the Signal Corps photographic division, about prospective service. Barnes and Lt. Edward Steichen (one of the original founders of the Photo-Secession), both with the Aerial Photography Division, explained to Struss that positions in the division were going only to enlisted men rather than draftees and urged him to enlist. The first class in aerial photography would begin soon, using techniques the British had developed from British Sergeant-Major Haslett, and Major Barnes gave Struss a letter for the recruiting officer in New York, recommending his enlistment as a photographer.[48]

Back home, Struss arranged for Paul Anderson to take over his studio and continue sales of the Struss Pictorial Lens and their photographic developer Kalogen under the name of Struss-Anderson Laboratories. He then enlisted on September 7 and reported nine days later for basic training at Camp Vail, New Jersey. Enthusiastically anticipating the exciting photographic work he expected to do, Struss reportedly gave daily informal lectures on photography to the men there. At the end of a month, he was among the twelve chosen to report to the School of Aerial Photography at Langley Field, Virginia, for Sergeant-Major Haslett's first course. Upon graduation a few months later, Sergeant Struss (fig. 20) was sent to instruct at the new School of Military Aeronautics, opening at Cornell University. He arrived in Ithaca, New York, in mid-December and began organizing everything so he could begin teaching classes in January. In all three military locations, he loaned his own photographic equipment for classes to use, since the army had not yet procured adequate equipment.[49]

Even before Struss started the course at Langley Field, however, forces working behind the scenes had ensured that he would not go much farther in the photographic division. Unbeknownst to him, his past remarks about American policy and Germany's actions had given him a pronounced pro-German reputation, and his enlistment coincided with the country's growing suspicion about German spies. On September 29, David Jones, an acquaintance of Struss' who was also a member of the Defense League, sent a memo to the Department of Justice Intelligence Bureau stating that "Carl [sic] Struss, an expert photographer whose place of business is at 5 West 31st Street, is a decidedly pro-German fellow, who is said to have recently joined the U.S. Aviation Corps and in that capacity might be in a position to do much harm."[50] With that, the Military Intelligence Department began to investigate Struss in the same manner as they investigated thousands of American soldiers and civilians suspected of unpatriotic sentiments. The department secured confidential reports on his photographic experience and loyalty from his

Figure 20. Karl Struss, *Self-portrait in U.S. Army Sergeant Uniform*, 1917, modern print from original glass plate negative, Amon Carter Museum

commanding officers, Major Kendall Banning at Langley Field and Major James Barnes, and the Military Intelligence office in New York spoke to Struss' associates there. On November 1, an investigator interviewed Clarence White at his studio at 122 East 17th Street, then contacted Edward Dickson (fig. 21) by telephone. In this first interview, White claimed to be unaware of any discussions with Struss relating to Germany but noted that he had heard indirectly that Struss was pro-German. Dickson, however, said that Struss "had always talked very pro-German—that

Figure 21. Clara Estelle Sipprell, *Edward R. Dickson,
Photographer*, before 1922, gelatin silver print,
Amon Carter Museum

since moved to Indiana, claimed that she had
heard Struss make pro-German comments, but
was unaware of pro-German meetings and
"thought if there had been any her sister would
have told her of them. She had, however, heard
. . . of German friends visiting Struss in his studio and of pro-German talk that had occurred
there."[51]

The investigative records show considerable confusion about what constituted a pro-
German "meeting" and what might be merely
visits from German-American friends or clients
whose comments could be construed as pro-
German. Furthermore, the statements against
Struss changed over time, possibly because the
investigators were trying to elicit a certain
response. For example, an investigator named
Holmes Mallory, who conducted additional interviews and obtained signed affidavits from
Clarence White, Edward Dickson, and Melvin
Palmer, paraphrased White's comments to say
that Struss had "always been very pro-German,
and has attacked the Draft on at least one occasion when [White] was present. Struss' attitude
toward the service was hostile and he expressed
himself as being unwilling to serve." In fact,
White's signed affidavit said only: "At a meeting
of friends at Keans Restaurant in 1914 as well at
Prince George restaurant in 1917—I heard Mr.
Karl Struss express strong pro-German feelings."[52]
Similarly, though a signed affidavit from Edward
Dickson stated only that "On several occasions
I have heard statements uttered by Karl Struss,
to me, which have been hostile to the United
States and pro-German in tendency or direction,"
Mallory's report paraphrased Dickson as saying
that Struss was "so very pro-German that neither
himself nor any of a group of Artists and Authors
of which he was a member would have anything
to do with him." Mallory also reported that
Dickson thought Struss had only enlisted a day or
so before he would have been drafted, and that

this talk did not cease upon the entry of the
United States in the War, and that even to casual
acquaintances, Struss had aired his views on the
subject of Germany." Dickson further stated that
all of their mutual acquaintances had been surprised when they heard he had enlisted. Shortly
after this, an investigator interviewed Melvin
Palmer, who had shared the studio with Struss in
1914-15, and Mary Brown, whose sister Margaret
was Corresponding Secretary of the Pictorial
Photographers of America and had worked for
Struss in his studio. Brown, whose sister had

he had continued to make remarks "hostile to the United States." According to Dickson, Margaret Brown, Struss' assistant, "lived in a perfect 'hell' as a result of these fanatical pro-German expressions of Struss on all occasions," and when her sister Mary learned that Struss had enlisted, she reportedly said "what, as a spy?" Mallory further reported that Dickson thought it would be "extremely dangerous for Struss to hold any position of confidence in our Army." Melvin Palmer, described by Mallory as "rabidly pro-Ally," surprisingly was not as forceful in his condemnation as Mary Brown had been; he said only that Struss had been distinctly pro-German and that Palmer had not seen any evidence of a change in Struss' attitude.[53]

Since the signed statements from Struss' colleagues criticized his pro-German attitudes, but were not as harsh as the investigators' paraphrasing, it is difficult to know whether the original statements were exaggerated. Clearly, Struss had been insensitive to the growing superpatriotism and the resulting suspicion of German-Americans. Extremely outspoken and even arrogant with his opinions and sometimes lacking diplomacy, he had made enemies at a time when he should have been wary about his professional reputation. He could not have predicted, however, how seriously his lack of discretion would affect his career.[54]

While Struss trained to teach aerial photography, the investigation intensified, and soon military memos stated that the entire Struss family had always been violently pro-German and anti-American, that he had entered the service only to escape the draft, and that he had held "secret" meetings in his studio throughout the previous year. Other photographers were implicated in these meetings, suggesting a possible conspiracy.[55] On November 10, a memo from the chief of military intelligence recommended that Struss be relieved of his duties as a photographer; by

December 6, an acting Judge Advocate General recommended conducting a court-martial or at least Struss' discharge, and putting him under surveillance for the duration of the war.

Struss never knew how close he came to being charged as an enemy of the country. Instead, on December 20, 1917, by order of the Secretary of War, Chief of Staff General Tasker Bliss sent Special Order No. 296 to all relevant parties, stating that "Sergt. Karl Struss, Signal Corps, on duty at the School of Military Aeronautics, Ithaca, N.Y., is transferred as private to the United States Disciplinary Barracks Guard and will be sent to Fort Leavenworth, Kans., for assignment to a company." In the ensuing series of miscommunications and examples of military ineptitude, Struss was confined in Ithaca for thirty-seven days while officials tried to figure out what to do with him.[56] As soon as he was able to communicate outside of the military, he notified Paul Anderson, who had been managing the photographic studio during his absence. Anderson in turn called Struss' brother, who "was plumb hot at the idea of anyone questioning the loyalty of any member of the family" and wanted to contact his congressman. Anderson, however, advised him to wait until they could find out what the charges against Struss were, since probably "some hysterical person—and there are unfortunately a good many of them in this country at present—has got excited over your name or over something that you or someone else has been reported as saying . . . I have thought for some time that there was a danger of someone taking you for disloyal, just on the strength of your name."[57] Anderson soon realized how seriously Struss was being investigated but still expected people to come to their senses and judge the man rather than the name. He probably remembered an article about Struss in the photographic journal *American Photography* in 1915, before the U.S. entered the war. In the article, the pictorial photographer and writer John Wallace Gillies had referred to Struss' German heritage but had come to an entirely different conclusion than the later military intelligence investigation, describing "[t]he imperturbable Karl Struss. . . . As may be inferred from the name, there is German blood present, . . . though for some generations the family has been in this country and is strictly unhyphenated. . . . Excitement is foreign to his nature. Last month I wrote about an Englishman who would not jar when a bomb was exploded under him, and now I find myself saying much the same thing about a German. Maybe that is why the war is lasting so long."[58]

The "bomb" that exploded under Struss in December 1917 certainly jarred him and his family. Although his relatives hesitated momentarily, hoping that it was all a misunderstanding, by the time Struss had been held for more than a month "pending a military investigation," they began to contact anyone who might provide assistance. In addition to New York Senators J. W. Wadsworth and William A. Calder and Oregon Senator George Chamberlain, Chairman of the Committee on Military Affairs, they contacted Judge James Drew of Pittsburgh, an old friend whom they had met on the boat to Europe in 1909 and with whom they had remained in close touch. Drew, who was well-connected, immediately wrote to New York's senators and representatives and a state supreme court judge and also offered to bring Struss' case to the attention of Secretary of War Newton D. Baker. The Struss family also contacted pictorial photographer and prominent lawyer Augustus Thibaudeau, Struss' friend and colleague from Buffalo, who also wrote Senator Wadsworth. After hearing from so many people about this strange situation and then receiving a four-page letter from Struss himself about his predicament, his photographic qualifications, and entire family history, Senator

Wadsworth initiated an investigation at the War Department.[59]

Struss considered going to the press with his situation, but Anderson urged a gentler touch, cautioning Struss that publicizing his situation and aggressively pushing his own defense might backfire with military officials. Anderson at first believed that the military was actually investigating someone else, perhaps a true German spy, and thus had to investigate everyone who might have associated with him as well. Attempting to be the voice of reason, he suggested: "you will be doing a better service to the country and to yourself as well by just keeping quiet about it and waiting for matters to develop."[60] Judge Drew also advised Struss that his letter-writing campaign might prejudice people against him. Thinking it preferable to leave the efforts in the hands of "one man of influence," Drew contacted a personal friend, Pennsylvania Congressman John Morin, who was on the Committee on Military Affairs and apparently "had the ear" of Secretary of War Baker.

Finally, after thirty-seven days of confinement, Struss was transferred to the Disciplinary Guards at Fort Leavenworth's Military Barracks, as directed by the Special Order of December 20, 1917, and was assigned to guard the prisoners rather than to be one.[61] Although he had originally disliked writing letters, he now found it helped his morale, so he wrote daily. These letters betray his moods, his close relationship with his family, and his status as the "baby" in the family as his mother and sisters comforted him. Demoralized by the urgings of his friends to be patient and "keep quiet," Struss nonetheless took their advice and asked his family to stop writing letters to officials. He thoroughly expected that the efforts of Judge Drew and the senators would clear his name and return him to photographic work in no time.[62] His family, however, was devastated and would not let the matter drop,

Figure 22. Karl Struss, *Paul Anderson*, 1914, platinum print, Amon Carter Museum

though Struss, who had begun to distrust everyone, begged them not to talk to anyone. Suspecting that his letters might have been read by military investigators, he pleaded with his family to stop writing about the situation and began to refer to other people in abbreviated code.[63]

Struss may have never suspected that two of his primary accusers were his good friends and colleagues Clarence White and Edward Dickson. He did, however, hear that White had advised Augustus Thibaudeau not to try to come to Struss' defense and that several of his photographic colleagues (among them White, Francis Bruguière, and critic Sadakichi Hartmann) were "spreading rumors" that exaggerated or fabricated his situa-

tion. Some of the stories claimed that he had been caught photographing sensitive manufacturing areas, or that he had taken his father into restricted areas at the Aviation School at Cornell (his father had never visited him there), or that he had been insubordinate to officers in Rochester, New York (where he had never been stationed). Most of the rumors, however, claimed that he had been interned at Fort Leavenworth as a German spy, rather than being stationed there as a guard; some people even heard that he had been sentenced to twenty-five years.[64]

Although several friends and members of Struss' family criticized Paul Anderson's reluctance to come actively to his defense, Struss maintained that Anderson "unquestionably is one of my best friends and sincere and true."[65] Anderson (fig. 22) soon had occasion to defend him in the context of their photographic careers. An accomplished writer who had published numerous articles on pictorial photography in the 1910s, Anderson was in the final stages of preparing a long article for the popular journal *The Mentor* in early 1918, just as Struss was transferred to Fort Leavenworth. The *Mentor's* editor, W. D. Moffat, heard the rumor that Struss was interned as a German spy at Fort Leavenworth and questioned Anderson's use of eight Struss photographs as illustrations, suggesting that they credit the photographs to Anderson instead, or possibly to "The Struss Studio." Citing "the rising tide of hostility to all things German," Moffat quoted one of his colleagues: "Why must a num-

ber on photography feature all thru [*sic*] its pages
Karl Struss, Karl Struss, Karl Struss—and not a
thing about Genthe or of some other well-known
photographer?"[66]

In a sharp response, Anderson defended his
own loyalty and patriotism and emphasized that
he did not "feel that it is the part of any loyal
American citizen to discriminate against another,
merely because his name happens to sound
German." He then pointed out that "two of the
photographers whose work you asked me to discuss—Stieglitz and Genthe—are, unless my
information is erroneous, German-born,"[67]
adding that he was not accusing Stieglitz or
Genthe of any disloyalty, but only showing the
lack of fairness to Struss. Although Moffat threatened to pull the article entirely, he eventually
printed it in August 1918 with full credit to Karl
Struss.[68]

Struss found that he had other battles to
fight. In May 1918, the Pictorial Photographers
of America, the organization he had helped form
with Clarence White and Edward Dickson, asked
him to resign, claiming to have been criticized
for keeping his name on their membership list.
Later that year they attempted to change their
constitution and by-laws in order to eject him.
Although Struss did know that the organization
asked him to resign, he did not know that four of
the organization's top officers—White, Dickson,
Margaret Brown, and Melvin Palmer—had all
spoken against him to military intelligence investigators.[69]

As spreading rumors began to erode his circle of support, Struss tried to contain the situation as much as he could at long distance. Since
he could not defend himself in person, he asked
his family to tell those who asked about him only
that he was instructing photography in the War
College and to say nothing of his situation or
location. In addition, they were to tell anyone
who had already been told the story "not to re-

peat it, under any circumstances, to anyone—it
doesn't matter who." Frustrated with his lack of
control, Struss began to lash out at his family.
"What's the matter with father, has he lost all his
intelligense? Surely if I wrote T.M. and she knew
nothing, why should he go out of his way to tell
her. It makes me out a liar and a fool, and having said so often not to say anything further about
it to anyone and [him] disregarding my wishes—
simply makes me sick. . . Can't I even trust my
own father?"[70] He even began to suspect that his
father was partly to blame for his dilemma. When
a friend informed him that his father had made
"some comment," Struss wrote to his mother that
he had never agreed with his father, but, "Like as
not someone has heard him making absurd and
silly, nonsensical remarks and you see where it
has put me." He also remembered a lieutenant
at Cornell asking if his father had been anti-
Britain before the U.S. entered the war. "I said
'No, never, so long as she respected our rights,
but he had always been pro-America (being
the land of his birth) and not pro-Britain or pro-
anything else, and that couldn't possibly imply
that he was pro-German. He didn't favor any of
the belligerents, but insisted on the recognition
of every American right by all the belligerents.'"[71]

Meanwhile, Paul Anderson was unable to
keep the studio business profitable. Advertising
commissions decreased measurably as businesses
entered a wartime economy, the developer Kalogen turned out to be a money-losing venture,
and the war-related coal shortage kept him from
doing any photographic processing through the
winter and spring because the water temperature
was barely above freezing. He tried to rent lights
to other companies, then started selling equipment that was not being used. As early as December 1917, only three months after Struss had
entered the Army, Anderson had written his partner that he intended to enter the Signal Corps
and had advised that they close the studio until

after the war. Five months later, he did just that, liquidating or moving out all equipment and stock, with help from Struss' family.[72]

Even some of Struss' earlier work came back to haunt him. Several of his nude studies had been published in a portfolio titled *The Female Figure* (see Bonnie Yochelson's essay), and about this time publisher Ferenz Kotausek had developed legal problems because of them. "Some Society of Prudes," as Struss referred to the people responsible for Kotausek's trouble, were offended by the nudes and did not understand their artistic merit. Kotausek wrote to Struss, asking to borrow the original plates for the portfolio in order to prove his case in court. Although he eventually settled out of court and was able to continue selling the portfolios without further trouble, it must have seemed to Struss that society's values were once again at odds with his own. He felt he had conducted the whole project in a very ethical manner, with the models even chaperoned by their mothers during the photography, and the ensuing controversy seemed needless.[73]

Throughout this period, Struss attempted to keep busy and to maintain his health and spirits. A very physical man, he did whatever he could to keep active, ice-skating throughout the winter, then playing tennis once summer arrived. Guarding prisoners offered no intellectual or aesthetic challenge, so he went to movies constantly, attending two or three each day. He seemed to take great joy in this and wrote to his family about each one he saw, asking them if they had seen the new Chaplin film or anything with a new actress who impressed him. While much of his interest in the movies was probably escapism, the films occasionally interested him aesthetically, and at least twice he commented on ones he felt were photographed well.

In June 1918, he was assigned to a new position that lifted his spirits and changed his perspective on his own situation. Assigned to special duty as a file clerk in the Department of Sociology and Psychiatry, Medical Examiner's Office, he processed reports on the histories of all military prisoners interned in Fort Leavenworth. His demotion and transfer had left him completely absorbed in his own dilemma, but now he became interested in the lives of others. "To get such an insight into the humans that populate this universe is really a privilege indeed . . . I am sure the benefit derived will [be] of inestimable value in judging others."[74]

His new appointment was more than a change of scenery; he had achieved a higher level of trust within the prison system. In addition to filing reports, he planned to take charge of the department's photographic section and to begin photographing all prisoners. In a letter to his mother, he displayed a boost of enthusiasm from his new appointment and vented his pent-up frustration: "You see what getting back to work means to me, after five months idleness, mental I mean. The things stored up during that time will someday come forth." Suddenly caught up in the stories of others, he realized that he was not the only person who had been treated unfairly by the country's patriotic fervor. As a board of inquiry judged hundreds of conscientious objectors, he observed: "Contrary to newspaper accounts which are untruthful, [they] obtain short shift, being sent up for five, eight or ten years, and they are American to the core having been here for generations."[75] Struss may have been sympathetic to many of the prisoners, but he had to remain objective or at least attempt to keep his opinions silent. Displaying a new philosophical attitude, he observed that "what we consider fundamental American principles, are suspended for the period of the emergency and this applies to everybody and everything. One's opinions must be nil or minus on all subjects; whether one thinks he is right, matters not. It is

Figure 23. Karl Struss, *Conscientious Objector Imprisoned at Fort Leavenworth*, 1918, gelatin silver print, Collection of the Grandchildren of Karl Struss

better to give one's brain a vacation and simply drift along with the tide."[76]

Struss' photographs of the prisoners were straight frontal and side-view documents that left no room for interpretation or clarification of the subject's character. Still, they suggest intriguing stories behind the faces (fig. 23). Happy to be photographing again, Struss looked forward with pride to photographing the entire prison population and reported: "Am going to have the darkroom altered and modernized so we can turn out the best work in the country."[77] He also hoped to begin taking movies; the department purchased a camera in July and Struss submitted a three-page summary of a scenario, but he then had to wait for film and for the military bureaucracy to authorize his plans.[78] By early September the Army rejected both his request to modernize the darkroom (fig. 24) and his plan to make movies.

Frustrated again, Struss attempted a multi-pronged attack on the military bureaucracy. He approached several officials, including the commandant of his company, to request a hearing on his case, and papers giving his view of the situation were referred to the Central Military Intelligence Branch of the War Department. Then he wrote a long proposal to organize a series of exhibitions of wartime photography that would tour the country and raise public awareness of the wartime needs; he pleaded: "If for some unknown reason . . . I am still denied service to my country in the capacity of a technician, then I ask to be allowed to serve it as an artist."[79] Meanwhile, Struss' company captain suggested that he apply for entry into the Officer's Training Camp, explaining that a rejection would require written justification. Struss immediately wrote his mother that he would need several letters of recommendation stating "that I am intensely loyal and come from a family who have always worked for the advancement of every American right and principle and so forth and make it as strong along those lines as possibly can be." He himself wrote to Paul Anderson and several other photographic colleagues. On October 9, he was accepted and transferred to the training camp as a corporal.[80]

A few weeks later the armistice was signed to end the war, but except for his promotion to corporal, Struss' situation remained unchanged. In response to his request for a hearing, the Military Intelligence Department assembled all papers relevant to the case, including the many letters that had been written in support of Struss, and determined that the original witnesses and those who had come out strongly in his defense should be reinterviewed. While that was going on, Struss wrote a moving plea to Major John Campbell of the General Staff of the War College Division, requesting the right to be heard and give his own defense. "I do not intend to have to go thru life, considering my international photographic reputation and all, with any unmerited stigma attached to my name, for such a thing, in its last analysis, would brand me as a man without a country—a man who couldn't be trusted by his fellow beings—as people will always remark that 'His country couldn't trust him in its hour of need', and such-like expressions. If I am not of good enough calibre to be an American, tell me, and I will, then, reluctantly renounce my citizenship. Upon your decision rests my future."[81] Whether Struss would have given up American citizenship or was merely making a desperate bluff, he realized correctly that he could not return to the life he had known before the war. His studio was gone and much of the equipment had been sold or returned to original owners. His reputation with advertisers and publishing contacts was severely damaged. Most of his photographic colleagues had turned away from him. Even his relationship with his family, specifically his father, was critically strained.

Meanwhile, the intelligence officers concluded their investigation and decided that their original actions had been warranted. They had not been able to find Clarence White, whom they erroneously thought had left New York to work in the Military Intelligence Office in Washington. Thus it remains an unanswered question whether he might have recanted or softened his comments; Struss knew that White had spread rumors about his supposed meetings with pro-Germans but did not know his old teacher's entire involvement. All the other original witnesses against Struss confirmed their original statements and had no knowledge of him since that time. Although Judge Drew had praised Struss' character and claimed that he was incapable of pro-German attitudes or conduct, the investigators discounted his knowledge of Struss because it was purely personal. The only relevant thing Augustus Thibaudeau recalled was

Figure 24. Karl Struss, *Darkroom at Fort Leavenworth, Kansas*, 1918, gelatin silver print, Collection of the Grandchildren of Karl Struss

hearing Struss take the German side in an argument at the beginning of the war; although Thibaudeau did not take this as any indication that Struss was disloyal, the investigators obviously disagreed. When everyone who worked with Struss in the military praised his character and maintained that he had never shown anything but loyalty, the investigators concluded that Struss had wisely learned to keep his anti-American attitudes to himself. On January 15, the Acting Director of the Military Intelligence Office advised the Intelligence Officer at Fort Leavenworth that "in light of the demobilization, the easiest course would be to discharge him." Struss received an honorable discharge from the Army on February 15, 1919,[82] but unlike most soldiers, he did not return home, even for a visit. Instead, within three days he was on a train bound for California and what he hoped would be a whole new life.

LOS ANGELES— "THE FUTURE IS BRIGHT"

Karl Struss had decided to begin again in the land of opportunity. His earlier career was over, and although he might have revived it with some effort and patience, he was too bitter even to try. He did not write about his decision to move to Los Angeles or to seek work in the booming movie industry, so it is difficult to know exactly when this path became clear. He had some family in California, however, and had made several professional contacts through various pictorial associations. In addition to finding work in the movies, he planned to do commercial photographic work in advertising, illustration, and portraiture. Though not sure of what to expect or even that his gamble would work, he had his family ship his things from New York, but told his mother just to let people know that he was out of the service and traveling in California.

He may have remembered the photographs that Alvin Langdon Coburn took on his 1910 trip to the West, because he made a side trip to the Grand Canyon on his way to California. He arrived at the canyon rim during an early morning snow. The light, color, and spatial composition were unlike anything he had experienced before in the East, in Bermuda, or in Europe, and he reported, "Well, I've never seen anything like it and I guess its the only one of its kind." After photographing for two days, he continued on to Los Angeles, very pleased with the photographs he had taken.

Although the side trip was brief, it rejuvenated him. The images he made of this landscape were different from anything he had done before, and they helped prepare him aesthetically and spiritually for the new world before him. While the landscapes Struss had produced of Europe, Nova Scotia, and the northeastern states were fairly simple compositions with few lines

describing the hills and trees, the Grand Canyon views more closely resemble his urban views of New York. The grandeur of the view, the scale of the mesas, and the distance across the scene all required the same decisions he faced with skyline views of the city. Complex compositions with a broad tonal range could give a sense of space and distance, while a narrow tonal range and very dark printing flattened the scene into an abstract design and suggested drama and mystery (see *The Canyon—Late Afternoon*, fig. 25, and *Detail— Grand Canyon*, p. 156). These photographs were new work for him to show people, demonstrating his skills in composition and his potential for illustration or other commercial assignments.[83]

When Struss arrived in Los Angeles, he knew that he had made the right choice. Overwhelmed by the contrast between his experience and his state of mind in Kansas and what he encountered in California, he wrote home: "This is a most wonderful country and I am just crazy about it. . . . The future is very bright, and I know I'll love the place. Everything is so green and bright and looks so refreshing after drear [*sic*] dirty Kansas. What I like about this West Coast is that everything is all so new and clean, and one doesn't meet the crowds or poverty that abound in the Eastern cities."[84] He immediately set about defining his new life and identity. Though he wanted to leave behind the bitter memories and the blemish on his reputation, he knew that his success depended upon the assistance of a network and support system of colleagues. He had built up contacts during his years as a photographer, and without delay, he began to strengthen these connections. Through Clarence White's classes in Maine and New York he knew Viroque Baker, a pictorial photographer from Los Angeles; Edward Weston had participated in many pictorial exhibitions with him and would have been familiar with his work. Struss had also exhibited in at least two West Coast pictorial exhibitions,

Many of the people he met had connections with the film industry and were happy to
give him advice on how to get work. He planned
to take his work around to all "the big producers
and get acquainted for future use," exploring all
the possibilities before settling on a job. He
selected photographs that would show his skills in
portraiture, advertising, and magazine illustration
and also included some innovative work he had
done with an experimental color print process
called Hess-Ives. He had written an article about
this procedure for *American Photography* and
had included examples of the process in the
Female Figure portfolio (see p. 8), and he thought
he might do "some color work on the side as the
'stars' are very much interested."[85]

He took his Grand Canyon negatives to a
lab to make several enlargements. Although the
processing cost him almost all the money that he
had left, he knew the prints would be valuable in
promoting his work and felt confident that he
would recoup their expense through quick sales.
In fact, newspapers bought several of his views
and agreed to print something about his being in
the area.[86] The art editor at the *Los Angeles
Examiner* told him to send prints of the best
views directly to William Randolph Hearst, who
might want some to advertise his hotel at the
canyon rim. Struss had Hearst send them on to
his family in New York and relied upon their
assistance to distribute his work to all the magazines who might be interested.[87] An art dealer
agreed to sell the Grand Canyon prints in his
store and expressed interest in the rest of Struss'
work as well.

Having found a new market for his images,
Struss wrote his family to send the negatives of
his Europe, Bermuda, and New York views; many
of his new friends had darkrooms that he could
use temporarily. An assistant director who was a
"camera bug" offered to help get him a job as an
extra on a film, so he could shoot scenery on the

Figure 25. Karl Struss, *The Canyon - Late Afternoon*, 1919,
platinum print, Amon Carter Museum

the 1915 Panama/Pacific International Expo-
sition Exhibit of Pictorial Photography in San
Francisco and the First Annual Photographic
Salon of Los Angeles, organized by the Camera
Pictorialists of Los Angeles in 1917.

way to the set and then sell the photographs. Struss also made an appointment with the owner of Santa Catalina Island to talk about doing advertising work for their tourist concerns.

He thought of taking an evening job to support himself temporarily, so that he wouldn't have to take a photography job prematurely. He wanted to give potential employers the impression that he was not desperate for employment, although he was virtually broke, with a bank balance of $1.31. He wrote his mother to deposit some money into his account immediately, promising to pay her back as soon as he "struck oil" and observing: "In what I am trying to land I have to look prosperous and be indifferent whether I accept or not what is offered me. I don't want to jump too quickly."[88] Two days later, he wrote that he had just shown his work to some people and when they expressed interest and asked him how much he expected to be paid, he responded, "Two hundred dollars a week!—just like that. I can say it now without any difficulty and next week, if I don't land anything, it will be three hundred a week to start. You wouldn't know your little sonny—he's changed quite a bit and nothing phazes [sic] him anymore. They are quite used to large figures here, and they seemed impressed enough to devote an hour's time to me with a dozen people outside waiting their appointments."[89]

His appointment may well have been with Famous Players-Lasky Studios, the largest concern in Hollywood at the time, and "a veritable city within a city." A year earlier, Jesse Lasky had sent a letter to all directors, including Cecil B. De Mille, urging them to pay more attention to the quality of the photographic stills that were made to promote their films. The stills were as important as the films themselves, Lasky explained, "because it is just as important to sell the film as to make it," and he strongly urged all directors to supply "such attractive, unique

and artistic photographs as will materially assist our work."[90]

Struss may have been just what they were looking for. Although he had not had any directly relevant experience, he knew how to relate his work to the needs of potential employers or clients. With his talents in lighting and portraiture, he could make the stars look good, and his experience crafting illustrations for fictional pieces suggested an instinct for capturing the one instant that would communicate a story's narrative or emotion. He brought with him several letters of recommendation, including one from John Chapman Hilder, the editor of *Harper's Bazaar*, for whom he had illustrated several fictional pieces. Hilder praised Struss' artistry and technical proficiency, calling him "one of the few photographers who have taken the trouble to go beneath the surface of his subject."[91] Struss convinced the Lasky Studio officials to take a chance with him.

Thus, just three weeks after arriving in Los Angeles, he began work on *For Better, For Worse*, which their biggest director, Cecil B. De Mille (see figs. 26 and 73), had almost finished. Although he did not immediately receive the big salary he had hoped for, Struss considered the job a way of "breaking into the game." Still concerned about what the people back in New York would think about his new employment, he wrote his mother that she could say that he was in the movies, but that it wasn't "necessary to say what company—'one of the big ones' is enough."[92] Though hired to make portraits of the stars and produce the all-important stills, he immediately began to assist with lighting as well. For the most part, he used the standard lighting techniques from his earlier commercial photography career, but his great talent was in the use of light and shadow to create dramatic compositions. Feeling confident of his abilities, he suggested an innovative lighting arrangement that allowed an actor's shadow to appear first, growing larger and larger until the actor himself entered the scene. More importantly, on only his fourth day on the job, Struss did his first movie filming and planned to use his pictorial lens on various scenes. Clearly, he wasted no time in showing De Mille and Alvin Wyckoff, his photographer, that he had multiple talents that would improve the visual effect of the film.[93]

Struss may have noted some irony in his first Hollywood assignment. In *For Better, For Worse*, set during the war, the heroine loves a doctor whom she believes to be a slacker, but who in fact declined a commission because he was the only doctor able to run the children's hospital in his hometown. Slackers had been a much-discussed subject and popular theme in fiction during the war (one of the pieces Struss illustrated in the *Bazaar* had dealt with the subject), so by showing that the man who did not fight on the front was not necessarily a coward, the movie attempted to heal some of the war's lingering wounds. Struss, who by that time was accustomed to self-censorship, did not discuss his own experiences during the war. Just as he had instructed his family to tell friends in New York that he was teaching aerial photography in the War College, he told his Hollywood acquaintances that he had been doing secret photographic experiments for the military (actually what he had hoped to do). Likewise De Mille probably did not discuss his own role as a member of the American Protective League. Frustrated at not being able to enlist in the war, the director had become a volunteer representative for the Los Angeles district of the Justice Department's Intelligence Office, secretly investigating individuals he employed, reporting on people he had met at parties, and using the network of studio offices to investigate people in other cities.[94] Whether Struss and De Mille ever knew of each other's experiences during the war is unknown.

Figure 26. Karl Struss, *Cecil B. De Mille, 1919*, modern print from original nitrate negative, Amon Carter Museum

However, Struss sufficiently impressed De Mille with his artistic sense and his knowledge of lighting that he became the director's third cameraman. They finished shooting the picture very shortly, and Struss began making promotional portraits of the stars for the studio's publicity department. De Mille seemed very pleased with the results, and so was the leading lady Gloria Swanson, who had just recently started work for

De Mille and was his current star. For someone who had seen two or three movies each day during his military career and displayed a typical fascination with the stars, Struss showed restrained enthusiasm at being able to talk to and please the "star-ess," saying "had she known me better she would have put her arms about your hero and given him a lovely smack! But no, she refrained." One of Struss' old colleagues, Otis L. Griffith of the Hess-Ives Corporation, was quite impressed with his new position and claimed that he would not have been as restrained. "If I were in Los Angeles, I would have had my picture taken with Mary Pickford at my knees, Anita Stewart and the Gish girls hanging on my shoulders, and Mabel Normand sitting on my head; however you are undoubtedly more dignified than I."[95]

Although still not making much money, Struss was glad to be on the studio's regular payroll and to have money coming in between pictures. Since the schedule was not as hectic as during filming, he could also earn extra money making portraits in people's homes, including De Mille's (fig. 26), and preparing photographs for some of the magazines he had worked with in New York. In the summer, he traveled with the entire cast and crew to the island of Santa Cruz to film scenes for *Male and Female*, which again starred Gloria Swanson. This was the first film that Struss worked on from start to finish, and he took great care to prove himself with it. He made elegant promotional portraits of Swanson and Bebe Daniels, another actress prominently featured in the film, showing them in both standard portrait mode and in costume and character (see fig. 74 and pp. 151-153). He also had increased chances to film as second cameraman. In the fall, following completion of the film, De Mille officially promoted Struss to second cameraman and gave him a raise. Soon after, he signed a contract for another two years with the studio.[96]

LAND OF THE LIVING AND SUNSHINE

Struss' risky move across the country had succeeded, and he had little need for his past life in New York. When his mother mentioned a former colleague, Struss responded with bitterness: "If he wants to write, let him send the letter to you for forwarding . . . He [has never] written me a single line since seeing him last Fall and even before and as I am making plenty of new friends, really am not interested in the old, as I don't consider them friends in the true sense of the word . . . Had they been real friends, [they] would have done something."[97] Although Struss was ready to cut ties with the people he felt had abandoned him, he did regret being at such great distance from his family. They had always been very close; in fact, he had still lived at home until he entered the service. Having committed to a permanent move, he displayed his bitterness towards New York as he tried to convince his entire family to follow him. "Certainly wish you could all move out this way . . . Don't waste your time and life trying to live up to what a big city 'expects'." As he anticipated a visit from his mother and sisters during his first summer in Los Angeles, he wrote: "Everyone wishes you were all out here in the land of the living and sunshine and leaving the land of the narrowness and shams behind forever."[98]

Struss remained bitter toward many of his New York colleagues for damaging his reputation, and he considered seeking compensation. In November 1919 he wrote several letters to Dr. Charles Jaeger, treasurer and one of the original founders of the Pictorial Photographers of America, to try to reactivate his membership in the organization. Apparently, Jaeger did not respond to his queries, for Struss became so frustrated that he asked his mother to see about bringing suit against the society. It wasn't until

1929, years after the death of both Clarence
White and Edward Dickson, that his membership was finally revived through the efforts of
John Stick, the PPA regional vice-president representing Los Angeles, and Ira Martin, then PPA
president.[99]

In the meantime, Struss became very active
with Los Angeles pictorial photographers and
organizations, which provided opportunities both
for furthering his photographic efforts and for
socializing. On Valentine's Day, 1920, a year following his release from the Army, he attended a
gathering of photographers at the home of his
friend Viroque Baker, whom he had known from
Clarence White's school. On that romantic holiday, he became completely captivated by a young
woman named Ethel Wall, who was twenty-two
years old. Ethel had been assisting in the studio
of a friend who had a Struss Pictorial Lens but
was not accomplished at using it. Hearing that
Struss was now living in Los Angeles and would
be attending this gathering, the two women
resolved to meet him and get personal instruction. Ethel later remembered that he was at
her side the entire evening.[100]

Although meeting Ethel on Valentine's
Day was a significant event in Struss' life, in 1920
the following day—February 15—was more important. In two letters written that day, he noted
that it was the anniversary of his release from
the Army. He reminded his mother: "It was
exactly a year ago, and snowing to beat the band,
that I got out of the army. How the time has
flown." Perhaps in one last effort to put his
wartime experiences behind him, he also wrote
to Secretary of War Newton D. Baker that he had
not yet "received the slightest satisfaction from
those who were directly responsible for the treatment accorded me while in the Service."[101] He
was not to receive the vindication he sought, however. When one of his friends and supporters at
Fort Leavenworth, Lieutenant Louis Humason,

Figure 27. Karl Struss, *Ethel Wall Struss, 1616 Vine St.*,
c. 1921, modern print from original glass plate negative,
Amon Carter Museum

reopened the investigation at Struss' request and
argued that he had never witnessed anything in
Struss' actions that could be interpreted as other
than loyal, he was admonished by the Director of
Military Intelligence, Brigadier General M.
Churchill, that the case was closed: "This office
firmly believes that it would serve no useful purpose to correspond with this man for the purpose
of enlightening him on his status . . . The motives and good faith of the authorities in acting
as they did are not open to question."[102] The only
response Struss received from the Secretary of
War was a brief note stating that "whatever action
was taken by the War Dept. was warranted by the

were standard production stills, used for advertising and promoting the film. However when his filming schedule permitted, he also made a few pictorial stills and presented copies of these to the producer and director as mementos of the film, and to publicity offices in both Los Angeles and New York. His talent for producing a more pictorial still became well known, and when a production company wanted something out of the ordinary, they hired him.[104] If the subject of an image inspired him sufficiently, as the theme of *Not Guilty* may have, and was attractive enough to appeal to a broad photographic audience, he also made platinum prints for exhibitions (fig. 28).[105] Sometimes he worked on only one or two scenes of a film. Called to help make the closing scene of *The Faith Healer* (see p. 148), he described the scene "after the light has come in on the two figures. It looks awfully good on the screen, as the light on the crowd dims, the ray opens up on the two."[106]

As Struss became accustomed to working in two mediums, he understandably explored connections and similarities between them. He used techniques he had developed in his New York photographic career to produce dramatic shots in his films, but he also experimented to see how the added element of motion affected a composition. On his days off from work, he began to take both a movie camera and a still camera on his excursions into the country, and there he experimented with shots he considered using later in his films. Building on his long-standing interest in dancers as figures in the landscape, he made several trips into the mountains with some dancers he knew, taking still photographs until sundown, then making movies of the dancers silhouetted against the sunset.[107] *Dancer, Hollywood Hills* (fig. 29) is similar to many of his earlier photographs of figures in the landscape. The solitary dancer is framed by trees on either side, and an aura of light created by the sunset

Figure 28. Karl Struss, *Richard Dix* [still from the film **Not Guilty**], 1921, bromide print, Los Angeles County Museum of Art, Gift of Sid and Diana Avery Trust

exceptional circumstances of that time."[103] Unable to clear his name publicly, Struss continued for the remainder of his life to use his fabricated story of military service "doing secret photographic experiments."

With his past behind him, he pursued Ethel Wall intently, and they were married in January 1921. She became his photographic partner, accompanying him on excursions into the California countryside and posing for photographs (fig. 27). They lived in a bungalow on the same block as the Famous Players-Lasky Studio, where Karl worked, and in the evenings, Ethel assisted him as he processed the negatives and made prints in the studio's darkroom. Most of the photographs Struss made on the movie sets

Figure 29. Karl Struss, *Dancer, Hollywood Hills*, c. 1919, bromide print, Amon Carter Museum

to remain active in pictorial photography, and he participated in six exhibitions in 1921, renewing his connections with the same European and East Coast salons to which he had submitted work before, and also becoming active with the California pictorial groups. In addition to displaying his old work from Europe, New York, and other eastern locations, he submitted prints of California landscapes, dancers, and stills from movies. Struss clearly saw his role in the photographic world as unique. While submitting prints for the annual exhibition of the London Salon of Photography at the Royal Society of Painters, he wrote, "I believe I am about the first of the [American] Pictorialists to have entered the field of [motion picture photography] with the view of improving the presentation of pictures photographically." He explained that his motion picture work was his primary occupation, but that he still enjoyed doing pictorial photography "to be worked up at leisure."[108]

When Struss' contract with Cecil B. De Mille expired, he was not retained (as Richard Koszarski discusses in his essay), but De Mille wrote a glowing letter of recommendation that praised his artistry. "There are few better photographers," De Mille wrote. "His still work is more than excellent. He is highly artistic, and I cannot too highly recommend him."[109] This letter may have helped Struss get free-lance assignments over the next few years. In 1925 he was hired to work on the movie *Ben-Hur*, which had been in production for over a year and was plagued with

outlines her body. The composition and pose are almost classical, the image suggesting sensuality at the same time as a spiritual celebration of nature.

In February 1921, just one month after he and Ethel were married, one of Struss' Grand Canyon views (*Detail—Grand Canyon*, see p. 156) won third prize in a prestigious national competition, the 15th Annual John Wanamaker Exhibition of Photographs in Philadelphia. He had previously won awards in this competition in 1915-17 but had not exhibited any photographs from 1918 through 1920. Now firmly settled in his career as a cinematographer, Struss also wanted

line, including a man at the ship's railing looking longingly at the city (fig. 30). He chose a viewpoint set back from the ship's edge to emphasize his intended meaning of the image—a view of New York from the outside rather than from within, as many of his earlier images had been. In a sense, Struss projected himself into the man who was looking back at the city (and the past) he had left behind. When he exhibited the print later, he titled it "City of Dreams," a phrase many people used to describe Los Angeles. However, Struss' dreams of success had eluded him in New York; his vision of a successful career with a camera had been realized in Hollywood instead, and in motion picture photography.

As he looked back at the New York he had left behind, he apparently felt no regrets about his decision. Returning home from Europe after completing the filming of *Ben-Hur*, Struss began work on F. W. Murnau's *Sunrise* as co-cinematographer with Charles Rosher, whom he had met eleven years earlier in Bermuda. Contemporary scholars considered *Sunrise* to be the "pinnacle of visual beauty in the cinema,"[110] and Struss and Rosher were invited to represent their field as founding members of the Academy of Motion Picture Arts and Sciences. At the organization dinner for the Academy, Struss listened as Fred Niblo (his director in *Ben-Hur*) related how the idea for the Academy had sprung from a dinner conversation about the past war and a general feeling that wars were caused by a lack of understanding. Struss' first employer in Hollywood, Cecil B. De Mille, spoke compellingly about the importance of the film business. "The world is more influenced by the little group in this room tonight than by any other power in the world. . . . Our ideals have got to be high." Responding to Niblo's comments about war, De Mille described the effect of their medium, "It is the greatest unifier in the world . . . It is our job to support the idea of unity and

Figure 30. Karl Struss, *City of Dreams, 1925*, modern print from original glass plate negative, Amon Carter Museum

problems. Struss was brought into the project because of his ability with innovative and dramatic compositions, and it is a measure of his success in his new career that the studio turned to him. Passing through New York to film on location in Europe, he was able to visit his family and to see Paul Anderson in New Jersey. Aboard ship in New York harbor, he photographed the sky-

Figure 31. Kenneth Alexander, *Karl Struss with his Cinematography Oscar for the Film* **Sunrise**, c. 1929, toned gelatin silver print, Amon Carter Museum

intelligently and efficiently communicate it to the world."[111]

Himself a victim of wartime misunderstanding and unable to use his skills to improve the situation, Struss probably was inspired by this speech. He realized that motion picture photography offered him a greater opportunity to influence the world than pictorial photography ever could. A few months later, at the first Academy Awards ceremony, Struss and Rosher shared the first award for cinematography—and Struss, at the relatively young age of forty-two, was recognized as a respected artist in his new field (fig. 31). As Richard Koszarski discusses in detail in his essay, in the the long career that followed, Struss continued to make contributions to image-making in photography, films, and eventually television. By the time he retired in 1970, he had photographed over one hundred films, two television series, and numerous commercials. He remained in demand into his eighties because of his commitment to the concept of pictorial beauty—a concept first developed with a still camera. A writer for *American Cinematographer* may have best summed up his contribution in a 1935 profile: Struss turned everything he worked on into "a glowing epistle of life and beauty."[112]

NOTES

The Amon Carter Museum holds the Karl Struss Collection of photographs, negatives, and miscellaneous papers and equipment, acquired from the Karl Struss Estate. In addition, photocopies of materials in sources listed below can be available to researchers. The following individuals have graciously allowed access to their collections of Struss-related papers:

Craig Struss Rhea, Karl Struss' grandson, has a large collection of letters between Karl and his family and Paul Anderson, written from September 1917, when Struss entered the U. S. Army, until shortly after he married Ethel Wall. Unless noted otherwise, Struss Family Papers are in the possession of Craig Struss Rhea, Los Angeles, California

Stephen White, Los Angeles, California, was Struss' photography dealer from 1976 until his death, then represented Struss' heirs until he closed his gallery in 1991. He has a large collection of exhibition catalogues, Struss' scrapbook, interviews with Struss, and other miscellaneous papers. Researchers need White's permission for access to this material.

John and Susan Edwards Harvith, Syracuse, New York, curated and authored *Karl Struss: Man with a Camera* and have a large amount of research material accumulated while working with Struss on these projects.

Other collections relating to Struss are:

Alfred Stieglitz Collection, Beinecke Library, Yale University, New Haven, Connecticut

Clarence White Collection, The Art Museum, Princeton University, Princeton, New Jersey

Cecil B. De Mille Collection, Harold B. Lee Library, Brigham Young University, Provo, Utah

Margaret Herrick Library, Academy of Motion Picture Arts and Sciences, Los Angeles, California

National Archives, Washington, D.C., U. S. Army Military Intelligence file on Struss. Containing all interdepartmental communication and correspondence with Struss and other parties regarding his case and synopses by both investigators and Struss, this file was helpful in reconstructing the events.

1. Unless otherwise noted, the biographical information on Karl Struss comes from taped interview sessions with John and Susan Edwards Harvith from December 3, 1974, through September 16, 1976, and with Stephen White on November 12 and 26, 1976.

2. Karl Struss' siblings, Lilian (1876-1965), Elsa (1878-1959), Harry (1880-?), Hilda (1882-1927), and William (1883-1906), were all born in a house on 15th Street near Eighth Avenue. Henry Struss designed and built the house at 126 W. 73rd Street. In later interviews, Karl fondly remembered the atypical design with bay windows on each of three floors, which was quite elegant and modern for its day. He always mentioned this house with evident pride and with admiration for his father as the architect.

3. Karl's mother may have spoken German at home, and in her letters to Karl, she frequently addressed him as Karlchen. However, the children went to public schools, and although they may have spoken some German to their mother, their status in New York society influenced them to drop this habit. Remaining letters from Karl to his mother, written when he was only fourteen years old, include phrases in French, but none in German.

4. The Strusses moved to 53 Convent Avenue, near 143rd Street; the area, known as Hamilton Heights, was named after the Alexander Hamilton homestead. At the time, this was almost a country setting, and Karl Struss remembered playing around the "thirteen trees" supposedly planted by Hamilton. In 1898, the Strusses purchased a house at 729 St. Nicholas Street, at 146th Street near Convent Avenue. Karl lived there with his family until entering the service in 1917, and this house remained the family home until well after Henry Struss died in 1940. The house on 73rd Street was torn down with the entire block to make room for a high-rise.

5. Karl expressed regret that his father never received "credit for his part in the development of the automobile" (Karl Struss to [editor], 1952, in Amon Carter Museum). The patented Struss automobile, produced in 1897, is listed in several histories of early American automobiles: Automobile Manufacturers Association, Inc., *Automobiles of America* (Detroit: Wayne State University Press, 1962), p. 100, and Editors of Automobile Quarterly, *The American Car Since 1775: The Most Complete Survey of the American Automobile Ever Published* (New York: L. Scott Bailey, 1971).

6. Struss to [editor], 1952, Amon Carter Museum.

7. Rochester Optical Company, *The Premo Camera* (1898), p. 65.

8. John Dorr, interviewer, *Recollections of Karl Struss: An Oral History of the Motion Picture in America* (Los Angeles: The Regents of the University of California, 1969), p. 5.

9. Dorr interview, p. 6.

10. *Los Angeles Times*, January 9, 1977.

11. In September 1908, *American Photography*, a journal devoted to the amateur photographer, included a notice on p. 526 that "The success of the photographic instruction course conducted by Mr. Clarence P. White at Columbia University, N.Y. last winter, was so great that the university authorities have engaged him to conduct two courses this year."

12. "Day and Evening Courses in Art Photography, School of Industrial Arts, Teachers College, Columbia University, 1911," in Amon Carter Museum.

13. "Have You an Artistic Impulse? If You Can't Paint Be a Photographer," *New York Evening Sun*, January 16, 1917.

14. Struss' Christmas gift list of 1911 lists photographs as gifts for Willa Collison, Amy Whittemore, Eleanor Pitman Smith, Mrs. Chas Byron Bostwick (Francesca), and others. He went on photography excursions to Metuchen, New Jersey (with Amy Whittemore and Grace Halsey) and to Tarrytown, New York (with Amy Whittemore and Eleanor Pitman Smith, who lived in Tarrytown). In 1922, when Struss was living in Los Angeles and Eleanor Smith in San Diego, Amy Whittemore visited with both of them.

15. *Catalogue, International Exhibition Pictorial Photography, February 2-20, 1909, National Arts Club, New York City*.

16. Struss also visited his family at the cottage at Arverne that summer, making many photographs.

17. This summary of Struss' trip to Europe is taken from Harvith interviews, inspection of photographic negatives of the trip, and from the Military Intelligence officer's synopsis of his interview with Judge James Drew [1st Lt. Grayson

Metz, Military Intelligence, Pittsburgh, to Director of Military Intelligence, December 19, 1918].

18. Willa P. Collison may have been one of the friends he visited. For Christmas 1910, Struss constructed an album of Nova Scotia views for a Willa Collison. Negatives in the Amon Carter Museum collection show Karl with Hilda, one older woman approximately Hilda's age, and a younger girl, perhaps Willa.

19. William Innes Homer, *Alfred Stieglitz and the American Avant-Garde* (Boston: New York Graphic Society, 1983), p. 145.

20. Harvith interview, September 1, 1975.

21. It is unknown whether Struss went up for the opening or after, but the fact that he met no other photographers implies that he was not there for the opening.

22. Augustus Thibaudeau to Alfred Stieglitz, November 7, 1910, in Alfred Stieglitz Papers, Beinecke Library, Yale University.

23. Albright-Knox Museum Archives, Clippings scrapbook, December 31, 1910. Neither the buyer's name nor the titles of the photographs purchased are mentioned.

24. Christmas list, 1911, Struss Family Papers.

25. Karl Struss to Alfred Stieglitz, September 17, 1912, in Alfred Stieglitz Papers, Beinecke Library, Yale University.

26. Karl Struss, "The Field of Modern Photography," in *Art and Industry in Education* (New York: Arts and Crafts Club, Teachers College, Columbia University, 1913), p. 37.

27. An advertisement in the December 1913 issue of *Platinum Print* listed Struss' address at his parents' home and said he was doing "illustrations for magazines, books, poems, advertising and calendars." Other than his *Saturday Magazine* covers, he actually did not publish much illustration work until the following year.

28. Charles Barnard, the original associate editor, left in early 1914 to return to Montreal.

29. D[onald]. B. MacMillan, Crocker Land Expedition, under the auspices of the American Museum of Natural

History and the American Geographical Society, March 14, 1913, Stephen White Papers.

30. Karl Struss to Alfred Stieglitz, June 13, 1912, in Alfred Stieglitz Papers, Beinecke Library, Yale University.

31. Alfred Stieglitz to Karl Struss, June 14, 1912, in Alfred Stieglitz Papers, Beinecke Library, Yale University.

32. John Wood, *The Art of the Autochrome: The Birth of Color Photography* (Iowa City: The University of Iowa Press, 1993), pp. 10, 34.

33. Richard Butler Slawzer(?), to Karl Struss, January 24, 1914, in Stephen White Papers. This letter clearly states that Struss had contacted Mr. Slawzer, who worked with the advertising firm that handled the tourist campaign for Bermuda, and implies that it was Slawzer who had seen his *Hamilton, Bermuda—Moonlight* at the Montross Gallery in 1912. However, Struss later claimed in an interview with John and Susan Harvith that B. Hope Willard, the godson of one of the chief officers in the Bermuda government, had seen photographs he had taken on a previous trip.

34. Although Struss later discussed this event repeatedly and reproduced a photograph of himself using this camera in advertisements for his business and his lens, the Struss Collection at the Amon Carter Museum includes no negatives that could have been taken with this camera. It is likely that the negatives were turned over to his employer to produce the guidebook. The photographs finally used in the tourist guidebook appear to have been taken with several cameras, including some with his 4x5-inch view camera.

35. In an advertisement in *Platinum Print* (November 1914), Struss stated he had been making his pictorial lens for artists for a while and now, certain that there was a value in them, was marketing them (*Platinum Print* 2, no. 1, p. 14). At the New York Exposition, held at the Grand Central Palace in March 1915, manufacturers of photographic products set up booths displaying their products and Struss was there promoting his lenses. He filed a patent application in June 1915, but similarities between individual elements in his invention and others would have required him to appear personally in Washington, D.C., in order to pursue his application. In October 1916, rather than file for an extension, he dropped his efforts. See Briesen & Knauth [& Schrenk] to Karl Struss, March 6, 1915, to October 27, 1916, Stephen White Papers.

36. Although Struss and Anderson had stationery made with the heading Struss-Anderson Laboratories, they were partners only in their marketing of Kalogen and never shared the studio any other way. When Struss entered the army during World War I, Anderson took over his studio. Harvith interview, August 31, 1975.

37. Mergenthaler Linotype Co. exhibition brochure, October 5-8, 1914, Amon Carter Museum.

38. Quoted in Frederick C. Luebcke, *Bonds of Loyalty: German-Americans and World War I* (DeKalb, Illinois: Northern Illinois University Press, 1974), p. 86.

39. Luebcke, *Bonds of Loyalty*, pp. 119-120, 229-231.

40. Ibid., pp. 211-212, and Emerson Hough, *The Web: A Revelation of Patriotism* (Chicago: Reilly & Lee Co., 1919), p. 23. *The Web*, "the authorized history of the American Protective League," was "published by authority of the National Directors of the American Protective League, a vast, silent army organized with the approval and operated under the direction of the United States Department of Justice, Bureau of Investigation."

41. Holmes Mallory, report on Carl [*sic*] Struss, November 16, 1917, quoting statements by Clarence White and Mary Brown, Military Intelligence Files, National Archives. This is discussed in detail later in this essay.

42. Martin Mayer, *The Met: One Hundred Years of Grand Opera* (New York: Simon and Schuster and the Metropolitan Opera Guild, 1983), pp. 135-136.

43. "The Call," *Pictorial Photographers of America* [Annual Report] (New York: Pictorial Photographers of America, 1917), p. 8; "Founders Meeting," *Bulletin of the Pictorial Photographers of America* (January 1937), n.p.

44. Ibid.

45. "The Effect of the War on Photography," *American Photography* (September 1914), p. 580; "Enlist Your Lens in the U.S. Army!", *Photo-Era* (November 1917), p. 319.

46. Luebcke, *Bonds of Loyalty*, p. 257; registration certificate, Struss Family Papers.

47. "The Visit of Major Banning," *Pictorial Photographers*

of America [Annual Report] (1917), p. 24.

48. Karl Struss to Responsible Authority [then Major John M. Campbell], December 20, 1918, Military Intelligence Files, National Archives.

49. Ibid.

50. J. M. Bischoff, report to War Department, Army Intelligence, Governors Island, "In re Carl Struss (Karl Struss), German Activities," October 10, 1917. The National Archives in Washington, D.C., holds the Military Intelligence file on the Bureau's investigation into Struss' supposed pro-German feelings and activities. My thanks to Meg Hacker of the Southwest Center, National Archives, for directing me to this file.

51. Nicholas Biddle, Office of Military Intelligence, New York, to Chief, Military Intelligence Section, November 5, 1917, National Archives.

52. Holmes Mallory, report on [Karl] Struss, November 16, 1917, National Archives.

53. Ibid.

54. There is very little known about Struss' personal relationship with his accusers that might explain their motives. Clarence White's diaries apparently imply that White was unaware of these developments. Little is known of Dickson, except that he left his career in engineering for the Otis Elevator Company in 1917 to pursue photography full-time. He died in 1922.

55. The memo mentioned that the meetings were held in the studio of the photographer Peter Juley.

56. The Military Intelligence file on Struss at the National Archives includes telegram communication almost daily from December 20, 1917, until February 19, 1918, between officials in the War Department in Washington, D.C.; the Signal Corps at Langley Field, Virginia; the School of Military Aeronautics, Cornell University, Ithaca, New York; and the Disciplinary Barracks Guard at Fort Leavenworth, Kansas.

On December 20, 1917, Special Order No. 296, from the Secretary of War, specified that Struss should be transferred as a private from Langley Field to the Disciplinary Barracks Guard at Fort Leavenworth, Kansas.

Officials at Langley responded that Struss had already left for the School of Military Aeronautics at Cornell University. Officials at Cornell must not have received correct orders, for they placed Struss in confinement and then asked what to do next. They were told to hold him until orders were forwarded to them. When they finally received a copy of Special Order No. 296 on January 5, they asked for the Quartermaster to furnish transportation and sustenance for Struss and guards to accompany him to Kansas, but this request was denied. After a number of additional requests were denied, on February 1, the officials at Cornell asked if they were to keep Struss in confinement indefinitely. On February 4, officials at Fort Leavenworth communicated that Struss had never appeared for duty as Special Order No. 296 specified. At this point, direct telephone calls instructed the Cornell officials to release Struss from confinement and transfer him to Fort Leavenworth. Struss reported for duty in Kansas on February 11.

57. Paul Anderson to Karl Struss, January 7, 1918, in Struss Family Papers.

58. John Wallace Gillies, "Amateurs I Have Known — Karl Struss," *American Photography* (September 1915), p. 533.

59. All of the letters are in the Military Intelligence file on Karl Struss, National Archives.

60. Paul Anderson to Karl Struss, February 15, 1918; Judge Drew to Karl Struss, February 28, 1918; Judge Drew to Congressman Morin, February 28, 1918, in Struss Family Papers.

61. Karl Struss to Hil [Hilda Struss], February 17, 1918, in Struss Family Papers.

62. Karl Struss to Elsa [Elsa Struss], February 18, 1918, in Struss Family Papers.

63. Karl Struss to Lil [Lilian Struss], February 23, 1918, in Struss Family Papers.

64. Karl Struss memo written to add documentation to his request for a military appeal, December 20, 1918, in Struss Family Papers and in Struss' military intelligence file in the National Archives. It was Imogen (Partridge) Cunningham who told Struss that both Francis Bruguière and Sadakichi Hartmann had informed her that Struss was interned at Fort Leavenworth.

65. Karl Struss to Lil, February 23, 1918.

66. W. D. Moffat to Paul Anderson, June 24, 1918, in Stephen White Collection.

67. Anderson was incorrect about this. Arnold Genthe was born in Germany, but Alfred Stieglitz was born in New Jersey.

68. W. D. Moffat to Paul Anderson, June 24, 1918; Paul Anderson to W. D. Moffat, June 26, 1918; Karl Struss memo, December 20, 1918, in Stephen White Collection.

69. Karl Struss memo, December 20, 1918.

70. Karl Struss to Mother [Marie Struss], May 16 and 19, 1918, in Struss Family Papers.

71. Ibid.

72. Paul Anderson to Karl Struss, December 3, 1917; January 4, 1918; and January 23, 1918, all in Struss Family Papers.

73. Karl Struss to Mother, April 14, 1918; Dorr interview, p. 72.

74. Karl Struss to Mother [Marie Struss], June 2, 1918, in Struss Family Papers.

75. Ibid. In all, 400 conscientious objectors, of whom 130 were German-American Mennonites, were sentenced to prison terms ranging from ten to thirty years at Fort Leavenworth (Luebcke, *Bonds of Loyalty*, p. 259). See Winthrop D. Lane, "The Strike of 2300 Prisoners at Ft. Leavenworth, Kansas," *The Survey* (c. February 1919), and *Political Prisoners in Federal Military Prisons* (New York: National Civil Liberties Bureau, November 21, 1918), in Struss Family Papers.

76. Karl Struss to Mother, June 2, 1918.

77. Karl Struss to Mother [Marie Struss], June 29, 1918, in Struss Family Papers.

78. Karl Struss to Mother [Marie Struss], August 4, 1918, in Struss Family Papers. Unfortunately, Struss did not disclose the subject of the scenario, and the summary no longer exists.

79. Karl Struss to Major Kendall Banning (head of Photographic Division, Signal Corps), "Photography's Part in the War," August 30, 1918, in Struss Family Papers.

80. Karl Struss to Mother [Marie Struss], September 13, 1918, in Struss Family Papers.

81. Karl Struss to Major John M. Campbell, General Staff, War College Division, Washington, D.C., January 1, 1919, National Archives.

82. Col. Dunn, Acting Director of Military Intelligence, to Intelligence Office, Fort Leavenworth, January 1, 1919, in National Archives.

83. Karl Struss to Mother [Marie Struss], February 21 and 22, 1919, in Struss Family Papers.

84. Karl Struss to Mother [Marie Struss], February 26, 1919, in Struss Family Papers.

85. Karl Struss to Mother [Marie Struss], March 1, 1919, in Struss Family Papers.

86. He had also hoped to sell the Grand Canyon images to the Santa Fe Railroad to advertise the area as a tourist destination, but he discovered that government regulations prohibited them from advertising. Karl Struss to Mother [Marie Struss], March 9, 1919, in Struss Family Papers.

87. He instructed his family to take the photographs to *Scribner's, Vanity Fair, Travel Magazine, Harper's Monthly*, and even *National Geographic* in Washington, D.C., and told them whom to talk to in each office and how much they should pay. Karl Struss to Mother [Marie Struss], June 11, 1919, in Struss Family Papers.

88. Karl Struss to Mother [Marie Struss], March 3, 1919, in Struss Family Papers.

89. Karl Struss to Mother [Marie Struss], March 5, 1919, in Struss Family Papers.

90. "A Bird's-eye View of the Lasky Studio at Hollywood, California," *Photoplay* 13, no. 6 (May 1918); Jesse L. Lasky, Vice-president of Famous Players-Lasky Corporation to Cecil B. De Mille, April 18, 1918, Cecil B. De Mille Collection, Brigham Young University.

91.   John Chapman Hilder to Whom it May Concern, February 6, 1919, Stephen White Papers; *Harper's Bazaar* (December 1916 and January 1917).

92.   Karl Struss to Mother [Marie Struss], March 17, 1919, in Struss Family Papers.

93.   Karl Struss to Mother [Marie Struss], March 22 and May 4, 1919, in Struss Family Papers.

94.   Cecil B. De Mille to Elek John Ludvigh, Legal Department of Famous Players-Lasky Studios, May 9, 1918, in De Mille Collection, Brigham Young University.

95.   Karl Struss to Mother [Marie Struss], April 1, 1919, and O. L. Griffith, Hess-Ives Corporation, to Karl Struss, c. 1919, in Struss Family Papers.

96.   Karl Struss to Mother [Marie Struss], October 5, 1919, in Struss Family Papers.

97.   Karl Struss to Mother [Marie Struss], March 14, 1919, in Struss Family Papers.

98.   Karl Struss to Mother [Marie Struss], April 5 and 22, 1919, in Struss Family Papers.

99.   On the twentieth anniversary of the Pictorial Photographers of America, the society held a founders dinner in New York City. Unable to attend, Karl Struss sent a telegram to Ira Martin, PPA president. He congratulated the members and said, "I am happy to have been able to contribute in a small way to its success." As evidence of the fond regard now felt for Struss, the PPA made the entire telegram the cover of their *Bulletin* for January 1937, under the heading "Anniversary Greeting by Western Union."

100.   Stephen White interview with Ethel Struss, November 12, 1976, Stephen White Collection.

101.   Karl Struss to Mother, February 15, 1920, and Karl Struss to Secretary of War Newton D. Baker, February 15, 1920, in Struss Family Papers.

102.   Brigadier General M. Churchill, Director of Military Intelligence, to Military Intelligence, Fort Leavenworth, April 12, 1919, National Archives.

103.   Secretary of War Baker, March 26, 1920, National Archives.

104.   Struss' photograph of *The Faith Healer* (see p. 148) is extremely soft-focus, only giving a sense of the crowd illuminated by the ray of light. He exhibited the image frequently for pictorial salons.

105.   Karl Struss, *The Pictorialist* (February 23, 1924). He was hired by Thomas Ince to make pictorial stills with an 8x10-inch camera for *Barbara Frietchie*.

106.   Karl Struss to Mother [Marie Struss], December 14, 1920, in Struss Family Papers.

107.   Karl Struss to Mother [Marie Struss], October 26, November 3, and November 24, 1919, in Struss Family Papers.

108.   Karl Struss to Mortimer, July 25, 1921, in Stephen White Collection.

109.   Cecil B. De Mille "To Whom it May Concern," November 22, 1921, in Cecil B. De Mille Collection, Brigham Young University.

110.   "Karl Struss, Co-Winner of First Lensing Oscar, Dies," *Variety*, December 18, 1981.

111.   Speeches at Academy Organization, May 11, 1927. Struss was seated at table 46.

112.   James L. Fritz, "Struss' Photography Luxurious," *American Cinematographer* (April 1935), p. 52.

PORTFOLIO I
EARLY WORK

Karl Struss' most prolific period of making photographs was from 1909 to 1917. When he first began studying with Clarence White in 1908, most photographers still subscribed to the soft-focus, moody aesthetic of pictorialism, the photographic movement that advocated acceptance of photography as a fine art. By the time Struss entered the Army in 1917, pictorialism had begun to decline, and the tenets of modernism were influencing photography as well as the other fine arts. Struss was a transitional figure between the two styles, refining his compositions, printing techniques, and subject matter—which ranged from portraits to pastoral landscapes to urban street scenes and architectural studies—while retaining a common stylistic quality of attention to composition and mood.

Until 1914 Struss worked six days a week in his father's factory, and his opportunities to photograph were fairly limited. At home he experimented with soft natural light while making portrait studies of family members and friends, but works like *Amy Whittemore at Window* and *Lilian Struss—Study—N.Y.C.* frequently function more as studies of mood and lighting than as

identifiable portraits of individuals. On Sundays and during the summer, when he accompanied his family to vacation spots outside of the city, he was able to concentrate on honing his technical and pictorial skills. Arverne, on the south shore of Long Island, was the family's favored vacation spot and provided Struss with basic compositional elements of sand, water's edge, and piers. *Arverne, L.I. Fisherman* and *Silhouette Row Boats—Moonlight—Arverne* illustrate his affection for photographing in low light to obliterate details of the scene and let the basic outline of his subjects construct the image. This compositional technique also displays Struss' understanding of the way to create drama and mystery in a scene, as in the dreamlike, shimmering qualities of *Reflections, Moonlight, Arverne.*

Struss' summer vacation to Europe in 1909, following his initial year of study with Clarence White, resulted in his first substantial body of work. Several of these images (like *Landing Place, Villa Carlotta*) are bucolic and inspired by early pictorialists in the Photo-Secession, especially White and Alvin Langdon Coburn. Yet in other works Struss began to display more originality. The careful composition of *Balcony, Sorrento* directs the viewer's attention to the cliffs in the distance and the sumptuous details of the tile floor and balcony railing in the foreground, yet displays a playful mood and an almost snapshot quality by capturing the tourists in a moment of frivolity. With *Meissen Rooftops,* Struss experimented with a vantage point that flattened space and concentrated on the geometric arrangement of angles. This body of work made Struss' reputation as a worker "with a vision of his own," as Alfred Stieglitz wrote in his introduction to the portfolio of Struss' images published in *Camera Work* in 1912. These images of Europe remained favorites of critics and of Struss himself, and he continued to include them in exhibitions throughout his life.

Struss' true forte, however, was in his ability to translate the jumbled experience of an ever-changing New York into challenging compositions that show the city's patterns and energy. His images repeatedly concentrate on the skyline, architecture, new construction, transportation arteries and street traffic, and icons of tourism like the Brooklyn Bridge to symbolize New York's vitality. Taken together, his images document the city as a living entity, constantly transforming itself as it moves into the future. His skyline images show the instantly recognizable body of the city, while bridges become arms outstretched, welcoming visitors and commuters. Images such as *Horse-drawn Rig beneath El. N.Y.C.* and *Station on Hudson, N.Y.C.* illustrate how the railroads course through all parts of the city, like the lifeblood that supports the body. One of his most dynamic images, *Pennsylvania Station, New York*, focuses on the central hub, the heart of the city. The cavernous station becomes cathedral-like, and the glowing light of the sun's rays stretches across the marble walls and reaches down towards figures hurrying to their destinations. In this document of the city as a living being, human figures are merely individual cells within the whole. Photographs of workers (*Two Men, Two Crates on Dock*; *Steel Workers*; and *Ice Delivery, East Side*) show figures joining their efforts, struggling together as one to keep the city functioning and growing.

Throughout this period, Struss perfected his tools of image-making, adding elements of irony, abstraction, and mystery to his repertoire. In *Man's Construction at Docks, N.Y.C.*, he framed the skyline of Manhattan within the structures in the foreground, suggesting the possibility that one could lose sight of the city behind the structures of technology and industry. *Arrival of Adm. Dewey* and *The Open Window—First Ave. and 36th St.* illustrate his attention to framing and to choosing dynamic vantage points to

produce constructivist-style abstractions. The celebratory parade for Admiral Dewey becomes a quiltlike pattern of shapes and lines as the figures march in formation on the street below, while *The Open Window* uses a frame within a frame both to draw attention to the geometric patterns of the bricks and windows and to suggest the small dramas played out daily wherever one looks in the city. Nighttime images illustrate that the city quiets yet never completely sleeps, still pulsing with points of electricity that suggest the reenergizing process. These nighttime images challenged Struss' print-making skills, pushing him to create shadow areas that are not empty space but become areas of rich black filled with detail. In *Manhattan at Dusk* (also titled *Fifth Ave. Twilight*) the street and sidewalk traffic becomes apparent as one's eyes adjust to the darkness, and the viewer is seductively pulled into the scene to discover the mysteries in the shadows.

During his time in New York, Struss pushed the photographic medium as far as he could. Aware that fine print-making could vary the mood communicated by an image, he frequently made several versions of the same image in different processes, even assigning separate titles to the different versions to emphasize the unique effect or emotion created by a specific print. In addition, publishers who printed Struss' images as illustrations frequently assigned their own titles to fit the particular story being told; thus *Pennsylvania Station, New York* was once published with the caption "Return of the Native." Struss expected his images to function as metaphors and illustrations for a number of purposes, so he frequently titled his images only with a brief descriptive phrase like *Two Men, Two Crates on Dock*. In the following portfolio, Struss' own descriptive titles are accompanied by variant titles under which the works were exhibited, where such information is known.

Portrait of Clarence White, 1912, platinum print,
The Art Museum, Princeton University. The Clarence
H. White Collection, assembled and organized by
Professor Clarence H. White Jr., and given in memory
of Lewis F. White, Dr. Maynard P. White Sr., and
Professor Clarence H. White Jr., the sons of Clarence
H. White Sr., and Jane Felix White

TOP
Lilian Struss—Study—
N.Y.C., 1911, platinum print,
Amon Carter Museum

BOTTOM
Amy Whittemore at Window,
1911, platinum print,
Amon Carter Museum

*Landing Place, Villa
Carlotta,* 1909, hand-coated
multiple platinum print,
Amon Carter Museum

Balcony, Sorrento, 1909,
platinum print, Amon
Carter Museum

*Meissen Rooftops [Over the Housetops,
Meissen]*, 1909, platinum print,
Amon Carter Museum

TOP
Meissen from the Albrechteburg, 1909, platinum print, Amon Carter Museum

BOTTOM
On Lake Como, 1909, platinum print, Amon Carter Museum

*Colby Hill, Salem,
Massachusetts*, c. 1912-13,
platinum print, Amon
Carter Museum

Windswept, Nova Scotia,
1911, hand-coated multiple
platinum print, Amon
Carter Museum

Sunset, Simplon Pass, 1909,
hand-coated multiple
platinum print, Amon
Carter Museum

Reflections, Moonlight,
Arverne, 1910, platinum print,
Amon Carter Museum

TOP
Arverne, L.I. Fisherman,
1909, platinum print, Amon
Carter Museum

BOTTOM
Silhouette Row Boats—
Moonlight—Arverne, 1910,
platinum print, Amon
Carter Museum

Hamilton, Bermuda—
Moonlight, 1912, platinum
print, Collection of the
Grandchildren of Karl Struss

Pennsylvania Station, New York, 1911, platinum print, Amon Carter Museum

*The Open Window—First Ave.
and 36th St.,* c. 1910-11,
platinum print, Amon
Carter Museum

TOP
Cold and Misty, NYC,
c. 1911-12, platinum print,
Amon Carter Museum

BOTTOM
Arrival of Adm. Dewey,
1909, platinum print, Amon
Carter Museum

Madison Ave., N.Y.C., 1912,
platinum print, Amon
Carter Museum

TOP
*Eastside, New York
[Chimneys, Consolidated
Edison, New York]*, 1912,
platinum print, Amon
Carter Museum

BOTTOM
*Horse-drawn Rig Beneath El.
N.Y.C.*, 1911, platinum
print, Amon Carter
Museum

Man's Construction at Docks,
N.Y.C., 1909, platinum print,
Amon Carter Museum

TOP
Two Men, Two Crates on Dock, N.Y.C., c. 1911-13, platinum print, Amon Carter Museum

BOTTOM
Steel Workers, Fifth Avenue Toward "291," 1911, platinum print, Collection of John and Susan Edwards Harvith

Ice Delivery, East Side, N.Y.,
1911, platinum print, Marjorie
and Leonard Vernon Collection

TOP
Back of Public Library,
1912, platinum print, Amon
Carter Museum

BOTTOM
Station on Hudson, N.Y.C.,
1911, platinum print, Amon
Carter Museum

*Lower New York, Vanderbilt
Hotel at Night*, 1912,
platinum print, Amon
Carter Museum

*Brooklyn Bridge from Ferry
Slip, Late Afternoon*, 1912,
platinum print, Amon
Carter Museum

*Vanishing Point II: Brooklyn
Bridge from New York Side*,
1912, platinum print, Amon
Carter Museum

*Claremont Inn, Riverside
Drive*, 1915, platinum print,
Metropolitan Museum of Art,
Warner Communications Inc.
Purchase Fund, 1977

*Manhattan at Dusk [Fifth
Ave., Twilight]*, c. 1914-15,
platinum print, Amon
Carter Museum

Lower N.Y., West Side,
1911, platinum print,
Marjorie and Leonard
Vernon Collection

*New York at Night—City Lights
from the Metropolitan Tower,
South,* 1916, gelatin silver print,
Collection of John and Susan
Edwards Harvith

Figure 32. Karl Struss, *Brooklyn Bridge, Nocturne*, c. 1912-13, palladium print, Amon Carter Museum

KARL STRUSS' NEW YORK

Bonnie Yochelson

"In Mr. Struss we present one of the younger photographers whose work we have watched with interest for some years. He first attracted public attention in the Open Section of the Albright Gallery Exhibition in Buffalo, in November 1910, where his prints marked him as possessing a vision of his own."[1] With this gracious introduction, Alfred Stieglitz presented eight photogravures by Karl Struss to readers of the April 1912 issue of *Camera Work*. The Buffalo exhibition, seen then and now as the crowning (albeit controversial) achievement of American pictorial photography, had included twelve Struss prints— an entire wall devoted to a novice unknown outside New York circles. And at the time of the 1912 *Camera Work* publication, Struss was named a member—as it turned out, the last member—of the Photo-Secession, pictorial photography's inner circle. Such enthusiastic support from Alfred Stieglitz, leader of the Photo-Secession, organizer of the Buffalo exhibition, and publisher of *Camera Work*, was nothing short of extraordinary. It was especially so since Struss commanded Stieglitz's attention at a time when the latter's interest in photography was waning and when pictorial photography was succumbing to repetitious formulas.

What was Struss' accomplishment that earned him the respect and support of photography's leading proponent? And why, given this recognition, is Struss so little known today?[2] The short answer to these questions can be found not in New York but in Hollywood: after World War I, Struss abandoned his promising start as a photographer and built such a distinguished career as a cinematographer that it eclipsed his earlier accomplishments. There is a longer, more complex answer as well, one that illuminates several obstacles to understanding Struss' importance.

One of the obstacles is that Struss' work defies today's accepted labels; neither purely pictorialist nor purely modernist, his photographs inhabit the netherworld of the "transitional." Struss retained several key elements of pictorialist style: soft focus, subtle tonal effects, and a preference for platinum paper. He quickly mastered pictorial photography's repertoire of pastoral subjects, but he also took to the streets of New York; in 1911 he was creating works as dynamic and unsettling in style and subject as those by his friends Alvin Langdon Coburn and the painter Max Weber. Coburn and Paul Strand hold places of honor in the development of American modernist photography, but Struss, by contrast, has been included only tentatively in discussions of photographic modernism. He never embraced modernist rhetoric, but many of his photographs were as radical as those of his more celebrated colleagues.

A second obstacle to understanding the scope of Struss' accomplishment is that his New York subjects have never been thoroughly identified and analyzed; "New York, c. 1911" is an all-too-common title for Struss' work. Dating his works within the years 1909 and 1916 remains highly problematic,[3] but a thorough review of the over four hundred negatives of his New York subjects in the Amon Carter Museum collection has yielded a clear Struss itinerary. Like many artists of his generation, Struss was enthralled with New York's turn-of-the-century building boom, in which new bridges, train terminals, subways, and skyscrapers transformed it into the archetypal modern city. His photographic portrait of New York would remain the most comprehensive until the work of Berenice Abbott in the 1930s.

A third hindrance not only to our understanding of Struss but very likely to his own development was the strife within pictorial circles during his most creative years. From 1908 to 1912, Struss studied with Clarence White at Columbia Teachers' College, seriously pursuing photography while working ten hours a day in his

father's bonnet wire factory. Stieglitz embraced Struss' photography at precisely the time when his leadership was challenged by White, and Struss had to choose between opposing camps. Although he chose White, Struss managed to maintain a relationship with Stieglitz, but the bitterness between his two mentors could not have helped his career. Nor has it helped his reputation with later generations, who have preferred Stieglitz's artistic judgments to White's.

A final obstacle to fully understanding Struss' contribution is his transition in 1914 into commercial photography, when he took over White's studio to specialize in the new field of photographic magazine illustration. By the fall of 1917, when he entered the army, Struss had established a solid clientele not only with product advertisers but with *Vogue*, *Vanity Fair*, *Harper's Bazar* (now *Bazaar*), and the Metropolitan Opera. He also had published a portfolio of artistic nude photographs and experimented (unsuccessfully) with the Hess-Ives color process. Struss abandoned this career after the war, leaving his potential unfulfilled, but his example was not lost upon a younger generation of White students, including Paul Outerbridge, Anton Bruehl, Margaret Bourke-White, and Ralph Steiner, who became leaders in magazine photography in the years after 1925. The importance of Struss' commercial years as a transition to his Hollywood career also should not be overlooked. His mastery of studio practice and his ability to tailor his artistic ideas to his clients' demands provided a practical foundation for his shift to another medium.

FROM THEORY TO PRACTICE

From 1908 to 1912, Struss took evening classes with Clarence White at Columbia University's Teachers College. White offered New York's only course in art photography, first at Columbia and The Brooklyn Institute of Arts and Sciences and then at his own School of Photography, which he opened in 1914. Teachers College was conveniently located near Struss' upper Manhattan home,[4] and White's field trips to Riverside Park were undoubtedly a pleasurable respite after Struss' factory workday.

White had been hired in 1907 by Arthur Wesley Dow, chairman of the Teachers College art department and author of the 1899 text *Composition*, which had revolutionized art education and was a classic in its field. Dow's design principles and exercises, derived from the study of French Impressionism, the Nabis, Whistler, and Japanese prints, were meant to free students from academic practice and to teach them the expressive potential of abstract composition. He analyzed works of art in terms of design principles, such as opposition, repetition, and symmetry, and he dissected composition into the component parts of line, *notan* (light and shade), and color. A proponent of the European arts and crafts movement, Dow aimed to elevate the applied arts, including photography, which he believed were subject to the same principles as painting and sculpture.[5]

Although Struss never took Dow's art appreciation course at Teachers College, he received a large dose of Dow's ideas through White, who taught his students the rudiments of photographic technique and turn-of-the-century symbolist aesthetics. When asked in a 1975 interview what he learned from White, Struss replied, "An interest in pictures, in space filling, that's the chief thing." He continued: "White wasn't a great technician. He was a little farmer boy from Ohio, and I don't know where he learned his photography, but he had a great sense of composition and space filling."[6]

Consistent with Dow's and White's teaching, Struss applied the same compositional principles to all arts. He remarked, "Composition is the same in any form of picture-making, whether it's oil painting . . . wood engraving or . . . etching." Accordingly, he regularly visited the art galleries which lined Fifth Avenue between 23rd and 59th Streets. Years later he recalled: "If composition means something, you're not imitating anybody, you're filling your space. . . . That's why I went around to art galleries to look to see what these people were doing, what they considered good art. I'm not talking about color at all, just the interest of the picture."[7]

Although Struss used the terms composition and "space filling" interchangeably, "space filling" was coined by neither Dow nor White but by the painter Max Weber. The relationship between Struss and Weber is significant in the photographer's aesthetic development. Weber, who had studied with Dow at the Pratt Institute and spent the years 1905–09 in Paris, returned to New York as one of the few American artists with direct knowledge of the art of Cézanne, Matisse, and Picasso. Stieglitz embraced Weber's work in 1910, showing his paintings at 291 and publishing his art criticism in *Camera Work*. Increasingly involved with photography, Weber helped hang the 1910 Buffalo exhibition and that same year lectured on photography to White's Teachers College students, Struss among them. After breaking with Stieglitz in 1911, Weber drew closer to photographers White and Coburn. In 1912, Weber and Coburn worked together, experimenting in their respective mediums with cubist depictions of New York City; with Coburn's help, Weber published his *Cubist Poems* in 1914. Weber taught art appreciation at White's summer school in Maine and after 1914 at his School of Photography; in 1916, a compilation of Weber's lectures was published as *Essays on Art*. He held his teaching position until 1918, when he was replaced by Charles J. Martin, a Dow protégé.[8]

Weber's phrase "space filling" derives from an essay he published in the second issue of

Platinum Print, a journal on pictorial photography that White and his colleagues began producing after Stieglitz's interests turned elsewhere.[9] Weber's message to art photographers was that 1) "Photography is flat space art, as is drawing, painting or printing. The page or the canvas is empty, but pregnant with birth as is space, waiting for the touch of the inspired mind"; 2) "The photographer's art lies supremely in his choice or disposition of visible objects, as prompted and guided by his intellect and his taste"; and 3) "The artist in photography . . . ha[s] equal access to enjoy, to study and to assimilate some unfailing principles of plastic beauty and truth in objects found in the best museums." In language more abstract and grandiose than Dow's, Weber reiterated his first teacher's precepts: that photography is a two-dimensional art relying on the selection rather than the creation of forms but sharing fundamental principles of composition with the great works of art of the past.

Struss and Weber traveled in the same artistic circles, and Struss' close association with Stieglitz from 1910 to 1912 coincided with Weber's. Both young men were intimately involved in White's efforts between 1912 and 1916 to replace the Photo-Secession with a new support system for pictorial photographers: the Clarence H. White School of Photography, *Platinum Print*, and the Pictorial Photographers of America. A photogravure of Struss' *Earl Hall, Columbia University, Night* (see fig. 16) was inserted and offered for sale (for twenty-five cents) in the same issue of *Platinum Print* that included Weber's "Filling of Space" essay, and with the next issue, Struss became associate editor of the journal.

Struss' 1914 portrait of Weber establishes a more than casual relationship between the two artists.[10] Sitting at a table reviewing a large pile of Struss prints, Weber examines (and tilts toward the viewer) *The Span at Twilight* (also called *Brooklyn Bridge, Nocturne*), a 1912 photograph of the Brooklyn Bridge (fig. 32). Propped up on the table facing the viewer is one of Weber's paintings, a Cézannesque still life of vases and fruit. Behind the table, a dimly lit hutch displays plates, bowls, and glinting pewter objects, another "still life" filling the middle distance; in the background at right, over Weber's head, is a framed portrait photograph. An homage to both men's art, the portrait shows Weber as both painter and critic (fig. 33).

The portrait provides ample evidence that Weber and Struss had a mutually supportive artistic friendship at least between 1912 and 1914; the relationship may have begun as early as 1910, when both were close to Stieglitz.[11] That Struss retained Weber's phrase "space filling" as the cornerstone of his lifelong aesthetic beliefs suggests that the two men actively discussed art theory during the most productive, experimental period of Struss' photographic career.

Struss' conflation of Dow's "composition" with Weber's "space filling" does not indicate semantic carelessness on Struss' part but the flexibility of his aesthetic thinking. Like White, Struss perceived no gulf between the older ideas of Dow and the newer ideas emanating from Paris. Younger and less formed than White, Struss entered new aesthetic territory with more assurance and success than his mentor.

With his theoretical premises set in the 1910s, Struss was never moved to revise them. He was, by contrast, a passionate technical experimenter, always striving for better ways to reach his aesthetic goals. As early as 1909, he developed a lens, marketed in 1915 as the Struss Pictorial Lens, that facilitated his compositional objectives. Most cameras were equipped with a lens whose focal length equaled the diagonal of the camera's negative; for Struss' 4 x 5-inch negatives, a standard lens had a focal length of six inches. Struss found that the images produced by this lens were too sharp-focused and too inclusive. By doubling the lens focal length to twelve inches for a 4 x 5-inch negative, Struss produced a telephoto effect, limiting the field of vision and reducing the illusion of depth. This allowed him to simplify his compositions in the viewfinder of the camera. As he explained it, "I just got the heart of that picture out."[12]

Struss also found the standard anastigmatic lens too "literal and harsh."[13] By leaving the lens uncorrected, he could produce softened contours and enhance the feeling of volume in his subjects. In an advertising brochure, he described the Pictorial Lens' effect as "a very delicate line, giving excellent modelling and an unusual quality of light, texture, depth of focus, reality and richness of tone."[14]

Simplifying compositions and softening contours with the lens itself enabled Struss to avoid cropping and soft-focus manipulations in printing and thus to contact print his negatives on platinum paper. This "straight" printing technique was favored by White, who by Struss' standards was not a "great technician"; indeed, Struss considered straight platinum printing a mere point of departure. He invented the multiple platinum process, in which a print was resensitized and re-exposed numerous times to achieve an extremely long tonal range, particularly in the shadows. It was this characteristic of Struss' work that first attracted the attention of Stieglitz, another master printer. Struss fondly recalled the story of Stieglitz wetting his finger and touching *Sunset, Simplon Pass* (see p. 70), a multiple platinum print, and remarking that he had never seen such blacks.[15]

Struss' penchant for technical experimentation provided the foundation for his relationship with Paul Lewis Anderson, another member of White's circle who in 1917 became Struss' business partner.[16] Anderson, whom White hired in 1914 to teach the technical classes at his school,

Figure 33. Karl Struss, *Max Weber [looking at Karl Struss' photographs]*, c. 1912, modern print from original glass plate negative, Amon Carter Museum

was an authority on the full range of pictorial photographic printing techniques—platinum, carbon, gum, oil, bromoil, and photogravure.[17] He also wrote technical and critical articles for several photographic journals and published two books, *Pictorial Landscape Photography* (1914) and *Pictorial Photography, Its Principles and Practice* (1917).[18] Anderson's aesthetics were more conservative than Struss', for he preferred the teachings of his mentor, Henry Rankin Poore, a landscape painter and well-published art professor, to Dow's symbolist aesthetics. Although he experimented with New York City subjects at the same time as Struss, his own best works were extremely refined but unoriginal pic-

Figure 34. Karl Struss, *Mother Struss Reflected in Mirror over Fireplace*, c. 1909-11, platinum print, Amon Carter Museum

torial landscapes and portraits.[19] Struss' interest in experimental printing and his friendship with the aesthetically old-fashioned Anderson once again demonstrates his lack of dogmatism in matters of art.[20]

In later years, Struss recalled that "[i]n the first year, White helped me a great deal, and then I went to Europe for ten weeks" in the summer of 1909.[21] The European trip marks the culmination of Struss' apprenticeship. He devised his Pictorial Lens in preparation for the trip, and in printing his European negatives, he invented the multiple platinum printing process. When he exhibited in Buffalo at the end of 1910, Struss

had mastered the pictorialist style and, as Stieglitz noted in *Camera Work*, "possess[ed] a vision of his own."

By the time he turned to pictorial photography, the movement's creative energies were spent. Pictorialists were generally well-to-do amateurs, and their subjects were drawn from their personal lives and leisure activities. Family portraits, domestic genre scenes, pastoral landscapes, and exotic vacation sites filled exhibitions and publications with increasing predictability after 1910. Despite this decline, Struss achieved distinction within the standard pictorial repertoire, drawing on such subjects to demonstrate his mastery of Dow's compositional principles and his careful study of works by White and other Photo-Secessionists. For example, the spatially complex portrait of Struss' mother reflected in a mirror over the fireplace (fig. 34) embeds the family matriarch in her domestic surroundings and shows his thorough understanding of White's renowned interiors. Spare, Japanesque compositions of water, trees, and tiny female figures in Riverside Park and Nova Scotia (see p. 69) are arrangements in the manner of Dow, while *Reflections, Moonlight, Arverne* (see p. 71) is technically brilliant, an evocative, Whistlerian study of the Struss family's Long Island vacation spot. European subjects such as *Reflections, Venice* (fig. 35) reveal his knowledge of similar works by Stieglitz and Alvin Langdon Coburn.[22]

Struss' most original photographs within pictorial norms depict architectural subjects. To commemorate the 1910 Buffalo exhibition, Struss photographed the newly built Albright Art Gallery, an austere, marble-clad, Doric revival edifice (fig. 36).[23] He intentionally ignored the building's symmetry, instead choosing oblique angles, fragmenting classical architectural members meant to be seen whole, and rendering the marble's texture. These photographs present a subjective, intimate experience of the building,

Figure 35. Karl Struss, *Reflections—Venice*, 1909, multiple gum print, Amon Carter Museum

Figure 36. Karl Struss, *Albright Art Gallery, Buffalo, New York, Colonnade*, 1910, platinum print, Amon Carter Museum

comparable to Frederick Evans' 1890s views of English Gothic cathedrals. In *Meissen Rooftops* (see p. 66), an overhead view of high-pitched, skylighted roofs abandons traditional perspective for the geometric play of forms on the picture plane. Struss' special talent for translating architecture into pictorial form became increasingly important when he tackled the more complex problem of photographing the skyscraper.

STRUSS' NEW YORK

It may be that Struss, returning to New York from Europe in 1909, saw it with new eyes; for many artists the contrast between the old cities of Europe and a rapidly changing New York proved stimulating.[24] New York was not only new, it was news, an emerging symbol of modernity. As the nation's leading commercial, financial, and manufacturing center, the city experienced unprecedented economic growth in the decades preceding World War I. The lower half of the eight-mile-long island of Manhattan was bursting at the seams, and the island's consolidation with its surrounding boroughs in 1895 set the stage for sensational changes in the city's infrastructure. The Williamsburg Bridge (1896-1903) and Manhattan Bridge (1904-09) spanned the East

River just north of the Brooklyn Bridge (1867-83). The subway system (first opened in 1904) offered commuters an underground alternative to the city's three elevated train lines. Two gigantic railroad systems burrowed under the east and west sides of Manhattan, culminating in the grandiose terminals of Pennsylvania Station (1904-10) and the Grand Central Terminal (1903-13). On the city's congested streets, motorized buses and cars competed with horse-drawn carriages, electric trolleys, and pedestrians. Most spectacular were Manhattan's skyscrapers, clustered on the southern tip of the island and crowning the intersections of Broadway and Fifth, Sixth, and Seventh Avenues at Madison, Herald, and Times Squares.[25]

Opinion on the moral and aesthetic character of the "new" New York was sharply divided, for the thrill in technological progress was blunted by the fear of the unknown. This ambivalent fascination was beautifully expressed by H. G. Wells, who toured America in 1906 to "find England's future":

> Noise and human hurry and a vastness of means and collective result, rather than any vastness of achievement, is the pervading quality of New York. The great thing is the mechanical thing, the unintentional thing which is speeding up all these people, driving them in headlong hurry this way and that, exhorting them by the voice of every car conductor to "step lively," aggregating them into shoving and elbowing masses, making them stand clinging to the straps, jerking them up elevator shafts and pouring them on to the ferry-boats. But this accidental great thing is at times a very great thing.[26]

This seemingly chaotic New York, with its architecture and rushing throngs, its underlying me-

chanical precision and disorderly appearance, became Struss' primary subject.

Between 1909 and 1916, Struss produced over four hundred negatives of New York and made exhibition prints from well over one hundred of them.[27] Arranging his New York negatives by location reveals Struss' itinerary, which conforms in large part to the tourist's. Struss was attracted to sites that were discussed in the popular press and that symbolized the city's dynamism. Like guidebooks that begin at the port of New York and move northward, he proceeded from the island's southern tip and walked along Manhattan's spine to the end of its commercial district at 59th Street, the southern edge of Central Park. He explored the harbor and photographed the ever-changing skyline from Brooklyn, from the ferries, and from the bridges. He prowled the docks, photographing the bridges and watching workers unloading cargo and ferries discharging commuters.

Walking through the congested streets from Wall Street to Newspaper Row, he contrasted new skyscrapers such as the Singer Tower (1905-08) with Victorian buildings such as the City Hall Post Office (1875) and with even older structures, such as the pre-Revolutionary St. Paul's Chapel and Federal-style City Hall. He took notice of the elevated trains at Bowling Green and Chatham Square (where the El met the Brooklyn Bridge) and the construction of the new subway in City Hall Park. And as the new Woolworth (1910-13) and Municipal Buildings (1907-14) transformed the skyline, he photographed them from every direction. At Madison Square, where Broadway and Fifth Avenue intersect at 23rd Street, Struss concentrated on the controversial Flatiron Building (1903) and the Metropolitan Tower, the world's tallest building when it was completed in 1909. On Fifth Avenue between 23rd and 42nd Streets, he explored the spectacle of elegant new storefronts, well-dressed shoppers, and a crowded thorough-fare filled with vehicles of all kinds. To convey the tumult of the street, he photographed the Avenue from the top of a bus.

Struss also focused on hubs of activity along the crosstown axes of 34th and 42nd Streets. He followed the construction, from excavation to completion, of the immense Penn Station on 34th Street between Seventh and Eighth Avenues. He captured the commotion of Herald Square (see fig. 37), where Broadway and the Sixth Avenue Elevated cross at 34th Street and where the fanciful Herald Building (1893) vied for attention with the new Macy's (1901) and a myriad of advertising billboards. At Times Square, he showed the new Times Tower (1904) soaring over the intersection of Broadway and Seventh Avenue at 42nd Street. East of Fifth Avenue at Park and 42nd Street, he observed the building of the Grand Central Terminal, photographing the soon-to-be-demolished open train yards to the north, the construction of the Beaux Arts southern facade, and the completed exterior and interior.

Struss was strongly drawn to the grand, neoclassical structures designed by French-trained architectural firms such as McKim, Mead & White.[28] His Fifth Avenue shopping scenes featured its new "white palaces," such as B. Altman's department store (1904, at 34th Street), Tiffany's (1906, at 37th Street), and the Knickerbocker Trust Company (1904, at 34th Street). He also lavished great attention on civic structures, especially the New York Public Library (1897-1911, at 42nd Street) and the two gigantic train terminals. These classical structures were intended to lend order and dignity to a city under heavy fire from its detractors for its lack of planning and its ill-proportioned "cathedrals of commerce."[29]

Struss was largely uninterested in sites north of 59th Street, which were primarily resi-

dential.[30] A notable exception, however, was his attraction to the new neogothic and neoclassical buildings in northern Manhattan and the Bronx: Columbia University on Broadway at 116th Street (1893-1913), where he began photographing with White; Audubon Terrace (1905-08) on Broadway at 155th Street; the College of the City of New York (1905) on Amsterdam Avenue and 138th Street; and the majestic amphitheater of New York University's Bronx campus (1894-1902).[31] He delighted in the "old world" architecture of these remote oases, isolated from the city's fast-paced rhythms,[32] and his relatively static and lyrical photographs show that Struss never lost interest in the less adventuresome pictorial subjects favored by White.

Struss' negatives afford the opportunity to study images that he considered failures as well as those he considered successes. When Struss found a subject to his liking, he photographed it from several points of view, sometimes in repeat visits. For example, he kept twenty-seven negatives of the New York Public Library, including overhead shots from nearby buildings to the north and south, the facade from various angles and from a bus, close-ups of the lions on the front staircase and of people leaning on the Fifth Avenue balustrade, and views at night, in the rain, and festooned with lights for a parade. By contrast, several subjects exist as single negatives with no known prints. Despite Struss' close adherence to a tourist itinerary, these "false starts" quite often include New York's most cherished landmarks. There are only three remaining negatives and one known print of Central Park, for example, although this location was popular not only with the public but with many artists, including pictorial photographers.[33] Several sites of antiquarian interest, such as the eighteenth-century Jumel Mansion in Washington Heights and the early nineteenth-century Greek Revival townhouses on Washington Square in Greenwich

Figure 37. Karl Struss, *Trolley, Horse-drawn Vehicle & El. New York City [Herald Square]*, 1911, platinum print, Amon Carter Museum

Village and on Willow Place in Brooklyn Heights, appear in single negatives for which no prints have survived. It may be that, despite their sentimental or historic value, these sites did not convey the city's dynamism sufficiently to capture Struss' pictorial imagination.

Taken as a whole, Struss' photographs of New York City comprise his most original contribution to modern photography. Although he continued to study with White through 1912, he found little guidance from White in exploring the artistic possibilities of the city's fast-changing visage. For that, Struss turned to the popular press, to painters and printmakers, and to Stieglitz and Coburn.

Struss' entire repertoire of tourist subjects was available in penny postcards—cheaply printed, often colored halftone reproductions. These tourist mementos, a relatively recent innovation, may have strengthened Struss' interest in well-known sites, but they were of little use to him compositionally. Postcards mark the culmination of what historian Peter Bacon Hales has termed "grand-style urban photography."[34] The postcard photographer, like his predecessors, favored high-angle street views—approximating an architect's elevation or bird's-eye perspective—to display an orderly vista of public buildings, transportation systems, parks, and monuments. Given the city's cramped spaces and soaring heights, this was no

Figure 38. Thaddeus Wilkerson, *Herald Square, New York*,
c. 1905, postcard, Museum of the City of New York

mean feat. The standard solution was to use a wide-angle, sharp-focus lens, find a perch in a nearby tall building, and seek a panoramic view.

Struss' rejection of this compositional strategy can be seen in a comparison of a postcard and a Struss photograph of Herald Square (figs. 37 and 38). Struss used his Pictorial Lens to compress space into a narrow and shallow field—the opposite effect of the postcard view—and sought to capture not an ideal view but the chaotic impressions of the pedestrian: trolleys and cars approaching, the owl-lined roof of the Herald Building peeking over the diagonal of the Sixth Avenue El, and a huge billboard and the Times Tower rising up in the background.

Of greater use to Struss was "the picturesque," an artistic tradition older than photography but commonly invoked by turn-of-the-century advocates of New York. From its romantic origins, "the picturesque" had evolved into the European traveler's aesthetic guide, allowing the

tourist to appreciate the unknown from a secure vantage point, "as if it were a picture." In the course of the nineteenth-century, the picturesque had absorbed many subjects and styles, from romantic sketches of ancient sites and paintings of rural peasants to mist-covered street scenes and working-class types by urban naturalist painters. The familiar conventions of art transformed the threat of the unknown into strange beauty. The picturesque point of view was that of an outsider, safe in his social station but open to new aesthetic experience.

Turn-of-the-century New York suffered a steady stream of attacks by illustrious tourists, among them expatriate Henry James and Russian socialist Maxim Gorky, who ridiculed the city as a vulgar New-World Mammon. In response, younger cultural critics sought to define New York in picturesque terms.[35] Both assaults and apologies were often written as travel guides, appearing first as magazine articles and then often collected as books, which took the reader on a vicarious journey from harbor to midtown, either reviling or savoring the city's startling sights, smells, and sounds. Censors upheld the history and decorum of Europe, while apologists pleaded with the traveler to abandon his expectations of "home" and consider New York an exotic adventure. A quintessential defense was in art critic John C. Van Dyke's *The New New York* (1909), a guide book of over 400 pages which described the city as "not classic . . . but picturesque."[36] In contrast to Henry James' condemnation of New York's skyline as "some colossal haircomb turned upward," Van Dyke likened it to the minarets of Constantinople and the walls of the Alps. He recommended the palliatives of mist, rain, snow, twilight, and electric-lit night to the jarring profiles of the new skyscrapers.[37]

Struss could hardly have missed this debate, which regularly filled the New York-based, nationally circulating magazines. Nor did he have to stray far from pictorial photography, for near the center of the "picturesque" debate was Stieglitz, who as early as 1897 published a portfolio of photogravures called *Picturesque Bits of New York and Other Studies*. Stieglitz's urban street types— ragpickers and street pavers—and his street scenes veiled in rain and snow show the European-trained photographer rendering New York in accordance with picturesque expectations.

Under Stieglitz's editorship in 1900, the Camera Club of New York's journal *Camera Notes* published "A Plea for Picturesqueness in New York," by art critic Sadakichi Hartmann. For Hartmann, the picturesque appreciation of his city meant following in the footsteps of the French impressionists[38]:

> I am well aware that much is lacking here which makes European cities so interesting and inspiring to the sightseer and artist. No monuments of past glory, no cathedrals spires of Gothic grandeur, no historic edifices. . . . [But] any person with his eyes open, and with sympathy for the time, place and conditions in which he lives, has only to take a walk or board a trolley, to find a picture worthy of depiction almost in every block he goes. . . . But who will be the first to venture on these untrodden fields and teach New Yorkers to love their own city as I have learned to love it, and to be proud of its beauties as the Parisians are of their city? . . . May he soon appear![39]

During the next several years, more and more artists heeded Hartmann's call. American impressionists and tonalists produced snowy and rainy Fifth Avenue views; the controversial Ashcan School offered keenly observed vignettes of tenement life; and Whistlerian printmakers adapted the conventions of travel illustration to the city's soaring skyscrapers. Stieglitz sought to establish his pioneer status in this trend, as attested by his prominence in the 1908 National Arts Club exhibition, which hung pictorial photographs with impressionist and Ashcan paintings.[40]

In 1910, Stieglitz produced a new series of New York photographs and published seven of them in *Camera Work* 36 (October 1911). His selection included five photographs of New York harbor, three featuring the Singer Building, then the City's tallest building; *Old and New New York*, which contrasts Fifth Avenue five-story Victorian buildings with a new skyscraper under construction; and *Excavating—New York*, which showed a steam-shovel crew preparing for a skyscraper's foundations. Although Stieglitz had depicted the skyscraper as early as 1903 with his meditative rendition of the new Flatiron Building,[41] he seems with the new series to have tried to integrate the skyscraper into a celebration of New York as a city of the future. To these seven New York images were added *The Aeroplane* and *The Dirigible*, photographs not necessarily taken in New York but reaffirming the futuristic theme. In addition, to establish his longstanding attention to what had become a fashionable subject by 1911, Stieglitz published a group of his older New York photographs, including his 1892 *The Terminal*, which shows a horse-drawn trolley at the end of its run, and his 1902 *Hand of Man*, featuring a train billowing smoke through the Grand Central yards.

Camera Work 36 included a photogravure of Picasso's analytic cubist drawing *Standing Female Nude* (1910), which Stieglitz had exhibited and purchased in 1911 and which made his own works appear old-fashioned by comparison.

Figure 39. Karl Struss, *Cables*, c. 1910-12, gum platinum print, Amon Carter Museum

The harbor scenes in particular conform to picturesque norms: the silhouette of the Singer Building emerges from clouds of steam and smoke to shimmer in the sun. *The City of Ambition*, a smoke-filled panorama of the skyline and today the most famous of the series, is remarkably derivative of picturesque travel illustration, especially the works of Joseph Pennell.[42]

Beginning in 1910, Struss regularly visited 291, where he recalled being recognized as a notable new talent: "I was interested in photography, and I would visit the gallery, and then I met him [Stieglitz] personally and all, and we had lots of talks together, and he seemed to like my work because he picked twelve of my best prints—hand-coated platinums . . . nobody in Clarence White's class had ever done anything like that."[43] Struss and Stieglitz were both photographing New York at this time, and the two men most likely shared their enthusiasm for the subject. Stieglitz provided a point of departure, however, not a model for imitation. When asked what influence Stieglitz played in his development, Struss replied: "No, there wasn't any. Any whatsoever. Just conversation, you know, to go over and see his shows and that sort of thing, because I was interested in those—progressive in that respect."[44]

Struss covered more territory in New York than did Stieglitz, but both concentrated on two of the city's most famous locations: the harbor and Madison Square. The Wall Street skyline, the port's maritime trade, and the three great bridges spanning the East River formed an unrivaled symbol of American power and wealth. Madison Square was central to fashionable New York, with elegant hotels, restaurants, and office buildings nearby. It was also a few blocks from Stieglitz's gallery, as well as other art galleries and photography studios, and was therefore a natural subject for many artists. Contemporaneous photographs reveal that Struss' work was often more compositionally challenging and playful in spirit than Stieglitz's.

Struss often relied upon the compositional device of framing a distant object with an unrelated foreground element, thus forcing the relationship of dissimilar elements and collapsing the space between them onto the picture plane. The best of these photographs function as visual puns. In *Man's Construction* of 1909 (see p. 79), the frame—industrial structures on the Brooklyn

Figure 40. Karl Struss, *Metropolitan Life Insurance Tower,* 1911, platinum print, Warren and Margot Coville Photographic Collection

docks—completely overwhelms the primary subject, the New York skyline at night. The viewer is left to decide what "man's construction" is: the unintended beauty of the dockside equipment or the glittering towers across the river.[45] In *Cables* (fig. 39), the diagonal grid of the Brooklyn Bridge's cables forms a screen over the skyline and traps the awe-inspiring vista—the same vista as in Stieglitz's *City of Ambition* (1910).[46]

Stieglitz had photographed Madison Square since the turn of the century, and Struss was certainly familiar with the older artist's many well-known images, including *Spring Showers* (1900) and *The Flatiron Building* (1903). Struss, however, found an original approach to a familiar subject. In *Metropolitan Life Insurance Tower*

Figure 41. Karl Struss, *New York [East 29th Street—Tower of Madison Square]*, n.d., modern print from original glass plate negative, Amon Carter Museum

Figure 42. Alfred Stieglitz, *Two Towers*, negative 1911, photogravure from *Camera Work* 44 (1914)

(1909), he again framed a distant subject with one nearby to comment wittily on a New York landmark. When the "campanile" of Cass Gilbert's Metropolitan Life Insurance Building was completed in 1909, it briefly held the laurels as New York's tallest skyscraper. Standing on the balustrade of B. Altman's department store, eleven blocks north on Madison Avenue, Struss framed the new clocktower, miniaturizing the latest winner in the city's publicity-driven competition (fig. 40).

A series of seven undated and unprinted exposures, taken while walking down Madison Avenue from 29th Street toward Madison Square, offers a different insight into Struss' compositional thinking.[47] In these images he compressed onto the picture plane three "towers" receding into space: a Victorian street lamp in the foreground, the Spanish-inspired tower of McKim, Mead & White's Madison Square Garden (1890)

in the middle distance, and the Metropolitan Tower in the background. The seven exposures, taken as dusk settled over the scene, show how Struss systematically experimented with the spatial relationships of the three towers on the picture plane: street lamp atop the Garden tower, atop the Metropolitan, and at various intervals between the two (fig. 41).

Stieglitz's 1911 photograph *Two Towers* is remarkably similar: the Madison Square Garden and Metropolitan towers in the background contrast with a snow-covered branch and stoop in the foreground (fig. 42). Because Struss' unprinted negatives are undated, it is impossible to establish the relationship between them and Stieglitz's print, which was exhibited at 291 in 1913 and published in *Camera Work* 44 (March 1914).[48] The comparison, however, shows that both photographers were exploring the disjointed visual experience of the modern urban street, in which

Figure 43. Karl Struss, *Passing Throng*, c. 1912, sepia-toned platinum print, Amon Carter Museum

Figure 44. Alvin Langdon Coburn, *The Knickerbocker Trust Company*, photogravure from *New York* (1910), Amon Carter Museum

huge structures looming over their neighbors appear toy-like in the distance. Both photographers also shared the pictorial predilection for the softening effects of snow or dusk. Of the two, however, Struss was more willing to sacrifice the illusion of depth, collapsing near and far space onto the picture plane in a manner foreign to Stieglitz.

Alvin Langdon Coburn, another leading pictorialist, was also more audacious than Stieglitz. Struss recalled that he and Coburn met quite often "at the Photo-Secession" and that he had seen much of Coburn's work, noting that Coburn "exhibited profusely."[49] As with Stieglitz, however, Struss was not a Coburn follower but

an equal. Because Coburn is credited with creating the first cubist-inspired photograph—a 1912 overhead view of Madison Square called *The Octopus* (see fig. 45)—Struss' relationship with him between 1910 and 1912 merits close scrutiny.

Coburn's earliest photographs of New York are masterful renditions of a picturesque, Europeanized New York. In 1905, in the *Metropolitan Magazine*, he published "Some Photographic Impressions of New York." All seven images depict famous tourist sites, but Coburn favored exotic buildings reminiscent of European architecture. Shrouding the structures in deep shadow, he transformed the "Tombs" jail into a French chateau and the Waldorf-Astoria into the Alhambra.

In 1909, on a trip to New York for an exhibition of his work at 291, Coburn produced a new group of New York negatives, and the following year, he published a portfolio of twenty New York photogravures as a pendant to his London portfolio. Again, most of the New York subjects were tourist sites—the skyline, bridges, and tallest skyscrapers—embellished with atmospheric hazes of mist, steam, and dusk. In his introduction to the New York portfolio, H. G. Wells described Coburn's achievement in picturesque terms: "Our time will go to our descendants heavily and even abundantly documented, yet still I fancy these records of atmosphere and effect will gleam, extremely welcome jewels, amidst the dust-heaps of carelessly accumulated fact with which the historian will struggle."[50] Coburn was in close contact with Stieglitz when he exposed his New York negatives, and the portfolio includes an homage to Stieglitz—a photograph of Holland House, the Fifth Avenue hotel where Stieglitz regularly dined with friends. Coburn's portfolio, which was advertised in *Camera Work*, might, in turn, have inspired Stieglitz's 1910 photographs.

Struss, who kept his copy of Coburn's New York portfolio all his life, would certainly have studied it carefully, for it appeared at the height of his interest in photographing the city. The difficulty in dating Struss' New York photographs, however, precludes establishing a clear relationship between the two bodies of work. In a few cases, Struss could have borrowed an idea directly from Coburn. *Passing Throng* (fig. 43), showing crowds of Fifth Avenue shoppers dwarfed by the gigantic Corinthian columns of the Knickerbocker Trust Company, is a near quotation of Coburn's version of the Fifth Avenue bank building (fig. 44).[51] In most cases, however, the two photographers depicted the same sites differently, as a comparison of their *Metropolitan Tower* photographs illustrates. Stieglitz, Coburn, and Struss all attempted several of the same subjects, such as *The Ferry Boat*, and their works present variations on a theme.

While these photographers were exploring the picturesque possibilities of New York in 1909–11, they also were immersed in an intensive education in modern art. Exhibitions at 291 included works by Cézanne, Picasso, Rodin, and the French-influenced American artists John Marin and Max Weber, whose penchant for theoretical debate had a noticeable effect on Stieglitz's exclusive soirees at Holland House.[52] *Camera Work* introduced a heady mixture of provocative ideas and images—post-impressionist, symbolist, cubist, and futurist—which the journal called "the modern Movement in art" and which today is termed modernism. The modernist challenge was technical and philosophical: by casting off the conventions of art-making and bourgeois social life, the artist could serve as society's avant-garde in the pursuit of authentic experience. Articles in *Camera Work* also suggest that Stieglitz encouraged speculation on photography's new role. Hartmann's "On the Possibility of New Laws of Composition" proposed that photography, because of its underdeveloped pictorial traditions, was especially suited to the new art, and Coburn, in "The Relation of Time to

Art," explained why photography was particularly suited to depicting New York City, the quintessentially modern subject.[53] It was not Stieglitz, however, who first achieved a new synthesis of modernist style and subject with the camera; it was Coburn and Struss.

The well-documented relationship of Coburn and Max Weber in 1911-12 shows without doubt that both were wrestling with cubism and modernity in their depictions of New York.[54] Struss was close to both men at this time, and although there is no written evidence that he participated in their dialogue, his photographs argue strongly for his involvement. Working side by side from the observation deck of the newly built Woolworth Building in 1912, Coburn photographed *House of a Thousand Windows* and Weber painted *New York (The Liberty Tower from the Singer [sic] Tower)*—overhead views that crush traditional perspective space and splinter the streets and buildings into clusters of cubic forms on the picture plane.[55] Coburn considered *House of a Thousand Windows* "almost as fantastic as a cubist fantasy,"[56] and a *Platinum Print* review of a 1914 exhibition called the image "Cubist Photography!"[57] In such works, Coburn and Weber gave the disorienting experience of New York's streets an equally disorienting formal structure. Unlike the picturesque photographs that softened and beautified the city's harshness and confusion, the modernist rendition amplified those very characteristics, challenging the audience to experience more intimately the city's chaotic sensations.

Coburn's 1911 essay titled "The Relation of Time to Art" argued that the photographer, who was required to act instantly in making exposures, was particularly well suited to capture the city's rushed life: "Just imagine anyone trying to paint at the corner of Thirty-fourth street, where Broadway and Sixth avenue cross!" In a revealing sentence, he inadvertently shifted from a picturesque point of view (surveying the skyline from the safe remove of a luxury ocean liner) to a distinctly modernist one:

> Now to me New York is a vision that rises out of the sea as I come up the harbor on my Atlantic liner, and which glimmers for a while in the sun for the first of my stay amidst its pinnacles; but which vanishes, but for fragmentary glimpses, as I become one of the grey creatures that crawl about like ants, at the bottom of its gloomy caverns.[58]

This experience—of catching fragmentary glimpses of skyscrapers from their "gloomy caverns"—was what Coburn strove to convey in his new photographs of New York.

Weber's *Cubist Poems* likewise describe the encounter between the modernist artist and city. In "The Eye Moment," Weber mixes disparate sensations and ideas—the high buildings, the noises of the street, the hundreds of windows, the calm of the river—trying to simulate the sensory challenge of New York.

> CUBES, cubes, cubes, cubes,
> High, low, and high, and higher, . . .
> Colours, lights, signs, whistles, bells,
>   signals, colours,
> Eyes, eyes, window eyes, eyes, eyes, . . .
> This for the eye, the eye of being,
> At the edge of the Hudson,
> Flowing timeless, endless,
> On, on, on on. . .[59]

Although the formal structure of *A House of a Thousand Windows* shows more clearly the imprint of cubism, Coburn's *The Octopus* (fig. 45) more successfully achieves the disorienting visual experience that was at the heart of modernist experimentation. Viewed from the top of the Metropolitan Tower, the walkways of Madison Square Park lose their identity, and by free association become the moving arms of a sea creature. Only the shadow of the famous tower, which covers the left half of the composition, tells the viewer that the photograph's site is familiar. Coburn's recollection of making *The Octopus* is a fascinating fusion of modernist provocation and Weber's art theory:

> At the time this picture was considered quite mad, and even today it is sometimes greeted with the question "What is it?" The answer is that it is a composition or exercise in filling a rectangular space with curves and masses; depending as it does more upon pattern than upon subject matter, this photograph was revolutionary in 1912.[60]

Two photographs, known only by the title "New York" and taken around 1911 from the top of the Metropolitan Tower, strongly suggest that Struss was thinking along similar lines. Both photographers transformed one of New York's most recognizable tourist sites into a strange urban vision.[61] In an overhead view of the northeast corner—the same corner seen in Coburn's *The Octopus*—Struss obscured the identity of the site by focusing on the park's corners, thus scattering over the picture plane fragments of park, streets, buildings, and their shadows (fig. 46). The sun's strong reflection off the edge of one building asserts the building's massive bulk, which dominates the top half of the composition and seems precariously perched over the ant-like pedestrians, toy-like cars, and open spaces of the park that fill the composition's bottom half.

A second photograph of Madison Square's southeast corner offers a clue to its famous site: the base of the Flatiron Building, outlined by its odd U-shaped sidewalk, fills the upper left corner

Figure 45. Alvin Langdon Coburn, *The Octopus*, plate from A *Portfolio of Sixteen Photographs by Alvin Langdon Coburn* (Rochester, New York: George Eastman House, 1962), plate 12

Figure 46. Karl Struss, *Overhead View, Lower Broadway, New York [Madison Square]*, c. 1911, platinum print, Collection of John and Susan Edwards Harvith

Figure 47. Karl Struss, *The Flatiron, Broadway and Fifth Avenue*, c. 1911, platinum print, Collection of John and Susan Edwards Harvith

of the picture (fig. 47). The building's huge mid-day shadow bisects the composition horizontally, isolating the traffic of Fifth Avenue at the top from that of Broadway at the bottom, while trolley tracks on 23rd Street form a pair of diagonal white lines through the Flatiron's immense shadow. The camera's angle of vision produces the illusion that the Fifth Avenue downtown traffic is headed uphill to avoid sliding off the picture's edge. Struss' Madison Square, rather than Coburn's, perhaps best illustrates the vision of "grey creatures that crawl about like ants, at the bottom of [New York's] gloomy caverns."

By looking down from such a great height, both Coburn and Struss sought to collapse traditional perspective and to lose human scale. Unrelated elements framed within their compositions replaced the functional relationships of everyday life with the formal relationships of art. In this way, both photographers succeeded in creating metaphors for the disorienting thrill of life in the modern city.[62]

The uncertain dating of Struss' two photographs renders futile any effort to establish precedence between Struss' and Coburn's photographs of Madison Square. More interesting than the competition for first place, however, is the great variety of Struss' other daring experiments in 1911-12. Coburn, for one, was extremely interested in Struss' work. In a letter from Los Angeles at the time of Struss' January 1912 exhibition at Columbia Teachers College, Coburn wrote: "I am very sorry that distance makes it impossible for me to come and see your show of New York pictures. The titles sound most alluring and I am sure from what I know of your work that the exhibition will be altogether delightful. When I come East however a few months hence, I will ask for a private viewing of them in your portfolio."[63]

The collapse of near and far space that Struss so favored was not his most innovative for-

Figure 48. Karl Struss, *The Ghost Ship*, 1912, platinum print, Marjorie and Leonard Vernon Collection

mal device. More challenging, and suggesting his understanding of cubism, was his penchant for intentionally confusing solid form with shadow, thereby throwing into question the literal subject of the photograph. In *The Ghost Ship* (fig. 48), the Wall Street ferry casts its shadow on a warehouse wall on the East River docks just north of the Brooklyn Bridge. The delicately graduated intersecting planes of bridge, wall, dock, water, and shadow transform this prosaic subject into a mysterious spatial conundrum. In *110th St. El Station* (fig. 49), which depicts a station stop famous for its great height, Struss cre-

Figure 49. Karl Struss, *110th St. El Station*, c. 1910, platinum
print, Amon Carter Museum

or waiting for the earth-bound trolleys.[64] In *Queensboro Bridge* (fig.
51), Struss aligned a tiny industrial
smokestack in the far distance with
the vanishing point of the bridge's
massive steel framework. Construct-
ing a totally abstract composition
from geometric industrial forms,
Struss touched upon an approach
later explored in the precisionist
cityscapes of Charles Sheeler.

All of these works are radically
new in composition and infinitely
subtle in effect. Struss explored a
much greater range of urban subjects than Coburn, sharing with him
the modernist goal of expressing dis-
concerting new sensations with a
new pictorial language. Struss was
an innovator who spoke softly, retaining the delicate gradations of
tone and the soft focus of pictorialism. His fusion of old and new has
led some to label him an "innate"
modernist, a nonsensical and unnec-
essary qualification.[65] Between 1910
and 1912, when he produced most
of his ground-breaking New York photographs,
Struss was in constant contact with Stieglitz,
Coburn, and Weber as well as White and became the first of several White students to find
his way to modernism without abandoning the
heritage of pictorialism.

With one important exception, Struss was
not interested in the tenements, small businesses,
and light industry that filled large segments of
lower Manhattan. The exception was the neighborhood surrounding his father's bonnet wire
factory, on the northeast corner of 36th Street
and First Avenue near the East River, where he
worked from 1903 to 1914.[66] He photographed
this working-class neighborhood from the factory

ated a flat, three-tiered composition—crowded
platform above, steel supports in the middle, and
street-scape below—in which the waiting commuters seem held aloft by a giant mechanical spider.

The overhead view that he and Coburn
used so effectively at Madison Square was only
one of the perspectival distortions that interested
Struss. In *Vanishing Point I* (fig. 50), Struss conveyed the dehumanized experience of standing
under the tracks of the elevated trains, a subject
that New York photographers, most notably Berenice Abbott, would exploit in the 1930s. The
overhead tracks and their spotty shadows created a
receding tunnel—a strange, futuristic habitat for
the tiny silhouetted pedestrians crossing the street

Figure 50. Karl Struss, *Vanishing Point I [Under the El]*, 1911, platinum print, J. Paul Getty Museum

Figure 51. Karl Struss, *Queensboro Bridge [Blackwell's Island Bridge]*, 1911, platinum print, Collection of John and Susan Edwards Harvith

windows, from the street, and from the nearby Second Avenue El, exploring it in greater depth than any other area and depicting it in all seasons of the year and at all times of day.[67]

Looking west, Struss surveyed the expanse of low-rise tenements that stretched from the industrial river's edge to the Park Avenue hotels south of the Grand Central Terminal. Directly across First Avenue was a tenement with a bill-board and a laundry-filled clothesline on the roof. Struss often photographed this western panorama, allowing the tenement to fill the right half of his frame and conflating the glittering towers of Park Avenue with the prosaic reality of First Avenue (fig. 52 and p. 83). Looking across

the street, Struss framed tenement dwellers lean-ing out windows; looking down, he photographed the corner tavern and "Quick Lunch" shop at mid-block (fig. 53). One of Struss' best-known photographs, *East Side Promenade* (see fig. 61) — a title which ironically suggests an amble in fash-ionable Central Park rather than a stroll near the East River — is an overhead view of the small park across First Avenue between 35th and 36th Streets. Of all Struss' New York photographs, those of the factory neighborhood come closest to the spirit of the Ashcan School.

Four looming smokestacks of the nearby Consolidated Edison electrical plant attracted Struss' attention, and he made several attempts to

Figure 52. Karl Struss, *Near H. W. Struss Factory, New York City*, c. 1911-13, platinum print, Amon Carter Museum

Figure 53. Karl Struss, *Street Scene—First Avenue and 36th Street*, c. 1910, platinum print, Amon Carter Museum

combine in one picture the plant and the nearby Second Avenue El, two technological systems vital to modern urban life. His most successful photograph taken from the El platform shows Struss using his characteristic device of collapsing near and far space: the El's delicate Victorian gridwork forms a decorative frame around the enormous cylinders of the distant factory (fig. 54).

Struss explored in depth one site outside both the factory neighborhood and the tourist's route—a stretch of Park Avenue looking south from 36th to 33rd Street, south of Grand Central. The location bears a special relationship to Struss' neighborhood views, however, because it was this part of Park Avenue that Struss saw looking west out the factory windows; it was his own New York skyline. The Vanderbilt Hotel (see p. 83), whose scalloped crown of lights highlights Struss' westward panoramas, is a dominant structure in the Park Avenue series.[68] One of several hotels which rose in the wake of the construction

Figure 54. Karl Struss, *Consolidated Edison from the Second Avenue Elevated. New York*, c. 1912, platinum print 1979 by Phil Davis, Amon Carter Museum

Figure 55. Karl Struss, *Construction — "Excuse Me,"* 1911, platinum print, Amon Carter Museum

Figure 56. Karl Struss, *"291." New York*, 1915, modern print from original glass plate negative, Amon Carter Museum

Figure 57. Alfred Stieglitz, *From the Back Window*, '291', 1915, platinum print, National Gallery of Art, Alfred Stieglitz Collection

of the nearby train terminal, the Vanderbilt was flanked by an interesting assortment of structures: the newly built "palazzo" of the 71st Regiment Armory (1905), a Victorian cast-iron warehouse, an ancient two-story building with a billboard on its roof, and the frame of a new skyscraper going up. Peeking out in the background ten blocks south was the pinnacle of the Metropolitan Tower on Madison Square. In *Construction—"Excuse Me"* (fig. 55) Struss brought all of these forms into equilibrium as a trolley car passed in front of his camera. He borrowed the billboard's advertisement for the photograph's title but might also have intended it to refer to his pictorial construction, masterfully achieved in an instantaneous exposure.

Just as he had photographed from the factory windows in earlier years, Struss continued to photograph from the window of White's former studio at 5 West 31st Street. Stieglitz also photographed from the windows of 291, located just across the street. Whether they were aware of each other's efforts is difficult to know, but their photographs share many of the same subjects and formal concerns. Several of Struss' views, including *"291." New York*, show an interest similar to Stieglitz's in the oblique geometry of nearby rooftops (figs. 56 and 57). The window view inspired an even more radical experiment, looking straight down onto Fifth Avenue, where a new building was rising on the corner of Fifth and 31st Street and a parade was passing by

Figure 58. Karl Struss, *[Aerial View of Parade]*, c. 1915, modern print from original glass plate negative, Amon Carter Museum

(fig. 58). Struss and Stieglitz both captured the geometric forms of the construction site and parade formation, anticipating constructivist overhead views by Alexander Rodchenko and Laszlo Moholy-Nagy in the late 1920s.[69] Struss also photographed construction workers hovering in space, balancing on an I-beam (see pp. 7 and 80).[70] A subject explored by Struss alone, it became common in the 1930s and is best remembered in Lewis Hine's celebratory photographs of Empire State Building construction workers.[71]

At precisely the moment when Stieglitz took an interest in Struss—showcasing his work in the Buffalo exhibition, naming him a member of the Photo-Secession, and planning to publish his work in *Camera Work*—the Photo-Secession

fell apart. In the aftermath of the Buffalo exhibition, Stieglitz broke with Weber, Gertrude Käsebier, Coburn, and ultimately with White—the last documented by angry letters they exchanged in May 1912.[72] In April, Sticglitz featured Struss' works in *Camera Work*, and in June, Stieglitz and Struss exchanged cordial letters about the publication.[73] In September, White, Coburn, and Struss began planning an October exhibition of pictorialist photographs at the Montross Galleries,[74] and Struss was given the task of soliciting work from Stieglitz. In a second failed attempt, Struss wrote: "I would regret very much not being able to show any of your prints, for in an exhibition of this character, there is no reason for the sake of good photography why you should not be represented, especially when one considers what you have done for photography."[75]

Feeling his leadership threatened in the aftermath of the Montross Galleries show, Stieglitz grew spiteful. In a November letter to Cornelia Sage, Acting Director of the Albright Gallery, who helped organize the Buffalo exhibition, Stieglitz voiced his resentment:

> Of course there is a collusion on between Weber, White, McColl [*sic*], Mrs. Coburn and Coburn to put 291 out of the field so that they might reap financial benefits from the work done there. This is the way these "friends" of mine repay me for Buffalo. Fortunately these matters no longer excite me. I look upon members as named above as rather pathetic instances of what pretty good fellows will stoop to when jealous and envious.[76]

Struss was truly caught in the eye of a hurricane, but he seems to have maintained friendships with White and Stieglitz throughout. From 1912 through the establishment of the Pictorial Photographers of America in 1916, he continued to help White create a support system from the remnants of the Photo-Secession. He recalled working on exhibitions for the Newark Free Public Library (1911), the Montross Art Galleries (1912), the Ehrich Art Galleries (1914), and the Brooklyn Academy of Arts and Sciences (1914); and he contributed to *Platinum Print*, from helping to found it in 1913 to becoming associate editor in 1914. His memory of these activities shows that Struss clearly saw White's group taking over the Photo-Secession's selective approach to membership and intentionally unstructured mission:

> Myself, Clarence White, and Edward R. Dickson [editor of *Platinum Print* and an organizer of the Newark exhibition], we were the three conspirators and we had no association of any kind with the local camera clubs. . . . We were more associated with members of the unorganized Photo-Secession which Stieglitz headed at the time. . . . [The P.P.A. had no] established rules of any kind, just congenial people [who] worked together and exhibited together and tried to help the art.[77]

He also regularly visited 291 during these years,[78] managing to bridge what one would have expected to be an unbridgeable chasm and producing many of his most important photographs during this stormy period.

This political maelstrom did not deter Struss from regularly and widely exhibiting his photographs, and the exhibition history compiled by Susan and John Harvith makes it possible to evaluate how Struss presented his work to fellow photographers.[79] After the Buffalo show of November 1910, Struss' next exhibition—his first and only solo show—was at Columbia Teachers College in January 1912. Struss was still attending White's classes, and undoubtedly White was

influential in providing this opportunity for his prized pupil. From 1912 through 1914, Struss showed in the various exhibitions organized by White's group, and in 1915, his work was represented when White started traveling group shows around the country. When Coburn selected and hung the 1915 exhibition of the Royal Photographic Society, he included works by himself, White, and Struss, and in the same year, these three men also submitted works to the Panama-Pacific International Exposition in San Francisco. In 1916 and 1917, Struss sent work to the Pittsburgh annual salon and the London Salon of Photography, two of the most prestigious forums for pictorial photography; he also submitted works to the competitions sponsored by the John Wanamaker Department Store, whose juries included Stieglitz.

For the Buffalo exhibition, Stieglitz chose twelve works, nine from Struss' 1909 European trip and three moody, romantic New York subjects. Many were multiple platinum prints whose rich tones had so impressed Stieglitz. In 1911 Struss assembled mounted four-by-five-inch platinum prints into albums that bear a striking resemblance to *Camera Work*.[80] Although not a public display, they were clearly intended for posterity and reveal his approach to his work at a dramatic moment of transition. Struss gave at least three albums as Christmas gifts, one to White and one each to two White students, Willa P. Collison and Amy Whittemore. He kept at least one, which contained seven New York City scenes and sixteen views of the exterior and interior of the Buffalo Art Gallery; he may have intended to give this Buffalo memento to Stieglitz but thought better of it as discord grew in the aftermath of the exhibition. The Collison album is lost, but the White and Whittemore albums are extant and suggest that Struss tailored each album's print selection to its recipient. The White album is a survey of Struss' work, favoring summer landscapes from Riverside Drive, Arverne, Europe, Nova Scotia, and Maine, where Struss visited White's summer school in 1910; it also includes two interiors showing White's work on display at the Albright Art Gallery. Of its twenty-five prints, only three depict city street scenes.[81]

The Whittemore album, by contrast, includes twenty-five New York City images, out of its total of thirty-three. Unfortunately, very little is known about Whittemore (1875-1959) or about her relationship with Struss, making it impossible to determine if her interests affected the print selection for her album.[82] In any event, the album is the only remaining document of Struss' own arrangement of his New York photographs. Opening with an overhead view of Fifth Avenue, it has a loose narrative structure, moving from the rush of city life to pastoral landscapes on Long Island, Nova Scotia, and Europe. The city subjects stress the technology of transportation, including five scenes of the elevated trains. Some of Struss' most dynamic compositions appear, such as *Herald Square* (a variant composition of fig. 37), in which a random array of stores, apartment buildings, streets, El tracks, and billboards rise up behind an on-rushing trolley; and *Queensboro Bridge*, an abstract composition of girders and smokestack (see fig. 51). *Metropolitan Life Insurance Tower*, which transforms the office tower into a New York icon, is the only static work in the series (see fig. 40).

Three weeks after Christmas, Struss hung a selection of forty photographs of New York at Teachers College. The checklist shows that he displayed a full assortment of his New York subjects, including the Wall Street skyline, Madison Square, First Avenue (the factory neighborhood), Park Avenue southward (near the Vanderbilt Hotel), and Columbia University. He also sought stylistic variety, including picturesque works such as *Earl Hall, Columbia University,*

Night (see fig. 16), which had been seen at Buffalo, and *Metropolitan Tower at Dusk*, and more dynamic experiments such as *Queensboro Bridge* (see fig. 51) and *110th St. El* (see fig. 49).[83]

The show at Teachers College, which was only on view for ten days (and which Coburn regretted missing), was the only time that Struss exhibited his most audacious images and the only time that he emphasized New York as his principal subject. His photographs were next seen in *Camera Work*, which came out in April. Stieglitz's selection was very similar to that of the 1910 exhibition: of eight photogravures, six were from the 1909 European trip and the only New York image was *On the East River*, which had been shown at Buffalo. That Stieglitz favored these 1909 works for a 1910 exhibition is not surprising. What is less understandable is that he favored a similar group of 1909 works for the 1912 issue of *Camera Work*.

Struss himself was disappointed. In an otherwise obsequious letter to Stieglitz thanking him for the privilege of appearing in his journal, Struss remarked, "No doubt a slightly different selection would have been more representative." In his gracious reply, Stieglitz acknowledged the point: "As for the selection, I too would have chosen somewhat differently were I to select today."[84] No doubt Struss wished to have his more recent New York photographs featured, but Stieglitz, who had just published his own New York views in *Camera Work*, may have been reluctant to offer strong work on the same subject by a newcomer.

Struss' exhibition submissions after his *Camera Work* debut became increasingly standardized and conservative. He combined a greater number of travel scenes—adding landscapes of Nova Scotia, New England, and Bermuda to his European inventory—with his more picturesque New York subjects. Among those most often shown were *On the East River*

Figure 59. Karl Struss, *Lower Broadway, New York,* 1912, gelatin silver bromide print on Japanese tissue, Amon Carter Museum

and *Earl Hall, Columbia University, Night* (see fig. 16), which had been exhibited at Buffalo; *Lower Broadway* (fig. 59), a somber scene of a shadowy silhouette passing by the exotic columns of the City Hall Post Office; *Pennsylvania Station* (see p. 74), a radiant vision of sunlight streaming over the new marble halls of the station's waiting room; and *The Span at Twilight* (see fig. 32), a Whistlerian nocturne of the Brooklyn Bridge.

As an artist Struss had ventured into modernist territory, but as an exhibitor he remained within pictorial expectations. He was not by nature a crusader, and he submitted works that he felt would be favored by juries and the photography audience. This is not to suggest that Struss was content with the state of pictorial photography, as his lament published in *American Photography* in 1917 makes clear:

> To those of us who follow the development of photography as an art, and indeed to almost any photographer who occasionally sees a pictorial exhibition, or the reproductions in the photographic magazines, it has been evident for some time that little progress in pictorial photography is being made. Although today there are many workers with pictorial aspirations as compared to a relatively small group ten years ago, and much better average technical work is being done, yet the best pictures being made today are of no higher quality than the work produced at that time.[85]

Even if he had wanted to promote his boldest work conspicuously, he would have found little encouragement. White was Struss' strongest advocate, but White's efforts were channelled into helping him leave his father's factory and launch a professional career. Stieglitz, who had the temperament and vision to nurture Struss'

experiments, chose not to do so. Although the tempestuous break between White and Stieglitz in 1912 did not seem to harm Struss' work, it may have hindered its promotion. In his letter concerning the print selection for *Camera Work*, Stieglitz reassured Struss that he planned to publish more of his work in future, but this never came to pass. As a result, Struss' modernist photographs remained little known even at the time they were made.

Instead, the honor for a modernist breakthrough in photography went to Paul Strand, whose images were published in the last issues of *Camera Work* in 1916 and 1917 and were heralded by Stieglitz as revolutionary. For the next fifteen years, Strand and Stieglitz enjoyed a fruitful artistic and personal alliance that advanced the art and reputation of both men. Comparison of Struss' and Strand's photographs in the early teens affords an opportunity to reevaluate Struss' achievement and to examine the effect of Stieglitz's patronage on the two emerging artists.

Strand, who was four years younger than Struss, took up photography in Lewis Hine's class at the Ethical Culture School in New York. Upon graduation in 1909, he began to earn his living as a commercial photographer while following pictorial photography. A group of prints from a trip to Europe show that he had mastered the pictorial style by 1911. Little remains of his artistically ambitious work between 1911 and 1915, the date of several photographs published in *Camera Work* 48. Strand seems not to have played a significant role in photographic circles during the difficult year of 1912, but in its aftermath, he achieved notice in Stieglitz's and White's circles. In 1913, he became a 291 regular, and in 1914 he joined White's group as well. His work was included in the January 1914 "International Exhibition of Pictorial Photography," which White organized for the Ehrich Art Galleries, and he attended a celebratory dinner in

Figure 60. Paul Strand, *New York*, 1916,
photogravure from *Camera Work* 48,
Gernsheim Collection, Harry Ransom
Humanities Research Center, The
University of Texas at Austin

Figure 61. Karl Struss, *East Side Promenade*, 1911,
platinum print, Amon Carter Museum

Chinatown; in December 1914, he was a member of a group that included White, Dickson, Weber, and Struss and that met informally once a month to critique prints.[86]

In 1915 and early 1916, Strand produced New York City views similar to Struss', creating abstract compositions from the dynamic subjects of the city's streets. Strand was certainly acquainted with Struss and may have seen Struss' New York photographs, most of which were taken several years earlier. One or two photographs by Strand bear direct comparison with Struss' work.[87] Most notable is an overhead park view, published in *Camera Work* 48 under the title *Photograph* (fig. 60), which might have been inspired by Struss' 1911 *East Side Promenade* (fig. 61): paths, railings, and lampposts form a curvilinear design, punctuated by pedestrians randomly scattered over the picture plane.[88] The link is tenuous, however. Most of Strand's street scenes, including the now famous *Wall Street* and three more of the six photogravures in *Camera Work* 48, were taken a few stories above street level from a diagonal point of view.[89] Strand's heavy reliance on this compositional device, which was uncharacteristic of Struss' work, argues against any meaningful influence. Struss and Strand also differed in the way they exploited the tonal range of platinum paper; Strand preferred higher contrast, giving up the narrow tonal range of pictorialism that Struss retained.

Sruss and Strand had very different artistic temperaments but fundamentally similar intentions. In a 1974 interview, Strand characterized his goals in words that could easily describe Struss' photographs: "One of the elements I wanted to work with then was people moving in the street. I wanted to see if I could organize a picture of that kind of movement in a way that was abstract and controlled."[90] By mid-1916, Struss had produced a very large body of varied photographs; Strand's work, at least what has survived, was meager by comparison, and tentative.

Stieglitz saw Strand's overhead street views as a radical breakthrough, the first photographs fully equal to the accomplishments of modern painting. He exhibited Strand's work at 291 "as a natural foil to the Forum Exhibition of Modern American Painters." Stieglitz had hung his own photographs at 291 during the epochal 1913 Armory Show; by hanging Strand's work at 291 during the Forum Gallery show, he deemed Strand his artistic heir. Devoting six plates of Camera Work 48 (October 1916) to Strand, Stieglitz wrote an ecstatic appraisal of his work, claiming that Strand was "in close touch with all that is related to life in its fullest aspect, intimately related to the spirit of '291.' "[91]

Stieglitz undoubtedly sensed a great talent in Strand, but his extravagant proclamations might be attributed at least in part to Stieglitz's own needs at that moment. He had endured years of splintered relationships and thwarted ambitions, and Strand, like Georgia O'Keeffe, would play a vital role in his regeneration. Whatever its source, Stieglitz's encouragement had a salutary effect on Strand. In the final double issue of Camera Work (nos. 49-50), published in June 1917, Stieglitz reproduced Strand's newer work. Completed during the summer of 1916 and early 1917, these street portraits and still life

abstractions were truly revolutionary and completely foreign to Struss' sensibility.[92] The photographs he had surreptitiously taken of indigents at Five Points, one of New York's worst slums on the Lower East Side, were "brutally direct," to use Stieglitz's phrase,[93] and proved pivotal for younger documentary photographers such as Walker Evans.[94] The abstractions, in which Strand sought a total break with representation by turning an image 90 degrees, presage constructivist and surrealist manipulations of the 1920s.[95] Stieglitz's claims for Strand's originality, perhaps exaggerated in 1916, were justified in 1917. Indeed, Stieglitz repeated verbatim his remarks from the earlier Camera Work in the later issue.

Over time Stieglitz's assessment of Strand's work has become regarded as historical fact, and the publication of Strand in Camera Work is commonly understood to begin a new chapter in the history of photography. Scrutiny of Strand's early works in light of Struss' accomplishment yields two adjustments to received wisdom. Of Strand's three groups of early modernist photographs—overhead street views, street portraits, and abstractions—it is the latter two that represent a radical break with the past.[96] Strand's street views were no more innovative than Struss', which preceded them by several years. Strand's breakthrough, furthermore, did not occur in a vacuum; it was nurtured by Stieglitz's devotion and promotion. That resolute support in 1916 stands in stark contrast to the muddled moment in 1912 when Struss fired Stieglitz's enthusiasm. Presenting a second selection in Camera Work, which proved decisive for Strand, was something Stieglitz had offered but never given to Struss.

STRUSS' PROFESSIONAL CAREER

In 1914, after eleven years in his father's factory, Struss at the age of twenty-eight decided to make photography his living. Taking over Clarence White's Fifth Avenue studio, Struss went into business with the blessing of White, who firmly believed that his students could adapt artistic photography to commercial practice. There were ample precedents for such a career: White himself took commercial assignments from time to time, and many of the best pictorialists—Gertrude Käsebier, Baron de Meyer, Edward Steichen, Arnold Genthe, and Coburn—were skillful society and celebrity portraitists.[97] The fashion in the teens for "home portraiture," in which a client was photographed in the familiar surroundings of home, gave the pictorialist more flexibility in composition and mood.[98]

White sensed that photography had even greater commercial potential for publication. The proliferation of popular illustrated magazines and the technological improvements in halftone illustration promised opportunities for artistically sensitive photographers. White envisioned pictorialist genre scenes replacing drawn illustrations in novels and magazines.[99] As early as 1901, he had illustrated the novel *Eben Holden*, and Stieglitz had thought enough of the illustrations to publish them in *Camera Work*.

White's belief in high-quality popular art was grounded in aesthetic principle. Steeped in a peculiarly American version of the arts-and-crafts philosophy, White was committed to bringing art and beauty into the lives of all Americans.[100] In the years following the break-up of the Photo-Secession, he began to transform his beliefs into a concrete program.[101] Struss was the first of White's protégés to test those beliefs. When asked in 1918 if "the pictorial photographer [could] make a living in America," White answered affirmatively: "The pictorial photographer in reality ought to be a financial success, for the tendency is strongly toward the development of the work in that direction."[102] White no doubt had Struss' example firmly in mind.

In 1913, even before he opened his studio, Struss began dabbling in illustrative photography. He produced a Teachers College calendar using photographs made for White's class. When the *New York Tribune* published an article on the Columbia summer school, the paper ran one of Struss' views.[103] Throughout 1913, he marketed his photographs to the newspapers for their weekend "rotogravure" sections, receiving twenty-five dollars for a full-page cover.[104] His working principle, inspired by White, was the interchangeability of art and commerce, and he was constantly thinking of ways to place his artistic photographs in a commercial context. In a 1913 issue of *Platinum Print*, he announced that he could provide photographs for "magazines, books, poems, advertising and calendars."[105]

Despite a preference for illustration, Struss' practice was, of necessity, broader. His studio stationery advertised: "Pictorial photography; home portraiture, architecture, marines, landscape, illustration." Inventory lists of negatives from his commercial practice suggest a full and varied schedule.[106] In his three-year stint as an emerging commercial photographer, Struss seems to have earned a respectable living, but he could not afford the luxury of specialization.

Before 1913, photographs were most often seen in fashion magazines such as *Vogue*, published by Condé Nast, and *Harper's Bazar*, published by William Randolph Hearst as *Vogue's* chief competitor.[107] These photographs of society and theater personalities were routine productions by unidentified photographers. In the spring of 1914, when Frank Crowninshield became editor of Condé Nast's *Vanity Fair*, a new era in magazine photography began. Crowninshield and his art director Heyworth Campbell, friends of White, immediately began printing full-page pictorial photographs, unconnected to a story and captioned with the title and the photographer's name.[108] Between September 1914 and

June 1917, *Vanity Fair* ran nine photographic features: one each by White, Anderson, Käsebier, and Coburn, and five by Struss. Struss' features included three of his most often exhibited picturesque New York views: *Cables* (see fig. 39), *The Span at Twilight* (see *Brooklyn Bridge, Nocturne,* fig. 32), and *Metropolitan Tower at Dusk.*[109]

Harper's Bazar very quickly adapted artistic photographs to its own needs, commissioning pictorial photographs to replace hand-drawn illustrations for its short stories. White may have played an encouraging role in this as well, since his students were among the first hired for the assignments. In late 1915, Struss and Amy Whittemore illustrated a two-part story, and from December 1916 until the summer of 1917, a Struss illustration appeared monthly.[110] He worked in various settings for these illustrations— home interiors, his studio, and, in one instance, the waiting room of Grand Central Station. The assignments required him to develop new skills in arranging models and planning lighting.

Even more plentiful than magazine illustrations were assignments in advertising, another field that was just beginning to exploit photography. To solicit work, Struss created a portfolio of what he called "illustration photographs," printing a variety of works on glossy silver paper and mounting them on board.[111] Many of his advertising jobs were anything but routine. His first was a tourist brochure for the government of Bermuda, a job that spawned several subsequent features in travel magazines.

Another was a brochure that accompanied an exhibit at the Waldorf-Astoria for the Mergenthaler Linotype Company. The company gave Struss unusual creative license, as a close-up of hands and machine parts shows (fig. 62). A half-covered lightbulb, suspended from above, fills the upper half of the composition and casts a harsh light on a worker's hands poised on the linotype controls. This industrial still life,

Figure 62. Karl Struss, *In War as in Peace* [from *Linotype Bulletin*], 1914, modern print from original glass plate negative, Amon Carter Museum

abstract and dramatically lit, anticipates the product advertisements pioneered by the next generation of White students, such as Margaret Bourke-White and Paul Outerbridge. Struss' night photographs may have originally attracted the Mergenthaler Company, since its brochure also included a glittering view of "bright, sleepless, newspaper row, where day and night, the world's adventure is cast into type for New York by two hundred Linotypes" (see fig. 19). A client most assuredly attracted to Struss' night views was the New York Edison Company, which published a series of them in the *Edison Monthly* (see fig. 15).[112] The journal included *Man's Construction at Docks, N.Y.C.* (see p. 79), Struss' idiosyncratic view of the Manhattan skyline seen through industrial structures on the Brooklyn docks.

Realizing the boon to its business that photographic advertising would bring, Kodak offered a yearly competition for the best Kodak advertisement. In 1916, Struss entered the competition, as a series of surviving trial-advertisements attests. Struss, Anderson, and Whittemore posed as well-dressed amateur photographers in front of the New York Public Library and inside Penn Station.[113] Struss won third prize, which carried a $350 honorarium, and Ansco, Kodak's chief competitor, used one of his overhead views of the public library in an advertisement published in *Harper's Bazar*.[114]

Struss also had several "bread-and-butter" accounts that required uninventive product display.[115] These typically showed a model using a product in a shallow, stage-like space (fig. 63). More innovative were narratives, which sought empathy between a potential buyer and the character in the advertisement. A soft-focus photograph showed a business executive in distress ("I was nervously bankrupt—my last scintilla of nerve force expended!"), who required the pacifying benefit of Sanatogen, "the food-tonic approved by science." Struss took his stylistic cue from hand-drawn Sanatogen ads in the popular style of illustrator Charles Dana Gibson (figs. 64 and 65).[116]

In 1916, Struss began to experiment in the studio with photographic silhouettes, placing figures against such strong backlight that they appeared as two-dimensional black shadows. They were an odd hybrid of portraiture and illustration and were clearly meant to be modern and entertaining, but what inspired the silhouettes is unclear. In March of 1915, *Vanity Fair* had published silhouettes by Käsebier, noting that "if there is a new photographic field, trust Mrs. Kasebier to find it."[117] It may be that Käsebier,

Figure 63. Karl Struss, *New Perfection Oil Cook Stove* [advertisement in *Good Housekeeping*, May 1917], Texas Women's University

who had been experimenting with this technique for years, inspired Struss' exploration of it.

Advertising may also have played a part. Hand-drawn silhouettes, which were clear and eye-catching, commonly appeared in advertisements, and Struss' own product display photographs may have served as a departure point (see fig. 63). Their simple, frieze-like arrangements led to more creative compositions such as the story illustration for "A Certain Poor Slacker" (fig. 66). In a scene where an artist at his easel is

Figure 64. *Sanatogen* [advertisement in *Vogue*, February 1915], Museum of the City of New York

Figure 65. Karl Struss, *Sanatogen* [advertisement in *The Outlook*, March 1917], Texas Christian University

interrupted by his girlfriend at the door, Struss shows two figures in strict profile in a shallow stage space. It is a short step from such work to the backlit silhouette.

Struss' silhouettes present a typical example of his *modus operandi* as a commercial photographer. The charm and artistic challenge of his silhouettes was that the effect was not total; three-dimensional detail could be seen around the edges of the figures. He assembled a small stage set, adorned its sides with bits of ivy that appear in every silhouette, and experimented with several models and a constant set of props: a Chinese plant stand, a vase of lilies, an early

American chair, and two potted boxwood plants. Struss then marketed a commercially viable artistic product.

In February 1916, the *Sun* published a pictorial feature, "Silhouette Photography the Latest Fad," with three Struss silhouettes, one of a mother and child and two of "Charlotte the Skater," a performer at the Hippodrome's ice show.[118] In March, *Vanity Fair* published his "Four Fantasies of Light and Shade," which included a skater, a standing nude, and two views of a seated woman at ease. The humorous caption claims that the "shadowgraphs" show Struss' "lamentable tendency to look at the dark side of

Figure 66. Karl Struss, *A Certain Poor Slacker*
[illustration for story in *Harper's Bazar*, December
1916], Fort Worth Public Library

Patience on a Monument
A Chiaroscuro, Illustrating the Danger of Putting a Woman on a Pedestal

Figure 67. Karl Struss, *Patience on a Monument*
[illustration in *Vanity Fair*, June 1917], Texas
Christian University

things." In a similarly droll vein, the June 1917 issue of *Vanity Fair* presents a nude perched on an ionic column, with the caption: "Patience on a Monument, A chiaroscuro illustrating the danger of putting a woman on a pedestal" (fig. 67). In March 1917, *Harper's Bazar* illustrated a story with a Struss silhouette that was a self-portrait.

Struss' nude silhouettes also appeared in another, less marketable artistic venture—his portfolio titled *The Female Figure*. By 1917,

Struss was financially secure enough to devote his energies to this artistically ambitious and technically experimental project, which had uncertain monetary gain. *The Female Figure* presented a series of nude studies for use by artists; the majority were black and white, but a few were produced by the experimental Hess-Ives color process. A regular edition included forty-eight black and white photographs and three color reproductions from Hess-Ives prints; a deluxe edition included twenty-one photographs printed on Japan tissue, two color reproductions, and one original color photograph.[119] Using ten different models and three artist-consultants to pose them, Struss produced 250 photographic studies from which forty-eight were chosen.[120] A second series of outdoor studies was planned but never executed.[121]

All the photographs depict a figure standing against a wall or fabric backdrop, sometimes draped in transparent gauze, sometimes holding a prop, such as a fan, a cup, or panpipes (fig. 68). Despite this restricted format, the overall impression of the portfolio is not unified, largely because of the varied lighting: strong backlight resulted in silhouettes; strong frontlight created clearly detailed, flattened forms; and dramatic, irregular lighting produced fully modeled forms emerging from darkness. The use of so many "consultants" may also have contributed to the disunity; there is no one consistent relationship established between model and photographer.

Struss' reason for embarking on the portfolio project is unknown, but its inspiration was almost certainly the modern dance movement, which was attracting a large heterogeneous audience in America and Europe. Performers such as Isadora Duncan, Ruth St. Denis, Loie Fuller, and Maud Allan explored non-western and folk dance forms for alternatives to classical ballet and conventional social dancing. Implicit in the movement was a critique of Victorian attitudes toward the body and, indeed, the confines of civilization itself. Liberating the female body from constraining clothing and conventional movement suggested a beneficent return to nature or to the golden age of classical Greece.

Modern dance proved enormously popular with pictorial photographers. Anne Brigman's California dancers *en plein air* were regularly reproduced in *Vanity Fair* in the teens. Semi-nude nymphs cavorting in the woods filled the

Figure 68. Karl Struss, *Untitled*, 1917, gelatin silver print, from *24 Photographs of the Female Figure*, The Art Museum, Princeton University, Museum Purchase, Gift of Mrs. Max Adler

photography exhibitions and journals. *Platinum Print* devoted an issue to the nude in 1914 and one to the dance in 1915.[122] But it was Arnold Genthe's 1916 *Book of the Dance* that most likely inspired Struss' portfolio. A highly respected pictorialist and theatrical portraitist, Genthe used soft-focus lenses and moody lighting to convey the feeling of movement and the mystery of performance. His book included color halftones made from his autochromes and a section called "Classic Dancers," which showed nudes posed against a cloth backdrop, simulating a frieze.[123]

Genthe, who had far more experience with models than Struss, succeeded in achieving the unity of vision and purpose that *The Female*

Figure lacks. Struss' nude studies now feel self-conscious and dated, betraying the tentative and defensive attitude that permeated the project. Struss introduced the portfolio with a textual justification of artistic nude photography, reprinting two articles and a poem from *Platinum Print's* 1914 issue on the nude.[124] By having three artists pose the models, he sought further to substantiate the portfolio's claim to "art."[125] This gathering of writers and artists contrasts sharply with the anonymous models, whose task was considered disreputable.[126] Yet Struss' defensive stance ultimately was justified, for the portfolio's publisher was apparently threatened with a lawsuit for distributing pornography.[127]

The color studies of nudes in *The Female Figure* attest to Struss' enthusiasm for the Hess-Ives process, an early attempt to make color separations through the use of colored filters. His experiments with the process reflected his abiding interest in color and his technical curiosity. When autochromes first appeared in 1907, many pictorialists (among them Stieglitz, Steichen, Coburn, and White) experimented with them, but the medium's limitations—including long exposure time and an inability to print on paper—proved frustrating. Both Genthe and Struss continued working in autochrome, looking for improvements (see pp. 1-8). In a 1917 article that appeared in *American Photography*, Struss also held out great hope for the Hess-Ives process, which allowed for paper printing and seemed to have potential for revitalizing pictorial photography. His hopes were dashed, however, by the chemical instability of the process.[128]

In 1916, the publicity department of the Metropolitan Opera Company hired Struss for photographic assignments that fell outside the company's regular requirements. For routine work, the Metropolitan had on-going relationships with two photographers: Luther S. White for on-stage photography and Herman Mishkin

for studio portraiture. Struss' approach to his unusual assignments was typically fresh and flexible.[129] To publicize a summer tour of *Siegfried*, performed outdoors, Struss photographed tenor Johannes Sembach at Edgemere, Long Island. Struss also traveled to Norfolk, Connecticut, to photograph soprano Melanie Kurt as Brünnhilde in *Die Walküre*. Although the singers relied upon standard operatic gesture, Struss' portraits still reveal considerably more of their personalities than routine studio photography.[130]

More promising was the assignment to photograph Sergei Diaghilev's Ballets Russes at the opening of its second American tour in October 1916. In a hurried, on-stage photo-session, using the only available arc lamp, Struss made two dozen exposures of Vaslav Nijinsky in two of his ballets.[131] Twelve exposures show Nijinsky and his partner Flores Revalles holding poses from his ballet to the music of Debussy, *L'Apres-Midi d'un Faune*, which was scandalous for its primitive, anti-classical movements and overt sexuality (fig. 69). Twelve other photographs show Nijinsky playing the puckish lead character in his new (and last) ballet, *Till Eulenspiegel*, which premiered a week late in New York.

Working with the 4x5-inch Century camera that he also used for outdoor work, Struss abandoned the proprieties of routine studio portraiture in the hope of creating a sense of immediacy and movement. As a result, many of the exposures are slightly blurred. The *Till Eulenspiegel* photographs show Nijinsky's expressive range as a character dancer, while the *Faune* photographs, described by dance historian Joan Acocella as "raw, unlovely" and "utterly unidealized," provide unique information about Nijinsky's body and the mechanics of his dancing.[132]

Struss made three more on-stage exposures of Adolph Bolm, another Ballets Russes star, wearing a Pierrot costume from the ballet *Papillon*.[133]

Figure 69. Karl Struss, *Vaslav Nijinsky and Flores Revalles in L'Apres-Midi d'un Faune*, 1916, gelatin silver print, Collection of John and Susan Edwards Harvith

Struss' only experience with film-making while in New York was a one-minute film of Bolm dancing. He had bought a Universal hand-cranked motion picture camera and fitted it with a Struss Pictorial Lens. He recalled using the camera only once, and the film is lost. Three autochromes and a series of eight negatives offer clues, however, to the film's appearance (fig. 70). Struss built a stage twenty feet wide and ten feet deep on the roof of his studio, hung a curtain fifteen feet high, and used box trees in planters and ivy (props from the silhouettes) to decorate the set.[134] The negatives show Bolm in costumes from two different ballets: *Sadko*, which Bolm himself choreographed, and *Thamar*, choreographed by Mikhail Fokine. Both ballets were based on Russian folktales, and in the *Thamar*

photographs, Bolm can be seen dancing on his toes, in the manner of Georgian folk dancers. The photographs, like the Nijinsky series, are simple spontaneous records (see p. 8). Struss described the lost film in similar terms, recalling that he made it "from one vantage point, just a nice full figure."[135]

World War I had a deleterious effect on American pictorial photography. With the war in Europe in 1914, critical supplies such as platinum paper and European-made photochemicals became scarce. When the United States entered the war in 1917, many photographers lost their belief in making art. In a 1918 interview, White bemoaned this change in attitude: "There has been a feeling that all activities should be directly connected with the war, and that photography should share in this; that pictorial photography should be devoted to . . . a sort of war propaganda, rather than purely pictorial work."[136]

For Struss, the period from 1914 to the fall of 1917, when he entered the Army, was remarkably productive. Although he continued to submit photographs to pictorial exhibitions, he established a solid reputation in the nascent field of illustrative photography. It was no exaggeration when John Chapman Hilder, editor of *Harper's Bazar*, wrote that, "Karl Struss is one of the most distinguished photographers in the country."[137] In a letter to Struss in 1918, Paul Anderson remarked that "there's going to be a rush into this business after the war," and he was right.[138] Had he returned to New York following his army stint, Struss undoubtedly would have attained a position of leadership in magazine photography.

Struss' commercial output—his advertisements, illustrations, silhouettes, nudes, and theatrical portraits—are not of lasting artistic value. But they reveal the step-by-step adaptation of pictorial photography to the emerging needs of the modern magazine industry. It was to Struss' creative advantage that editors and clients had

raphy, which also lacked trained artists. When he arrived in California in 1919 without work, he asked his family to send him *The Female Figure*, his color portraits, and the Bolm film to show to Hollywood filmmakers. His first assignment, publicity stills for Cecil B. De Mille's *Male and Female*, launched his Hollywood career. The stunning platinum prints that he kept from this assignment are dramatic proof of the lessons of his commercial years (see pp. 151-153).

CONCLUSION

Struss explored a great subject— New York in an era of exciting but wrenching change—and produced a larger, more varied, and more unified body of work than any other photographer of his generation, including Coburn and Strand. Struss and his peers were preoccupied with the city as a symbol of modernity, with its skyscrapers, transportation systems, and crowds. His style was a unique synthesis of pictorialism and modernism, combining the soft focus and narrow tonal range of the former with the anti-rational spatial experiments of the latter. Struss' vision of New York was not harsh or loud; it was subtle, witty, and intellectually challenging.

Figure 70. Karl Struss, *Adolph Bolm in Thamar*, 1916, modern print from original glass plate negative, Amon Carter Museum

uncertain expectations, for he was able to help shape them.

Struss' years as a studio photographer also prepared him for his future. He had learned to approach a new photographic field creatively and to earn a living from it. That experience gave him the confidence to try his hand at cinematog-

In the 1930s, when Berenice Abbott photographed New York at a different moment in its history, another building boom had again transformed the city with taller modernistic skyscrapers in the Art Deco style and an even larger system of tunnels, bridges, and subways. Abbott's documentary photographic style marks the end of the period of modernist experimentation, and her portrait of New York forms a fascinating generational contrast with Struss'.

Struss was also prescient enough to explore photography's potential in New York's publishing industry, which was as much a part of the city's dynamism as was its new architecture. His commercial photographs are the first substantial demonstration of White's tenet, grounded in the arts-and-crafts movement, that artistically accomplished photography can be enjoyed by a large public.

Struss' reputation, both in his day and our own, has fallen short of his accomplishments. He was twice the victim of poor timing. He first gained recognition as an amateur when the pictorial movement's leadership was in crisis and its creative impetus largely spent. Then his wartime experience led him to relinquish his foothold in magazine photography a decade before the field blossomed. Ironically, Struss' reputation suffers today because Stieglitz, one of his strongest early supporters, proclaimed in 1916 that Paul Strand had found photography's answer to modern art, which he and Strand came to define as straight photography. Borrowing a concept that had been discussed among pictorial photographers for years, they transformed it into a modernist credo. By the 1930s, Stieglitz had become the guardian of this restrictive approach, which condemned both pictorialism and commercial photography and defined a good photograph as a black and white, sharp-focus print made with great deliberation in the name of art. Straight photography, however, was not the only form that modernism could take, and Struss and others found alternative paths that allowed for manipulative printing, color, and commercial application.

When Struss was rediscovered in the 1970s, the prestige of straight photography was at its height and pictorialism was in disrepute, making Struss' work impossible to evaluate on his own terms. Despite recent challenges,[139] Stieglitz's values continue to have a pronounced effect on opinions about Struss and other Clarence White protégés. Struss' pictorial preferences have kept scholars from fully acknowledging his assimilation of modern art,[140] and his creative adaptation of pictorial photography to commercial practice has been seen as an abandonment of a high calling for a base one.[141] For Struss, however, pictorial photography was just a beginning. His technical curiosity and instinct for new horizons placed him in the vanguard of two industries—magazine photography and Hollywood films—whose transforming effect on modern American culture has been far greater than that of photography produced as fine art.

NOTES

1. *Camera Work* 38 (April 1912), p. 22.

2. Struss was virtually unknown to photography scholars and collectors before Susan and John Harvith's *Karl Struss: Man with a Camera*, a 1976 traveling exhibition with catalogue, which originated at the Cranbrook Academy of Art/Museum. Since then, Struss' work has entered the discussion of American pictorialism and modernism, albeit on the margins. See John Pultz and Catherine B. Scallen, *Cubism and American Photography, 1910-1930* (Williamstown, Mass.: Sterling and Francine Clark Art Institute, 1981), p. 12; William Innes Homer, *Alfred Stieglitz and the Photo-Secession* (Boston: New York Graphic Society, 1983), pp. 149-153; Lucinda Barnes et al., eds., *A Collective Vision: Clarence H. White and His Students* (California State University, Long Beach: University Art Museum, 1986); Sarah Greenough et al., *On the Art of Fixing a Shadow, One Hundred and Fifty Years of Photography* (Washington, D.C.: National Gallery of Art, 1989), pp. 151, 213. While this essay was in preparation, Toby Jurovics' "Karl Struss Composing, New York" appeared in *History of Photography* 17, no. 2 (Summer 1993): 193-203.

3. Struss signed and dated many of his prints at the time they were made. He signed and dated many more prints in the 1970s when his work was rediscovered; these dates are not very reliable. Struss annotated many but not all of the sleeves of his negatives with titles and dates. These are not entirely reliable either, as suggested by contradictions between dated prints and negatives.

4. From 1898 until well after he left New York, Struss' family lived at 729 St. Nicholas Avenue, near 145th Street. The centerpiece of the neighborhood is Hamilton Grange, Alexander Hamilton's 1802 country house. The elevated train built in the 1880s ended at 145th Street; it created a prime location for high-quality city houses which have since been designated a landmark historic district. The Struss family lived in a new home built in this well-to-do neighborhood.

5. For Arthur Wesley Dow, see Frederick C. Moffatt, *Arthur Wesley Dow (1857-1922)* (Washington, D.C.: National Collection of Fine Arts, 1977). For the influence of Dow's ideas on White's teaching, see Pultz and Scallen, *Cubism and American Photography*; Bonnie Yochelson, "Clarence H. White Reconsidered: An Alternative to the Modernist Aesthetic of Straight Photography," *Studies in Visual Communication* 9 (Fall 1983): 26-44; Barnes et al., *A Collective Vision*; and Peter C. Bunnell, *Clarence H. White: The Reverence for Beauty* ([Athens]: Ohio University Gallery of Fine Art, 1986).

6. John and Susan Harvith, interview with Karl Struss, August 30, 1975 (hereafter cited as Harvith interview).

7. Ibid.

8. For discussions of Weber, see William Innes Homer, *Alfred Stieglitz and the American Avant-Garde* (Boston: New York Graphic Society, 1977), pp. 124-138; and Percy North, *Max Weber, The Cubist Decade, 1910-1920* (Atlanta: High Museum of Art, 1991).

9. "The Filling of Space," *Platinum Print* 1, no. 2 (December 1913): 6.

10. The only known print of the Weber portrait belongs to Joy Weber, Max's daughter. It is undated, but a variant composition also belonging to Weber is signed and dated 19KS14.

11. A letter from Paul Anderson to Struss, written while Struss was in the army and Anderson was running their studio, suggests that relations between Weber and Anderson had cooled by 1918: "I understand White and Weber have had a row and Weber leaves at the end of the term. Happy days! He—Weber—is going to start and [sic] art school somewhere in the Berkshires; wanted to know if he could get board for his pupils in East Canaan [the site of White's summer school]. Absolutely impossible." The letter was dated simply "Sunday night," but Weber left White's school in 1918. Struss Family Papers.

12. Harvith interview.

13. Ibid.

14. Struss Pictorial Lens brochure, 1915.

15. Harvith interview.

16. When Struss entered the army, Anderson took over his studio and took charge of the sale of the Struss Pictorial Lens. Together they manufactured and sold Anderson's invention Kalogen, a developer meant to replace the

German-made Rodinal. In 1918, Anderson closed the studio and stopped teaching photography. Although very supportive of Struss during the war, Anderson lost touch with Struss shortly after the latter moved to California. See Terence R. Pitts, "Paul Lewis Anderson, A life in Photography," *The Archive* [Center for Creative Photography, University of Arizona], no. 18 (May 1983): 4-14.

17. The bulk of Anderson's photographs were given to George Eastman House. Because Anderson's work offers such an excellent example of pictorial printing processes, the staff of Eastman House organized the Anderson Collection by medium rather than by subject and regularly uses it to teach students a wide range of photographic techniques.

18. Anderson's first book derived from a series of articles published in the *American Photographer* between 1912 and 1914. His account of "The Development of Pictorial Photography in the U.S. During the Past Quarter Century" (8 [1914]: 326-334) is an invaluable account of pictorial politics from the point of view of White's circle. Anderson's second book was drawn from his teachings at White's School.

19. H. R. Poore (1859-1940), a Paris-trained painter and professor at the Pennsylvania Academy of Fine Arts, lived near Anderson in Orange, New Jersey. His book, *Pictorial Composition and the Critical Judgement of Pictures* (New York: Baker and Taylor, 1903), went through many editions and greatly influenced Anderson. It included a chapter on "The Place of Photography in Fine Art," which may well have resulted from discussion with Anderson. For Anderson's remarks on Dow, see *Pictorial Landscape Photography* (Boston: Wilfred A. French, 1914), p. 20. My opinion of Anderson's photographs is based on a survey of his collection at George Eastman House and at the Museum of Modern Art, which has a large and excellent selection.

20. The undoctrinaire spirit within White's circle is further demonstrated by the friendship between ultra-conservative Anderson and avant-garde Max Weber; the George Eastman House collection contains a beautiful 1914 portrait of Weber by Anderson; Joy Weber owns a variant of this work.

21. Harvith interview.

22. See Stieglitz's *Venetian Canal* (1894), recently on view in several variant prints in the exhibition *Stieglitz in the Darkroom* (National Gallery of Art, 1993), and Coburn's

Shadows and Reflections, Venice (1905) in Helmut and Alison Gernsheim, eds., *Alvin Langdon Coburn Photographer, An Autobiography* (New York: Dover Publications, Inc., 1978), pl. 35, p. 81.

23. The Albright Art Gallery's new building opened in 1905. In 1911, Struss made an album that contained sixteen photographs of the Gallery's exterior to commemorate the 1910 exhibition. For further discussion of the album, now in the Amon Carter Museum, see n. 80 below.

24. Within Stieglitz's circle, this reaction was commonplace. Stieglitz himself was initially crestfallen upon his return from Europe but soon turned to New York as the central subject of his art. John Marin and Max Weber had similar experiences. Outside Stieglitz's circle, Whistlerian printmaker Joseph Pennell was another artist who seized upon New York as his primary subject upon returning from Europe. See n. 36 below for Pennell's published prints of New York.

25. For an encyclopedic treatment of New York's architecture and urban planning at the turn of the century, see Robert A. M. Stern et al., *New York 1900: Metropolitan Architecture and Urbanism 1890-1915* (New York: Rizzoli, 1983).

26. H. G. Wells, *The Future in America* (New York and London: Harper & Bros., 1906), p. 37.

27. The Amon Carter Museum, which owns Struss' negatives, has made contact prints from them. By studying the nearly 400 contact prints of Struss' New York subjects, I was able to identify most of them. While there are far more negatives than extant vintage prints, there are many prints for which negatives are missing. The largest holdings of Struss prints are in the Amon Carter Museum, the J. Paul Getty Museum, and the collection of Susan and John Harvith, Syracuse, New York. Unless otherwise noted, the images discussed in this essay are ones that Struss chose to print.

28. Struss' photographs serve as a virtual guide to McKim, Mead & White's public buildings in New York, including Madison Square Garden, the Herald Building, Columbia University, New York University's Bronx campus, the Knickerbocker Trust Company, Tiffany's, and Pennsylvania Station.

29. Thomas Bender and William R. Taylor offer an inter-

esting analysis of turn-of-the-century New York architecture. They point out that civic leaders responded to the public's concern about the appearance of commercial skyscrapers by sponsoring massive horizontal structures, such as the city's train stations and the New York Public Library. Bender and Taylor, "Culture and Architecture: Some Aesthetic Tensions in the Shaping of Modern New York City," in *Visions of the Modern City, Essays in History, Art and Literature*, ed. by William Sharpe and Leonard Wallock (New York: Columbia University Press, 1987), pp. 185-215; reprinted in William R. Taylor, *In Pursuit of Gotham, Culture and Commerce in New York* (New York and London: Oxford University Press, 1992), pp. 51-68. Stern's *New York 1900* expands on Bender and Taylor's thesis.

30. A few negatives and a few prints depict residential neighborhoods; two are near his St. Nicholas Avenue home, and the rest remain unidentified.

31. Many of these complexes were not far from his home, especially the College of the City of New York.

32. In his 1914 photographs of Washington, D.C., for the Mergenthaler Linotype Company, Struss similarly depicted the city's federal and neoclassical buildings—the White House, the Capitol, Union Station, the Library of Congress, and the Senate Office Building. In a brief catalogue essay, Kevin Grogan rightly notes the "European" quality of Struss' Washington photographs, but misdates the works. See Grogan, *Karl Struss: Washington, D.C., July 1912* (Washington, D.C.: The Fine Arts Center, 1980).

A noteworthy exception to Struss' "old world" handling of stately, revival-style buildings are his photographs of the Cathedral of St. John the Divine (1899-1911) at Amsterdam Avenue and 112th Street. In two photographs, Struss placed the 110th St. El station in the foreground, with the looming structure of the cathedral under construction behind.

33. The Park views show the new Plaza Hotel (1907) rising above the trees at its southeast corner. In the same years that Struss was photographing New York, Czech-born photographer Dr. D. J. Ruzicka rose to prominence in pictorialist circles with pastoral photographs of Central Park. See Christian A. Peterson and Daniela Mrazkova, *The Modern Pictorialism of D. J. Ruzicka* (Minneapolis: The Minneapolis Institute of Arts, 1990).

34. Peter Bacon Hales, *Silver Cities, The Photography of*

American Urbanization 1839-1915 (Philadelphia: Temple University Press, 1984), chapter 2.

35. In 1906, Henry James visited New York after a twenty-five-year absence. His impressions (ranging from dismay to horror) were published in *Harper's Monthly* and collected in *The American Scene* (New York and London: Harper & Bros., 1907). For the socialist Gorky, whose objections were more ideological than aesthetic, see "The City of Mammon," *Appleton's Magazine* (August 1906), pp. 177-182.

For further discussion of the "picturesque" debate about New York, see Wanda A. Corn's seminal article, "The New New York," *Art in America* 61 (July-August 1973): 58-65; Alan Trachtenberg, "Image and Ideology, New York in the Photographer's Eye," *Journal of Urban History* 10, no. 4 (August 1984): 453-464; Merrill Schleier, *The Skyscraper in American Art, 1890-1931* (Ann Arbor, Michigan: UMI Research, 1986), chapter 1; and Marianne Doezema, *George Bellows and Urban America* (New Haven and London: Yale University Press, 1992), chapter 1.

For a broad-stroked essay on the political conservatism of artists' renderings of turn-of-the-century New York, see Sam Bass Warner, Jr., "Slums and Skyscrapers, Urban Images, Symbols and Ideology," in *Cities of the Mind, Images and Themes of the City in the Social Sciences*, ed. by Lloyd Rodwin and Robert M. Hollister (New York: Plenum Press, 1984), pp. 181-195.

36. John C. Van Dyke, *The New New York, A Commentary on the Place and the People* (New York: The Macmillan Co., 1909), p. viii. Van Dyke's book is the most extensive defense of New York as a picturesque subject. It is illustrated with twenty-five color and ninety-eight black and white sketches by Joseph Pennell. Pennell combined a light Whistlerian touch with standard architectural rendering to create a widely imitated style of travel illustration. He published numerous prints of New York, including a portfolio of six etchings in the *Century* (March 1905), and *The Great New York*, a 1912 book of twenty-three lithographs. Typical of Pennell's followers was Vernon Howe Bailey, who illustrated H. G. Wells' *The Future in America* (1906).

37. Van Dyke devotes entire chapters of *The New New York* to the sights and sounds of New York at various times of day and seasons of the year. Also see William Sharpe, "New York, Night, and Cultural Mythmaking, The Nocturne in Photography, 1890-1925," *Smithsonian Studies in American Art* 2, no. 3 (Fall 1988): 3-21. Before the age of

the automobile, New York, which had banned the burning of soft coal, was famous for its unusually clean air. This was a liability for artists, for whom soot softened the edges of urban structures; London, the sootiest of Old World capitals, was a model of pleasing smog. New York artists had to resort to mist, rain, snow, twilight, and night to soften the clarity of its relatively clean air.

38. Camille Pissarro's urban paintings of Paris and Rouen in the 1890s are examples of a French Impressionist's exploration of the picturesque city. Pissarro beautified and unified chaotic street life and raw dockside industry using atmospheric veils of rain, mist, and soot. See Richard R. Brettell and Joachim Pissarro, *The Impressionist and the City: Pissarro's Series Paintings* (Dallas: Dallas Museum of Art, 1993).

39. *Camera Notes* 4 (October 1900): 91-97; reprinted in Sadakichi Hartmann, Harry W. Lawton, and George Knowx, eds., *The Valiant Knights of Daguerre, Selected Critical Essays on Photography and Profiles of Photographic Pioneers* (Berkeley: University of California Press, 1978), pp. 56-63. Stieglitz was editor of *Camera Notes* from 1896 to 1902, and without him, the journal soon folded. Its last issue contained an article by Sidney Allan (Hartmann's pseudonym) on "Picturesque New York, The Esthetic Side of Jewtown" (6 [December 1903]: 143-148). Intended as a response to his earlier "plea for picturesqueness," Allan claimed that "the Hebrew quarter is undoubtedly the most *picturesque* part of New York City, *i.e.*, the one which lends itself most easily to artistic interpretation" (Allan's emphasis, p. 145).

40. Stieglitz's hand in orchestrating his reputation can be seen in the writings of J. Nilsen Laurvik, a member of the Photo-Secession and an organizer of the 1908 National Arts Club exhibition. Stieglitz printed Laurvik's review of the exhibition in *Camera Work* 26 (April 1909): 41, which singled out Stieglitz's New York photographs for special praise. Laurvik claimed that Stieglitz's photographs "ha[ve] furnished many of our younger photographers the inspiration for a whole series of New York street scenes, besides being responsible for opening the eyes of the painters to the pictorial possibilities of so-called ugly New York." When Laurvik became a reviewer for *International Studio*, his praise for Stieglitz grew: "His *Winter—Fifth Avenue*. . . created a sensation, not only in photographic circles, but in the world of art, and blazed the way for a whole school of painters, who set themselves the task of depicting the streets and life of New York"; see *International Studio* 44 (August 1911): 25.

The latter review was cited by Sharpe in his "New York, Night, and Cultural Myth-making," p. 20, n. 21.

41. In *Camera Work* 4 (October 1903), Stieglitz defended the much-ridiculed Fuller Building, just completed in 1902 and given the pejorative nickname the Flatiron Building. In addition to his now-famous photograph of the building, suitably softened by snow, Stieglitz published a celebratory poem and essay by Sadakichi Hartmann.

42. Compare *The City of Ambition*, in Dorothy Norman, *Alfred Stieglitz, An American Seer* (New York: Random House, 1973), pl. xxiv, to Pennell's *Docks and Slips*, pl. 7 in Van Dyke, *The New New York*.

43. Harvith interview, March 30, 1975.

44. Harvith interview, December 30, 1974.

45. In a 1976 interview, Struss discussed *Man's Construction*. He often crossed the river at twilight to photograph the Manhattan skyline and was particularly interested in the illumination of the World Building. He felt that the industrial structures in the foreground lent interest to the image and pointed out the triangular formations in the composition, explaining that he often looked for triangles in composing his photographs. Stephen White interview, November 12, 1976, roll 6. Sharpe discusses *Man's Construction* in "New York, Night, and Cultural Myth-making," in *Smithsonian Studies in American Art* 2 (Fall 1988): 14, but misses the title's pun.

46. The diamond-shaped grid of the Brooklyn Bridge cables over the skyline became a modernist cliché in the 1920s and 1930s. For several examples, see Leslie Nolan, *Shared Perspectives: The Printmaker and Photographer in New York, 1900-1950* (New York: Museum of the City of New York, 1993), cat. nos. 51-54. Struss' appears to be the earliest version.

47. Struss' negatives show two other series that employ the same strategy of walking toward a subject, juggling the compositional elements of near and far. They are of the Flatiron Building, looking south on Fifth Avenue, and the Times Tower, looking south on Broadway. There are no known prints of these series.

48. The *Camera Work* photogravure of *Two Towers* is undated, but Stieglitz apparently exhibited a print in his

1913 exhibition at 291; that print was dated 1911. I thank Julia Thompson, Department of Photographs, National Gallery of Art, for this information.

49. Harvith interview.

50. In *Alvin Langdon Coburn, Symbolist Photographer 1882-1966, Beyond the Craft* (Millerton, New York: Aperture and George Eastman House, 1986, pp. 33-42), Mike Weaver offers an interesting discussion of Coburn's city views, noting Coburn's relation to travel illustration (especially Pennell) and impressionism.

51. Although originally commissioned by the Knickerbocker Trust Company, the McKim, Mead & White building changed hands in 1907, when the Knickerbocker failed. The company's failure caused Coburn (and Gertrude Käsebier, among others) serious financial loss, a fact that was certainly in Coburn's mind when he photographed the imposing edifice. See Coburn to Stieglitz, November 17 and 20, 1907, Stieglitz Archive, Beinecke Rare Book Library, Yale University.

52. See Temple Scott, "Fifth Avenue and the Boulevard Saint-Michel," *Forum* 44 (July-December 1910): 665-685, for a thinly veiled fictional account of such a supper. From 1910 to 1916, *Forum* was published by Mitchell Kennerley, owner of the Anderson Galleries and a Stieglitz intimate.

53. Hartmann, *Camera Work* 30 (April 1910), pp. 23-25; reprinted in *The Valiant Knights of Daguerre*, pp. 132-134, and in Jonathan Green, ed., *Camera Work, A Critical Anthology* (Millerton, New York: Aperture, Inc., 1973), pp. 199-202. For Coburn, see *Camera Work* 36 (October 1911), p. 72-73, reprinted in *Camera Work, An Anthology*, pp. 215-216.

54. See Percy North's essay "Max Weber, The Cubist Decade," pp. 30-39 in the exhibition catalogue of the same name, for Weber's and Coburn's 1911-12 relationship.

55. In "The Cubist Decade," p. 33, n.65, Percy North determined that Weber's *New York* was painted from the Woolworth Tower, not from the Singer Tower as the painting's subtitle states.

56. Catalogue essay for 1913 Goupil Gallery exhibition, *New York from Its Pinnacles*, cited in Gernsheim (eds.), *Coburn, An Autobiography*, p. 84.

57. Edward R. Dickson, review of the International Exhibition of Pictorial Photography at the Ehrich Galleries, *Platinum Print* 1, no. 3 (March 1914): 9.

58. Alvin Langdon Coburn, "The Relation of Time to Art," *Camera Work* 36 (October 1911), p. 72.

59. *Cubist Poems* (London: Elkin Mathews, 1914), p. 11; reprinted in North, *Max Weber, The Cubist Decade*, p. 97.

60. Gernsheim, eds., *Coburn, An Autobiography*, p. 84.

61. The only known prints of these two views are in the Harviths' collection; the works were left undated at the time they were printed, and the Harviths have titled and dated the works "New York, ca. 1911." The negative of the park's northeast corner is in the Amon Carter Museum, but it was left unidentified and undated by Struss. The negative of the southeast corner is lost.

These two prints have been singled out for special attention before and grouped with Coburn's *The Octopus*, although it has not previously been recognized that they were all taken from the top of the Metropolitan Tower. Pultz and Scallen included them both in *Cubism and American Photography*, nos. 61 & 62. Kirk Varnedoe reproduced the northeast corner view and Coburn's *The Octopus* in "The Overview: Flight of the Mind," *A Fine Disregard, What Makes Modern Art Modern* (New York: Harry N. Abrams, Inc., 1989), figs. 255 & 256.

62. In "Overview: The Flight of the Mind," Varnedoe argues that overhead views by early modern artists such as Struss and Coburn were simply aimed at describing the world from the novel vantage point afforded by the observation decks of skyscrapers (p. 243). He writes that artists pursuing a more developed form of modernism in the 1920s, such as Rodchenko and Moholy-Nagy, placed an "emphasis not on what art could say about reality as we experience it, but on the ways art could change the way we perceive it" (p. 259). As discussed below, Struss and Coburn were not simply recording new points of view but were altering the way we perceive reality.

63. Alvin Langdon Coburn to Karl Struss, January 24, 1912, Stephen White Collection.

64. *Vanishing Point II*, taken from the Brooklyn Bridge, is a more complex composition: overhead tracks and their shadows frame the bridge and an oncoming train.

65. Pultz and Scallen, in *Cubism and American Photography, 1910-1930*, label Struss an "innate" modernist, along with Stieglitz, Haviland, White, Anderson and Coburn. They distinguish this group from a second group which includes Stieglitz (after 1915), Strand, Schamberg, Sheeler, and Steichen, who "self-consciously" experimented with cubism.

66. There are one or two other exceptions. *Water Street* (1910), which shows people shopping from a street vendor near the Brooklyn Bridge, is a rare Struss photograph of the city's lower classes. A more extensive series depicts the area near Washington Market, on the Lower West Side. Today's Tribeca, this was a bustling commercial district which mixed early nineteenth-century three-story buildings and late nineteenth-century cast iron warehouses. Struss was drawn to the neighborhood, just as Berenice Abbott was in the 1930s. The print of the Butterick Publishing Company, on Varick Street between Spring and Vandam Streets, which was included in *On the Art of Fixing a Shadow*, pl. 191, belongs to this group.

67. Over thirty images—negatives and/or prints—in the Amon Carter collection depict the factory neighborhood, including many previously unidentified New York images.

68. Stieglitz also photographed the Vanderbilt's scalloped lights, which appear in several of his 1915-16 series *From the Back Window 291*. See the Stieglitz Collection, National Gallery of Art, 49.3.401 and 49.3.403.

69. A group of negatives (nos. 3130, 3132, 3134, 3137) includes the construction and the parade. The compositions are wonderfully complex and dynamic, but there are no extant prints.

70. Struss managed, despite the long exposure time required, to make an autochrome of this subject.

71. See Nolan, *Shared Perspectives*, nos. 9-12.

72. See Clarence H. White to Alfred Stieglitz, May 15, 1912, and Stieglitz to White, May 23, 1912, Stieglitz Collection, Beinecke Library, Yale University.

73. See Karl Struss to Alfred Stieglitz, June 13, 1912, and Stieglitz to Struss, June 14, 1912, Stieglitz Collection, Beinecke Library, Yale University.

74. See Letter from Coburn, Struss, and White to Alfred Stieglitz, typed on stationery with the Struss factory address, September 14, 1912, Stieglitz Collection, Beinecke Library, Yale University.

75. Karl Struss to Alfred Stieglitz, September 19, 1912, Stieglitz Collection, Beinecke Library, Yale University.

76. Alfred Stieglitz to Cornelia Sage, November 13, 1912, Stieglitz Collection, Beinecke Library, Yale University. "McColl" is William D. MacColl, an art critic who supported modern art and photography. "Mrs. Coburn" is Alvin Langdon Coburn's mother.

77. Harvith interview, September 12, 1975.

78. Struss recalled how convenient it was for him to visit 291 during the years 1914-17, when he occupied White's old studio across the street; Harvith interview.

79. The Harviths produced two invaluable research aids: worksheets for the prints in their 1976 Struss exhibition and an exhibition chronology. The worksheets recorded Struss' memories about each print, including exhibition history. The chronology lists the titles of works mentioned in Struss' collection of exhibition catalogues and press clippings. It is not always possible to determine which print a title represents, but those exhibited repeatedly are easily identified.

80. The Struss album is in the Amon Carter Museum collection; the White album is in the Clarence H. White Collection, Princeton University; the Whittemore album belongs to Warren Coville of Bloomfield Hills, Michigan, a collector who specializes in students of the White School.

81. The three scenes are themselves something of a survey, depicting very different aspects of New York life: the park across from Struss' father's factory; the intersection of Fifth Avenue and 42nd Street; and a skyline view from the commercial district near Washington Market.

82. Whittemore was apparently a prominent White student, for her work was included in the Newark, Montross, and Ehrich exhibitions. On several occasions, she modeled for Struss. She worked together with Struss and Anderson to submit entries to the Kodak advertising competition of 1916: a series of prints depicts Struss instructing Whittemore with the camera in front of the New York Public Library and in Pennsylvania Station; these are in the Paul Anderson Col-

lection, George Eastman House. Whittemore and Struss were the models for Struss' silhouette illustrating "Woman's Place," a story by Parker Fillmore in *Harper's Bazar*, March 1917, p. 63. Whittemore illustrated the first installment of Temple Bailey's "Bread and Honey" in *Harper's Bazar* (November 1915), p. 33, and Struss illustrated the second (December 1915), p. 51.

83. From the list of titles, it is difficult to identify the works fully. Some are easily recognized from their titles: *Chatham Square*; *Earl Hall, Columbia University, Night*; and *Metropolitan Tower, Dusk* were kept in later exhibitions. Others, such as *Hotel Plaza, Night*, are of identifiable subjects, but the prints are lost. Still others, such as *First Avenue*, *Park Avenue Southward*, and *The Sky-Line, Wall Street Ferry*, identify a group of images but not specific prints. Struss also used typically picturesque titles, such as *New York, Past and Present*, and *Sunlight, Snow, Steam and Shadow*, which offer no clues to the photographs' locations.

84. Struss to Stieglitz, June 6, 1912, and Stieglitz to Struss, June 14, 1912, Alfred Stieglitz Collection, Beinecke Library, Yale University.

85. "Color Photography," *American Photography* 11, no. 8 (August 1917): 437.

86. *Platinum Print* 1, no. 3 (March 1914): 12, ran a complete list of those attending the Chinatown dinner. *American Photography*, March 1915, p. 179, in its "Notes and News" column, announced the meeting of "a very enthusiastic group of photographic workers, without a name or definite organization, which meets on the second Thursday of each month at the Little Book Shop, 2 East 29th Street, New York City, to look at lantern slides and pictures, to exchange ideas, and to get together generally for mutual benefit." Both Struss and Strand attended the December 1914 meeting, at which Max Weber criticized pictures.

87. Strand's 1915 photograph looking out a window onto snowy rooftops, which was published in *Camera Work* 48 (pl. IV), bears comparison to Struss' *291 New York* (1915) and similar works by Stieglitz.

88. Struss' and Strand's street views drew Stieglitz's praise at the 1917 Wanamaker exhibition, which he judged. Strand's *Wall Street* (1915) won first prize and Struss' *East Side Promenade* (1911) won fifth. Nineteen seventeen was Struss' third and last year exhibiting in these exhibitions,

which were sponsored by the Philadelphia-based department store. Struss' strong showing in them, which routinely drew over a thousand entries and which Stieglitz judged from 1912 to 1920, is the only clear indication that Stieglitz valued Struss' work after 1912. In 1915, Struss won third prize, two lesser prizes, and an honorable mention. In 1916, he won a fifth prize and seven honorable mentions. And in 1917, when Steichen was also a judge, Struss won fifth prize for *East Side Promenade*, another unspecified prize, and two honorable mentions.

89. A wonderful exception is *Fifth Avenue* (1915), which audaciously truncates two pedestrians who turn to look back at the photographer; see Sarah Greenough, *Paul Strand: An American Vision* (New York: Aperture Foundation with National Gallery of Art, Washington, 1990), p. 16.

90. Calvin Tomkins, "Profiles: Look to the Things Around You," *New Yorker* (September 16, 1974), p. 46; quoted in Greenough, *Paul Strand*, p. 165, n. 27. Greenough uses this quotation to characterize the revolutionary nature of Strand's street scenes.

91. *Camera Work* 48 (October 1916), p. 11; repeated verbatim in *Camera Work* 49-50 (June 1917), p. 36.

92. In his 1917 article "Color Photography" (p. 437), Struss complained of the stale repetitiousness of pictorialist photography and did not mention Strand's newest work, which had just appeared in the June issue of *Camera Work*, along with Stieglitz's lavish praise, although he certainly would have seen it. He did comment on Coburn's abstract Vortographs, also of 1917: "Others have in seeming desperation gone to all sorts of extremes (as, for instance, Coburn's highly original and amusing 'Vortographs')" (p. 437).

93. *Camera Work* 49-50 (June 1917), p. 36.

94. Walker Evans' 1929 reaction to Strand's street portraits shows how radical and disturbing the images could be. Evans remarked: "I came across that picture of Strand's blind woman and that really bowled me over. . . . That's a very powerful picture. I saw it in the New York Public Library files of *Camera Work*. That's the stuff, that's the thing to do." Alan Trachtenberg, *Reading American Photographs, Images as History, Matthew Brady to Walker Evans* (New York: Hill and Wang, 1989), p. 312, n. 15.

95. The most famous of Strand's abstractions turned 90 degrees is plate X in *Camera Work* 49-50, now called *Porch Shadows*. Less known but no less radical is plate VIII, an overhead view of girder shadows and pedestrians. Later in his life, Strand renounced his experiments in abstraction as peripheral to his realist orientation to photography.

96. Greenough, in *Paul Strand*, p. 35, declares all three groups revolutionary. In discussing Strand's street views, she distinguishes them from earlier New York City views by Stieglitz, Steichen, Coburn, and Struss; Strand's alone, she writes, combine "both a strong formal concern and an interest in movement and dynamism." I would draw the dividing line differently, with the early picturesque works of Steichen, Stieglitz, and Coburn on one side, and Coburn's and Struss' modernist photographs of 1911-12 and Strand's and Stieglitz's photographs of 1915-16 on the other.

97. In 1914, Struss worked at night developing negatives for Baron de Meyer, who was forced by the war to work as a portrait photographer. De Meyer opened a studio in the new Biltmore Hotel across from Grand Central Station.

98. In an interview with Henry Hoyt Moore, White remarked that "probably the greatest development of photography is in home photography or home portraiture"; "Progress of Pictorial Photography," *Pictorial Photography in America* (New York: Pictorial Photographers of America, 1918), p. 9.

99. In his early years in Ohio, White had looked to popular illustration for his own compositional ideas. For White's interest in popular magazines, see Bunnell, *Clarence H. White*, pp. 6, 16-17.

100. Dow's aesthetics stressed the importance of bringing beauty into the lives of the common man. White was also influenced by socialist Eugene Debs, whom he photographed and met socially in Terre Haute, Indiana. See Maynard P. White, Jr., "Clarence H. White: Artist in Life and Photography," in *Symbolism of Light: The Photographs of Clarence H. White* (Wilmington: Delaware Art Museum, 1977), pp. 18-19.

101. White developed a three-part program: the Clarence H. White School of Photography; the Pictorial Photographers of America; and the Art Center, an umbrella organization for several commercial art groups, including the PPA. These organizations provided young photographers with classes, a national network of fellow art photographers, and a local center for meetings and exhibitions. See Yochelson, "Clarence H. White Reconsidered."

102. White, "The Progress of Pictorial Photography," p. 15.

103. August 15, 1915.

104. Struss' photographs appeared on the covers of the *Evening Post, Saturday Magazine* on June 14, July 12, July 19, and November 1, 1913. They also appeared on the cover of the *Independent Weekly Magazine* on August 2, December 13, and December 27, 1915, and on January 31, 1916. The *Independent* reproduced Struss autochromes as colored halftones on March 6, 1916, and May 12, 1917.

105. *Platinum Print* 1, no. 2 (December 1913), inside front cover.

106. Struss was successful enough to hire a darkroom assistant and secretary (Stephen White interview, November 12, 1976, roll 1). Among Struss' papers are a series of lists of commercial assignments from the New York studio. He also marketed the Struss Pictorial Lens, and along with Paul Anderson, sold the developer Kalogen.

107. *Harper's Bazaar* was originally spelled with one "a"; the title changed in 1929 to the current spelling.

108. Barbara L. Michaels speculates that *Vanity Fair*'s photographic features were arranged with the help of Baron de Meyer, who was close to Condé Nast's staff and worked regularly for the magazine beginning in 1914; Michaels, *Gertrude Käsebier: The Photographer and Her Photographs* (New York: Harry N. Abrams, Inc., 1992), p. 152.

109. These works ran under several other variant titles, including *Twilight and the Vanishing City* (in *Vanity Fair*, January 1915, p. 18); *Manhattan at Night* (*Vanity Fair*, April 1915, p. 56); and *The Metropolitan Tower by Twilight* (*Vanity Fair*, July 1915, p. 62).

110. See Temple Bailey, "Bread and Honey," *Harper's Bazar* (December 1915), p. 51; Wallace Irwin, "A Certain Poor Slacker" (December 1916), p. 58, and (January 1917), p. 49; Cosmo Hamilton, "The Great Competition" (February 1917), p. 45; Parker Fillmore, "Woman's Place" (March 1917), p. 63; Temple Bailey, "Lady Crusoe" (April 1917), p. 50; May Edginton, "Heart—Trumps" (July 1917), p. 29. In August 1916, *Harper's Bazar* ran a three-quarter-

page photograph by Struss of Fifth Avenue traffic in its "What's Going On" column, p. 27.

111. Susan and John Harvith own a series of these mounted illustration photographs.

112. The company published a "New York at Night" series of uncredited penny postcards which look very much like Struss' work and may have been commissioned from him; Prints & Photographs Department, Museum of the City of New York.

113. A series of prints of Struss, Whittemore, and Anderson on their camera outing is in the Paul Anderson Collection, International Museum of Photography, George Eastman House.

114. *Harper's Bazar* (May 1915), page preceding table of contents.

115. Clippings in Struss' papers, Stephen White Collection, include Bonwit Teller, Grand Rapids Furniture Co., New Perfection Oil Cook Stove, Lea-Perrin Worcestershire Sauce, and Grape-Nuts Cereal.

116. In the Sanatogen advertisement, Struss' style resembles that of Lejaren a Hiller, his only serious competitor. Trained as a painter, Hiller began publishing photographic illustrations as early as 1908. His carefully orchestrated, soft-focus tableaux perfectly captured the Gibsonesque style. Hiller went on to become a leading advertising photographer in the 1930s and 1940s. For a brief biography of Hiller, see Robert A. Sobieszek, *The Art of Persuasion, A History of Advertising Photography* (New York: Harry N. Abrams, Inc., 1988), p. 194.

117. *Vanity Fair* (March 15, 1916), p. 34. Barbara Michaels mentions "the popularity of silhouette designs in commercial art during the teens" as a source for the fad, in *Gertrude Käsebier*, p. 152.

118. Struss' first attempt at silhouettes may have been for a brochure advertising a skating show at the Hippodrome.

119. There are two copies of the deluxe edition in public collections, one in the Art Museum, Princeton University, and one in the Visual Studies Workshop, Rochester. Five of the twenty-five images in the two versions are different. I have not seen an example of the regular edition.

120. The three artists were Herbert Martini, F. Winold Reiss, and Willy Pogany. All were muralists, illustrators, and decorative painters. Struss may have met Pogany at the Metropolitan Opera, where he worked as a stage designer in 1916-17.

121. An advertising flyer for the portfolio describes the project and mentions plans for the open-air series; Department of Photographs, Metropolitan Museum of Art.

122. *Platinum Print* 1, no. 6 (November 1914), and 2, no. 2 (1915). The trend in dance photography inspired Frederick Lewis Allen to write the spoof, "Terpsichore, The Present Rage for Rhythmic Dancing and Blurred Art" for *Vanity Fair* (March 1915), pp. 47-48. Allen describes his attempt on vacation to photograph his wife at dawn in Grecian garb, only to be spied upon by a scoffing brother-in-law.

123. Arnold Genthe, *The Book of the Dance* (New York: Mitchell Kennerley, 1916). Genthe's book may have served as a corrective to *Dancing and Dancers of Today, The Modern Revival of Dancing as an Art*, by Charles Caffin and his wife Caroline (New York: Dodd Mead and Co., 1912). A critic of modern art and pictorial photography, Caffin illustrated his book with stiff formulaic studio photography. In 1929, Genthe published *Isadora Duncan, Twenty-four Studies* (New York and London: Mitchell Kennerley), which reproduced his photographs of Duncan taken during her American tours of 1915-18. Another dance book from pictorialist circles was Edward R. Dickson's *Poems of the Dance, Anthology 1500 B.C.-1920 A.D.* (New York: Knopf, 1921), which was illustrated with Dickson's photographs of dancers in the woods.

124. The three texts were an interview by Coburn with George Bernard Shaw, "On the Nude in Photography"; an article "Nude or Undressed," by Dr. Frank Crane; and a poem by Edward H. Pfeiffer, "Hymn to the Body of Man."

125. An unsolved mystery is the possible involvement of Nickolas Muray, a Hungarian-born photographer who came to the United States in 1913, worked as a color-separation printer and became a leader in commercial photography. One of the prints in the portfolio (a crouching figure holding panpipes) can be found in Muray's collection at George Eastman House. A catalogue card for the photograph tentatively identifies the dancer as Muray's wife. Perhaps Muray was involved in the color printing of the portfolio or his wife was one of the models chosen for the project.

126.   Genthe's book shows the taboo on nude modeling: all the dancers are identified by name except those in the chapter on "classic dancers," the book's only nudes.

127.   F. K. Ferenz to Karl Struss, March 20, 1919, Stephen White Collection.

128.   After lamenting the state of art photography, Struss wrote, "And now, almost at the psychological moment, comes the newest form of color photography by the Hess-Ives method"; "Color Photography," p. 437. Accompanying the article are two Struss Hess-Ives nudes reproduced by colored halftone.

129.   Struss routinely mined his commercial negatives for potential exhibition prints. Two examples bear mention: he made a platinum print from one of the five exposures taken backstage at a vaudeville show starring Henrietta Crossman, at the Palace Theater at Broadway and 47th Street, and a platinum print from one of his ten exposures of an as-yet-unidentified Chekhovian play. Both prints are in the J. Paul Getty Museum.

130.   Struss photographed Sembach on the estate of Charles Ward, Struss' uncle. The Opera's account books show no payments for Struss but have entries for a hotel for Sembach in Edgemere and for Kurt in Norfolk.

131.   The Metropolitan Opera Company sponsored the tour, but it opened at the Manhattan Opera House, where the photographs were taken, perhaps on two different days. The backdrop for the *L'Apres-Midi d'un Faune* photographs is the set for that ballet; the backdrop for the *Till Eulenspiegel* photographs is for *Spectre de la Rose*.

132.   "Photo Call with Nijinsky: The Circle and the Center," *Ballet Review* (Winter 1987), pp. 49-71.

133.   The Pierrot costume was used in more than one ballet, but the two female dancers with Bolm are wearing costumes from *Papillon*.

134.   Harvith interview, September 1, 1975.

135.   Ibid.

136.   "The Progress of Pictorial Photography," p. 6.

137.   Letter of recommendation "to whom it may concern," dated February 6, 1919, Stephen White Collection.

138.   Anderson to Struss, dated "Sunday night," Struss Family Papers. The letter, which discusses Weber's break with White, must have been written in 1918.

139.   Since the late 1970s, a spate of articles have attacked Stieglitz's premise that photography is a fine art medium. The endurance of Stieglitz's legacy for a generation after his death reflects in large part the influence of historian Beaumont Newhall and the Museum of Modern Art. For Stieglitz's institutional influence, see Christopher Phillips, "The Judgement Seat of Photography," *October 22* (Fall 1982), pp. 27-63; reprinted in Richard Bolton, ed., *The Contest of Meaning, Critical Histories of Photography* (Cambridge, Mass.: MIT Press, 1989), pp. 15-48; and Maria Morris Hambourg, "From 291 to the Museum of Modern Art: Photography in New York, 1910-1937," *The New Vision, Photography Between the World Wars, Ford Motor Company Collection at the Metropolitan Museum of Art* (New York: Metropolitan Museum of Art, 1989), pp. 3-63.

140.   See notes 62, 65, 90, and 96.

141.   In "From 291 to the Museum of Modern Art," p. 33, Hambourg retains Stieglitz's low estimation of commercial photography. She writes that Stieglitz and Strand "could no more translate their art into a popular idiom than abandon their souls, so they shunned commercial photography and mass reproduction." By contrast, White's students were "like translators diligently transcribing grammar and syntax, while ignoring the poem's significance."

PORTFOLIO II
LATER WORK

By the time Karl Struss left New York to join the army in 1917, he had mastered the skills of composition, mood, metaphor, and printmaking and was ready to translate these skills to a new medium. When he moved to California, his new career placed the movie camera first, but he continued to produce and exhibit masterful still photographs, both as a way to remain sensitive to the individual image and to inspire his work with moving pictures. In 1921 he resumed submitting photographs to pictorial salons; by the end of the decade, he had participated in over forty exhibitions (frequently entering five a year) while pursuing his career as a cinematographer. He continued to exhibit his earlier New York and European views but also included examples from his life in the West. After hours, Struss concentrated not on city streets, as he had in New York, but on the western landscape and seascape. His work in Hollywood also provided him with many fascinating possibilities, including publicity portraits, figure studies, studies made on the studio lot or movie sets, and stills made during filming. Although he used bright lighting and a sharp lens to produce stills for the studio's promotional needs, Struss frequently made photographs for his own purposes using his soft-focus lens and soft lighting.

His first experience with documenting the performing arts was in New York, although none of those works suggest the talent he displayed once he arrived in Hollywood. His photographs of dancers Vaslav Nijinsky and Flores Revalles (see fig. 69) and Adolph Bolm (see p. 8) are simple documentation. His backstage view of Henrietta Crossman in a play at the Palace Theater, while displaying an interest in the immediacy of live performance and the drama of onstage lighting, is so unevenly lit that the subject is difficult to understand. When Struss went to work for Cecil B. De Mille in Hollywood, however, he gathered all of his understanding of composition and lighting and quickly began capturing the atmosphere and character of the scene.

His first movie assignment was to produce film stills and publicity portraits for De Mille's domestic drama *Male and Female*, which featured his newest stars, Bebe Daniels and Gloria Swanson. Struss' luminous portraits glorify these symbols of romance and glamour. His film still of Gloria Swanson, showing the fantasy sequence in the lion's den, captures both the luxurious detail of her dress fabric and the dramatic action of the lion's roar and communicates an exhilarating mixture of sensuality and danger.

Struss' other film stills frequently play with the confused morality communicated in early silent films. *The Faith Healer* uses a beam of light from above to symbolize heavenly intervention in a tent revival scene. Fantasy sequences—a frequently utilized technique—gave filmgoers temporary relief from a heavy moral tone through an excursion into a fairy tale. In the Cinderella fantasy scene in *Forbidden Fruit*, Agnes Ayres sits forlorn in an empty ballroom, seemingly regretting her misfortune. The unidentified film still of a scene within a picture frame (which might be a technique to communicate the story within the story) seems to tell an exotic tale of overt sexuality and murder and might be a reference to *Othello.*

When not making films or film stills for work, Struss often photographed landscapes for pleasure. His images of the Grand Canyon, taken on a side trip during his move to Los Angeles, defined his new orientation to the land. Unlike the simple silhouetted lines of hills and trees he had encountered in Nova Scotia and New Hampshire, the Grand Canyon detail and composition demanded the same kind of complex visualization he had used in photographing the "canyons" of New York City. In his constant fascination with photographic technology, Struss experiment-

ed with the simplest of lenses—the pinhole—to create the soft edge he had enjoyed with his pictorial lens. His two studies of rocks and water— *Pinhole, Monterey Coast* and *Pinhole, Breaking Wave*—convey a brooding sense of drama and mystery much like his earlier, symbolist-inspired night views in New York. His photographs of the Hawaiian jungle in thick fog, taken in 1933 while filming another Cecil B. De Mille film, *Four Frightened People*, seem to recall his earlier pictorial and modernist styles, now transferred to landscape work. The fog lends a soft-focus effect, obscuring much of the detail but leaving a sense of depth and complexity of composition that approaches some of his most abstract street scenes of New York.

Struss displayed a number of his later photographs in pictorial salons, and just as his New York views had in the 1910s, these works won him acclaim among the remaining practitioners of pictorial photography. *The Faith Healer* took second prize in the Third Frederick & Nelson Exhibition of Pictorial Photography, held in Seattle in 1921, and he showed *La Danseuse* at least twice. *Detail—Grand Canyon*, which he exhibited at least four times, was awarded third prize in the 15th Annual John Wanamaker Exhibition of Photographs, presented in Philadelphia in 1921. Some of his other favored landscapes were *Ookala, Hawaii*, which he exhibited once; *Outward Bound*, included in two exhibitions; and *Sails* (a personal favorite of his), featured in six exhibitions.

Henrietta Crossman,
Backstage at Palace Theatre,
1915, gum platinum print,
J. Paul Getty Museum

La Danseuse, 1919, platinum
print, J. Paul Getty Museum

The Faith Healer, 1921,
gum platinum print, New
Orleans Museum of Art

Agnes Ayres [Cinderella—
Fantasy Sequence from the
*film **Forbidden Fruit**],*
c. 1919-20, platinum print,
Museum of Fine Arts, Boston,
Lucy Dalbiac Luard Fund

*Fantasy scene still from
unidentified film,* c. 1921,
gelatin silver bromide print,
Amon Carter Museum

Bebe Daniels [The Siren—
Fantasy Sequence from the
*film **Male and Female**], 1919,*
gelatin silver print, Amon
Carter Museum

Portrait—Gloria Swanson,
c. 1919, gelatin silver bromide
print, Collection of John and
Susan Edwards Harvith

*Gloria Swanson in the Lion's
Den [Fantasy Sequence from
the film **Male and Female**],*
1919, gelatin silver print,
Amon Carter Museum

Poisoned Paradise *[Still
from the film]*, 1923, gelatin
silver print, Amon Carter
Museum

*Carmel Myers [Still from
the film **Poisoned Paradise**]*,
c. 1924, platinum print,
Amon Carter Museum

Detail—Grand Canyon,
1919, platinum print, Amon
Carter Museum

*Pinhole—United Artists
Studio Lot,* 1929, gelatin
silver bromide print, Amon
Carter Museum

TOP
Santa Barbara, 1921,
platinum print, Herbert F.
Johnson Museum of Art,
Cornell University

BOTTOM
White Cloud, 1922, gelatin
silver bromide print,
Museum of Fine Arts, Boston,
Sophie M. Friedman Fund

Eiffel Tower with Elephant,
1925, gelatin silver bromide
print, Collection of John
and Susan Edwards Harvith

Outward Bound, 1928,
gelatin silver bromide print,
Amon Carter Museum

Pinhole, Monterey Coast, 1921,
gelatin silver bromide print,
Hallmark Photographic
Collection, Hallmark Cards, Inc.,
Kansas City, Missouri

Pinhole, Breaking Wave, 1921,
gelatin silver bromide print,
J. Paul Getty Museum

Sails: En Route to Catalina,
c. 1929-30, gelatin silver
bromide print, Amon Carter
Museum

Ookala, Hawaii, 1933,
gelatin silver bromide print,
Amon Carter Museum

Hawaii, 1933, gelatin
silver bromide print,
Amon Carter Museum

Figure 71. Edward Weston, *Karl Struss—Los Angeles*, c. 1922-23, toned platinum print, Amon Carter Museum. Weston photographed Struss at the Schulberg Studios.

THE CINEMATOGRAPHER

Richard Koszarski

In June 1919 Karl Struss felt secure enough in Hollywood to order some new stationery. Four months after his arrival in Los Angeles, he was comfortably settled into a studio apartment at 6602 Yucca Avenue, a block north of Hollywood Boulevard and just a ten-minute walk from the Lasky studio, his new employer.

Until then Struss had been using his old New York business letterhead ("The Struss Pictorial Lens ... Especially Adapted for Pictorial Photography") as well as a stock of his old personal stationery, which still offered "Portraits by Photography" at his 31st Street studio. But all that was long behind him now, and Struss was making pictures for Cecil B. De Mille. His Hollywood stationery proudly proclaimed: "Karl Struss/Artist Photographer" (fig. 72).

If Struss really thought of himself as an artist, then what was he doing in Hollywood? Despite the achievements of men like D. W. Griffith, Charles Chaplin, Thomas H. Ince, and Cecil B. De Mille (all of whom he would eventually work with), the cinema was then scarcely recognized as a legitimate vehicle of artistic expression. The powerful theater critic George Jean Nathan, for example, had recently denounced the motion picture as "exhibiting still nothing that lifts it above the artistic and aesthetic level of Chinese cooking or German ballet."[1] Most New Yorkers of Struss' background would have agreed with Nathan, but Struss could see beyond the cinema's temporary problems with exposition and characterization. Like Sadakichi Hartmann, he understood that the motion picture's true potential lay in its poetic and pictorial qualities, and he had come to Hollywood to play his part in shaping its development.[2]

While pursuing his career as a commercial photographer in New York from 1914 to 1917, Struss had had ample opportunity to observe the motion picture industry firsthand. Although

Figure 72. Struss created self-promotional trade advertisements that superimposed a list of his movie credits over his own photographs. In this advertisement, prepared as late as 1930, Struss was still identifying himself as 'Artist Photographer.' Gelatin silver print, Collection of the Grandchildren of Karl Struss

most American film production had already relocated to the West Coast, there were still quite a few major and minor studios scattered around New York and New Jersey before the war. These studios employed still photographers as well as motion picture cameramen, and Struss would have been familiar with the circuit of photo labs and equipment houses shared by everyone in the trade. Perhaps it was through one of these supply houses that he acquired his Multiple Tourist Camera, a still camera using 35mm motion picture negative stock, which he used to photograph Bermuda for a tourist brochure in 1914 (see fig. 17). Indeed, when Struss ran out of film in Bermuda he turned for resupply not to the local

photographic dealers, but to a visiting motion picture company; there he first met the cinematographer Charles Rosher, who would be a crucial influence on his career in Hollywood a decade later.

After he returned to New York, Struss began to experiment with motion pictures on his own. Under the glass roof of his portrait studio, he filmed the dancer Adolph Bolm, possibly as an adjunct to still photographs he was then taking of various Metropolitan Opera artists. But Struss' most prominent connection with the motion picture industry at this time came as supplier of a Struss Pictorial lens to cinematographer John Leezer, who used it to photograph *The Marriage of Molly-O* at the Fine Arts studio in 1916. The event was widely promoted in the trade press, although credit for this development was given to one "Carl Strauss."[3]

Struss' professional career was interrupted by his enlistment in the U.S. Army Signal Corps on September 6, 1917. The Signal Corps became heavily involved with motion pictures during the war and even opened a school for cinematographers at Columbia University (although Struss did not attend). A voracious filmgoer while in the army, especially during his tedious posting at Leavenworth, Struss spent all of his free time watching movies or playing tennis. He would often go into town and see two or three different shows a day, and his letters home are filled with appreciations of William S. Hart, Charlie Chaplin, Douglas Fairbanks, and Harold Lloyd (Theda Bara he did not care for, however). His comments on these films are surprisingly uncritical and reflect the complete concentration on movie stars characteristic of any film fan of this period. He did praise the photography of *Pershing's Crusaders*, a documentary feature compiled from old Signal Corps footage ("considering the difficulties under which most of the films were taken"), but otherwise his correspondence evinces almost no professional interest in the medium.[4]

During the summer of 1918 Struss gained access to a motion picture camera and wrote a three-page "summary of a scenario to show the whole works," apparently intending to document the activities at Leavenworth. His letters in July and August express a real eagerness to begin work on the project, "the work being so interesting, I don't care now how long I remain here."[5] But in September his request for a new darkroom and developing equipment was turned down and the project abandoned. He did no filming at Leavenworth that winter, and on February 17, 1919, newly discharged from the army, he boarded a train for Los Angeles.

Struss had no contacts in the film industry and no motion picture experience worthy of the name. But looking over his options, he still chose Hollywood over New York and a career in advertising photography. "I felt that the cameramen that they had were not photographers. I could see that very clearly," he remembered in one 1976 interview.[6] Reasoning that he could transfer his skills from still to motion picture work, Struss planned to sell his talents to the studios on the strength of his photographic portfolio. He became part of a vast postwar migration to Hollywood, which had all but eclipsed New York as a production center by the winter of 1918-19.

HOLLYWOOD AND DE MILLE

Within days of his arrival in Los Angeles, his hopes were buoyed by an article he saw in the April issue of *Photoplay* magazine. Antony E. Anderson, a painter and an art critic for the *Los Angeles Times*, wrote that the motion picture as an artistic medium had finally won him over. But unlike some other recent converts, he did not see the director guiding the new medium: Anderson's article was headlined "The Next

Genius—A Cameraman?" Anderson wrote that pictorial beauty should take precedence over staging and story. Each image called for the correct balance of light and shade, proper distribution of masses, an artistic completeness involving depth, atmosphere, and rhythm. Struss was delighted and wrote to his mother that the article "will help me considerably in putting over what I want." Anderson was hardly the first to publish such a manifesto, but it was his article, featured in the country's most widely read movie magazine, that hit the newsstands just as Karl Struss appeared on Hollywood Boulevard.[7]

As soon as he arrived, Struss made the circuit of all the studios, seeking to impress production managers with his portfolio and asking for a salary of two or three hundred dollars per week, but with little initial success. "I went to different studios and they all said the same thing," he recalled, "well, you've never shot a picture, we can't engage you."[8] Although there were no craft barriers to hiring a cameraman off the street, few in authority would be so rash as to place an untested novice in charge of the most crucial technical aspect of any film. Struss began considering "some sort of a job for the evenings so as to pay expenses."[9]

Finally, after a month of fruitless job-hunting at Ince, Universal, and other studios, Struss compromised his original intentions and on March 17 accepted the best offer to come along: still photographer for Cecil B. De Mille at the Lasky studio (fig. 73). "That was the only way I could get into the industry," he later recalled. "The salary wasn't a fifth of what I wanted to start, but I said the heck with the salary, I wanted to get into the industry."[10] He still wasn't a cinematographer, but at least he was on the lot.

Struss' success with De Mille might have been that during the previous few weeks he had made friends with an assistant director at Lasky, a "'bug' on photography" named Horwitz, who

Figure 73. Karl Struss, *Cecil B. De Mille in His Studio Office*, 1919, toned gelatin silver print, Amon Carter Museum

helped him get his foot in the door.[11] More likely, however, it was the special nature of the De Mille company at this moment must have made Struss seem an appealing addition to the staff. For the past five years De Mille had worked with one cinematographer, Alvin Wyckoff, who was responsible for directing photography on the set, overseeing miniature and trick work, taking still photographs, and supervising the laboratory. Together they had introduced a crude but effective lighting scheme known in the trade as "Lasky lighting," in which an actor was picked out by a

strong single light source and dramatically highlighted against an inky background.[12] Sometimes
referred to as "Rembrandt lighting," this style had
reached its peak of popularity in 1915-16 and had
already been abandoned by most cinematographers by 1919. But Wyckoff did not have the
technical knowledge of lighting—especially the
capabilities of filters, lenses, and improved film
stocks—to create a softer, more modern look. In
a 1917 article, De Mille had written: "we are
beginning to pose our people as a painter would
pose them in his painting, with consideration for
the perfect balance of the scene, with more
thought given to lighting."[13] Like Antony
Anderson, De Mille was looking for someone
with a strong artistic sensibility—someone like
Karl Struss.

Although hired to relieve Wyckoff of the
responsibility for photographing stills and publicity portraits, Struss found himself behind a motion
picture camera three days after he appeared on
the lot. When he came on the staff, the De
Mille company was in the final days of shooting
For Better, For Worse, a homefront drama featuring their resident star, Gloria Swanson. De Mille
rehearsed each scene carefully and photographed
it simultaneously with three cameras. Wyckoff
would light the set and handle the master shot,
while two other cameras would film closer views
of the principals. De Mille felt that such coverage would afford him better editorial control and
result in smoother continuity, though most directors preferred to work with one camera angle
at a time.[14]

For the next seven months Struss did a little of everything for the De Mille camera department. He shot portraits and stills, occasionally
turned second camera for Wyckoff, and devoted
most of his time to filming inserts and art titles.
Inserts were isolated shots, usually not involving
the principals, that were filmed separately and
later interpolated into the final editing of a

Figure 74. Karl Struss, *Gloria Swanson with Ball*, 1919,
gelatin silver print, Amon Carter Museum

sequence. Today they would be considered part
of post-production. On *Why Change Your Wife?*,
for example, the inserts consist mainly of close-
ups of clocks, phonograph record labels, or hands
holding theater tickets, assignments not very different from Struss' advertising work in New York.
Struss also photographed the films' numerous

title cards, which during this period were frequently lettered over painted or photographic backgrounds and called "art titles." Title cards needed to fade in and out at the correct moment and sometimes called for other optical tricks as well. That part of the job was mostly mechanical, but occasionally Struss used his own photographs as the backgrounds for these cards. For example, on *Something to Think About* he used "a lot of New Hampshire & Nova Scotia landscape shots," which he printed from his old negatives. He spent an entire month working on the 120 art titles for this film.[15]

For a time, Struss was very ambivalent about his work in Hollywood, and nowhere was this more clear than in his studio portraiture. It was obviously his plan to continue selling photos to his contacts at New York picture magazines, and his letters home are filled with instructions on how such transactions were to be handled. But what were Frank Crowninshield and the others in New York to be told? "It's all right to say I'm travelling in Cal but don't say I'm in the movies," he wrote just before landing his job at Lasky. "You don't know when I'll be back. If they ask, say I am out of the service." The day he signed with Lasky he grudgingly allowed, "I guess you can say I'm in the movies, but it isn't absolutely necessary to say what company—'one of the big ones' is enough."[16]

The days had long passed when film workers felt embarrassed about earning their living in the motion picture industry. Struss was trying to keep his exact employer a secret because editors would then perceive his photographs as publicity material for which they need not pay. Apparently Struss had obtained permission to photograph the Lasky stars and place the results himself, retaining any publication fees. Indeed, his perceived access to these journals may even have been one of the inducements for De Mille to hire him in the first place. In May, for example, he put together a series of prints of Wanda Hawley and other stars who were completing a version of *Peg o' My Heart* for Cecil's brother William de Mille, and instructed his mother on how to place them with *Vanity Fair* or *Harper's Bazaar.* "Of course, they probably know now I'm in the movies & may not want to pay anything for them on that account but you can say I do portraits on the side."[17] Struss did not control all of the photographs he shot, however, and material taken on the set or recording the staging of individual scenes was clearly owned by the studio publicity department. "So glad you liked the Lion picture," he wrote to his mother regarding a scene still from *Male and Female* (see p. 153). "I could sell copies but the original is in New York. If it were my own or belonged to me instead of the company I could put them out as my own."[18]

As Struss continued to advance at Lasky, earning regular raises and greater responsibility, he appears to have devoted less time to his "on the side" activities. In October 1919 he was officially promoted to second cameraman, a spot that would allow him to share screen credit with Alvin Wyckoff so long as he worked on at least 51 percent of the scenes.[19] Two months later he signed a long-term contract with the studio, running until the end of 1921. Although Wyckoff was still receiving top billing, it was clear that Struss was moving up in the organization. *Something to Think About,* in production during the first months of 1920, was the first film to carry their shared credit, but *Forbidden Fruit,* filmed that summer, most clearly shows Struss' influence.

Forbidden Fruit was a remake of one of De Mille's early hits, *The Golden Chance,* which Wyckoff had shot for him in 1915. While the first version has a gritty, realistic texture not uncharacteristic of films of its era, *Forbidden Fruit* is elegant and glossy, a slick piece of work very much the product of classic Hollywood. It was also De Mille's most expensive film to date, very ambitious in terms of design, photography, and technical work. It used a sophisticated combination of wipes and cross dissolves to bridge sequences, and a bizarre "Cinderella" fantasy sequence (see p. 149) sparkled with glass, self-illuminated costumes, and glistening white-on-white decor. The narrative sequences are considerably less stark than in the original version. For example, in the key dramatic sequence in both films, a burglar prowls about an apartment carrying a flashlight. Wyckoff's "Lasky lighting" of *The Golden Chance* shows nothing but what the beam of this light illuminates: the screen consists of light areas and dark areas with no intervening gray scale. In *Forbidden Fruit*, however, the severe contrasts between black and white areas have been softened so that the flashlight is still the brightest thing in the frame, but fill light allows us to see something of the rest of the space as well. This "high key," less obviously dramatic effect was what De Mille was after, and he could not get it from Wyckoff alone.

Struss continued to share credit with Wyckoff on *The Affairs of Anatole* and *Fool's Paradise*, lavish productions that clearly bear his mark and were also great box office hits. But while De Mille's films were making money, the industry as a whole hit a major slump in the summer of 1921, and Struss was asked to take a considerable pay cut for the final six months of his contract. According to Struss, the studio intimated that if he refused the cut he would be terminated at the end of his contract, while if he agreed, they would "do the right thing" by him when the time came to renegotiate. He worked on *Saturday Night* under this reduced salary, then was summarily dismissed as "too expensive" when his contract expired. Feeling that he had been tricked into accepting the pay cut (which amounted to $600), he petitioned De Mille, the Lasky Company, and even the new czar of

Hollywood, Will Hays. It is unknown if he ever received any satisfaction.[20]

There were three tiers of photographic workers in Hollywood in those days: those lucky enough to have long-term working relationships with a single star or director, like Wyckoff with De Mille, Rosher with Mary Pickford, or Billy Bitzer with D. W. Griffith; those regularly employed under long-term studio contracts, like Joseph Ruttenberg at Fox or Hal Rosson at Paramount; and everyone else. Struss now found himself in this free-lance market, a vicious competition in which cameramen would audition for a film much as actors did, with the assignment often going to the lowest bidder.

While he knew he had made valuable contributions to some of De Mille's most successful films, most people in the industry automatically would have given credit for them to Wyckoff, who had been associated with De Mille since 1914. Struss realized that he should draw on whatever networking he had established since arriving in Hollywood three years earlier or risk more months of fruitless pavement pounding. In 1922, he worked as co-cameraman on two films for director Marshall Neilan—a job he probably landed due to his friendship with Neilan's previous cameraman, Henry Cronjager. Neilan did not have a permanent spot for Struss at his studio, but he did provide him with a warm letter of recommendation, and Struss used the reference to help land a position with Preferred Pictures, B. P. Schulberg's low-budget operation.[21] This would have been a new experience for Struss, who was used to the elaborate production standards of De Mille's films and the more modest, though still respectable circumstances at Neilan's studio. Preferred made films quickly and cheaply, but Struss was entirely in charge for the first time.

There was an audience for such films because moviegoing was a neighborhood habit, and neighborhood theaters often changed their programs every day. Large quantities of film were needed to service this undiscriminating market, and for a time Preferred was one of the more successful suppliers. Producers like Schulberg made money only by cutting costs, because low rental fees were their main selling point. To hold down budgets, they spent very little on stars, stories, and sets and sped through production as quickly as possible. On the other hand, a good cinematographer could make these inexpensive resources look reasonably good on screen and take the lead in moving production along. The skills Struss developed here would serve him well later in his career, making inexpensive B-movies during the 1950s.

The only one of these films available for study, *Poisoned Paradise: The Forbidden Story of Monte Carlo* (see pp. 154-155), shows Struss doing his best under trying circumstances. The film opens with stock footage clipped from Universal's earlier Monte Carlo epic, *Foolish Wives*. The interior of a gambling hall is indicated through a well-executed glass shot, a special effect that required building only the lower part of a set while the top was painted onto a glass plate positioned before the camera. Struss' job was not made any easier by the rest of the Preferred staff. The uncredited art director covered some of the sets in darkly patterned wallpaper, forcing Struss to use more backlighting than usual to keep the actors from disappearing into the backgrounds. His lighting is generally high key, which not only was fashionable but could be done quickly; dramatic effects took a little time. Multiple shadows on the wall occasionally reveal the hurried placement of too many lamps in too small a space, an inelegant touch that might have been improved on with a little extra time. It seems hard to justify Struss' later claims that these films had shooting schedules of as much as five weeks.[22] When Schulberg shut

down his operation in early 1924, Struss was unemployed again. He quickly found work at the Ince studio, but Ince's death on November 19, 1924, ended his prospects there.[23]

SILENT SCREEN CLASSICS

Finally, and again almost by chance, came the opportunity of a lifetime. The Goldwyn Company had been working on *Ben-Hur* since the end of 1923, but the lavish Italian production, never properly prepared, had become a nightmare. Millions of dollars were being spent on footage judged to be unusable. Louis B. Mayer, who became head of the newly merged Metro-Goldwyn-Mayer in May 1924, inherited the mess. He immediately threw out the script, substituted Ramon Novarro for George Walsh in the title role, and brought in a new director, Fred Niblo. That September Mayer himself traveled to Rome to assess the damage and ordered up another director and yet another cameraman. Mayer had once shared studio space with Schulberg at the old Selig Zoo Studio on Mission Road, and he was certainly aware of Struss' work for Preferred. He cabled Irving Thalberg to send Struss and director Christy Cabanne to Italy immediately.

Years later Struss remembered that he and Cabanne were being sent to take over the picture from Niblo and his current director of photography. That may or may not have been the intention, but by the time Struss arrived there was no longer any talk of replacing Niblo, and the chief cinematographer's job had been given to Rene Guissart, already on the job as a Technicolor specialist and laboratory expert. Struss and Cabanne formed a second unit in Italy (fig. 75), where they worked for three months on various scenes, including the chariot race, which Struss filmed with an Akeley, a newsreel camera with a floating gear tripod head specially adapted for filming

substituted, the makeup failed to register at all, and the lepers were "cured." Struss found that Niblo was the only director he ever worked with who resisted the introduction of panchromatic stock. Niblo enjoyed the traditional blank skyscapes of the orthochromatic days and prevented Struss from employing panchromatic film for exteriors.[25]

Throughout the silent period Struss found himself caught in an unusual number of split-credit situations—in fact, for nearly all his major productions. This was a reality of the business, and he accepted most such decisions with equanimity. But some of these credits he would later contest vehemently, and on *Ben-Hur*, as he told one interviewer nearly fifty years later, "I was gypped again!"[26] The screen credits listed Rene Guissart first and Struss second, followed by Percy Hilburn and Clyde De Vinna. Numerous other camera men received no credit at all. Struss later said, "I shot more than 50% of the picture," and sometimes claimed as much as 60 to 65 percent of the finished film. According to Struss, Guissart had negotiated the first cameraman's credit when Niblo asked him to take over the troubled production, and there was nothing that could (or would) be done to redress the billing.[27] Although Struss completed the principal photography with Niblo in Culver City (including at least some of the Technicolor sequences), he left the picture before the restaging of the chariot race. Nor did he work on the sea battle, which had been done before he arrived in Italy and was one of the few sequences carried over from the European footage. Nevertheless, Struss did have some cause to be bitter: he prob-

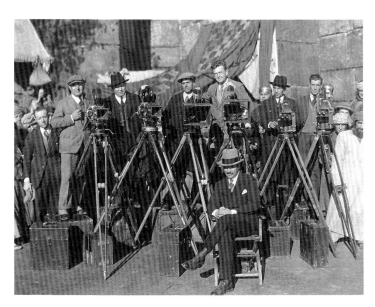

Figure 75. Karl Struss with Italian camera crew during the production of *Ben-Hur*. Director Christy Cabanne is seated in the foreground. The two cameras at right are Akeleys. Gelatin silver print, Collection of the Grandchildren of Karl Struss

rapid movement. The Italian production finally collapsed in January 1925, however, and the cast and crew were brought home to restart the picture in Culver City. Nearly all of the Italian footage would be scrapped.[24]

Struss now shifted to Niblo's unit and filmed such episodes as the Jerusalem street scenes and the healing of the lepers, for which he drew on his knowledge of filters and panchromatic negative stock. To achieve this "miracle," Struss had red "leprosy makeup" applied to the actors, then photographed them through a green filter. The makeup registered on the panchromatic negative as black. When a red filter was

ably had more footage in the final production than Guissart, most of whose work was scrapped with the rest of the Italian scenes, and he certainly could have used the first cameraman's credit.

Struss's next major assignment was another split credit, but here he accepted a secondary billing without complaint. Charles Rosher was Mary Pickford's cameraman, and for *Little Annie Roonie* (1925) he had brought in freelancer Hal Mohr to work on second unit and special effects. On their new picture, *Sparrows*, Rosher brought in Karl Struss as well. When asked which of the three had responsibility for lighting the set, Struss answered, "Charlie. And I was right there with him." And Hal Mohr? "Hal was doing special effects. He didn't do any of the major photography." Mohr remembered it differently, feeling that Rosher was not around very much and had left most of the work to him and Struss. "I took Charlie's place, and Karl took my place. . . . Struss shot stuff on his own, and I shot stuff on my own. Sometimes we worked together, but most of the time we worked separately." In later years Struss was not very possessive about *Sparrows* and was quite willing to acknowledge Rosher's lead, unlike the situation on their next film.[28]

One reason that Rosher may not have been around much was because he was preparing to film *Sunrise* for F. W. Murnau. It was Rosher who brought Karl Struss onto the project, although it is unclear if this had been decided before or after they worked together on *Sparrows*. Rosher had known Murnau since 1925, when he provided technical advice on the director's German production of *Faust*. Because of his connections with Murnau he clearly had the inside track, and Struss was quite prepared to share a credit, just as he had done with Alvin Wyckoff on films like *Forbidden Fruit*. But when he saw his name on screen, it was not only in second place, but in noticeably smaller type, an indication of

considerably reduced responsibility. As a consequence, Struss gave numerous interviews over the years to bolster his case for authorship, and he argued his position before history in far greater detail than for any of his other split credit assignments. For his part, while discussing *Sunrise* with Kevin Brownlow, Rosher's first thought was for his "excellent, and very helpful" assistant, Stewart Thompson. He referred to Karl Struss as "my friend and associate [who] operated the camera."[29]

The credit for photographing *Sunrise* was worth contesting. Not only did the film win the first Academy Award for Cinematography, but it was a landmark in bringing expressive photographic techniques to the American screen. In a 1928 essay on "Dramatic Cinematography," Struss wrote, "I believe . . . that *Sunrise* is the fore-runner of a new type of picture play in which thought is expressed pictorially instead of by titles."[30] While previous Hollywood films had been well illustrated by men like Rosher, Bitzer, or Struss himself, *Sunrise* served as a lesson in how technique alone could fulfill an expressive function. The script, written by Carl Mayer and further annotated by Murnau himself, gave preliminary guidance as to the film's visual style.[31] Murnau's art director, Rochus Gliese, whom Struss referred to as the "visualizer," took this document and produced two hundred sketches representing every scene in the picture. Three-dimensional plaster models were built of all the key sets, in order to test lighting and camera position. Within these rather specific constraints, both Rosher and Struss felt free to deal with the details of lighting. "That was absolutely up to us," Struss remembered. Rosher claimed that Murnau seldom even bothered to look through the camera, confident of the effects he would see on screen.[32]

There were three major sequences in *Sunrise* for which Struss claimed responsibility.

The first was the introductory portion shot at Lake Arrowhead (fig. 76), filmed while Rosher was ill.[33] This footage includes the graceful crane shot in which the camera drifts down just as the boat is entering the slip. Here Struss made heavy use of panchromatic negative, although orthochromatic was still used on the studio interiors. This mixing of film stocks required considerable knowledge of the effects of various filters and lighting sources, since everything had to match in the final print. The second of Struss' contributions was a complex lap dissolve in which an image of the lake water is gradually brought in around George O'Brien's bed as he contemplates drowning his wife—a photographic means of visualizing a thought process, which previously might have been described in a title card. Struss recalled, "That was all my idea, my shot, not Rosher's."[34]

The most important was the famous moving camera shot that travels with O'Brien as he makes his rendezvous in the marsh with Margaret Livingston. This set was built in a studio, and the shot accomplished by suspending a platform from an overhead track. Struss was positioned on the camera platform along with his Bell & Howell, to whose viewfinder he had attached a primitive magnifier (the image in this viewfinder, it should be noted, was inverted). Crouching over the machine, he attempted to hold the correct framing while the studio grips pushed the platform through the marsh set. As it happened, overcoming the inertia of this movement proved to be the most difficult part of the shot, since the camera needed to glide up to Margaret Livingston and come to a dead halt. There were three takes, and the scene was completed in an afternoon.[35] In later interviews, Struss always said that he was called on to film this shot because his motorized Bell & Howell left him with two hands free to operate the tripod head's pan and tilt handles, something which

Figure 76. Karl Struss with *Sunrise* film crew on location at Lake Arrowhead, c. 1926, modern print from original glass plate negative, Amon Carter Museum

Rosher, using a hand-cranked Mitchell camera, was unable to manage. But in a contemporary account he wrote that his camera was mounted on an Akeley head, the same specially geared mount he had employed on *Ben-Hur*.[36] This enabled the cameraman to obtain very smooth panning and tilting motions with the use of only one hand, and a look at the film suggests this to be the correct explanation.

Struss emphasized these three episodes most strongly in his interviews, but he mentioned many other sequences as well, suggesting that responsibility for them was shared. "We took turns doing the various dolly shots," he told John Dorr in 1968. "I don't know. We didn't toss a coin or anything. Just in some cases it was better to use my Bell & Howell, and other cases to use his Mitchell."[37] Among the sequences Struss always referred to as Rosher's were the "vacation

Figure 77. Karl Struss with director F. W. Murnau and camera crew filming scene for *Sunrise*, c. 1926. Standing next to Murnau, Struss keeps a record of the exact footage shot for a complicated trick effect. Before the introduction of the optical printer, all such effects had to be done directly on the original camera negative. Modern print from original nitrate negative, Amon Carter Museum

time" montage at the beginning of the film, and a complicated moving shot in which O'Brien and Janet Gaynor leave the church. To film this, grips had to walk in front of the actors while carrying a black velvet backcloth, which would allow the later superimposition of trick effects.[38] In production stills recording the filming of this scene, Struss can be seen walking beside the camera and taking notes (fig. 77).

The production of *Sunrise* was a sensation. Not only did the film win the first cinematography Oscar, but in a year when there was no "best picture" category, it was acclaimed by the

Motion Picture Academy as the "most unique, artistic, worthy and original production." Even before those awards were distributed on May 16, 1929, Struss was enjoying some of the celebrity that came to anyone associated with the picture. *Sunrise* had been completed in February 1927, and on May 11 Karl Struss was one of only fifteen cameramen invited to the organizational banquet of the Academy of Motion Picture Arts and Sciences.[39] On August 12 Charles Rosher nominated him for membership in the craft's most exclusive club, the American Society of Cinematographers (something he would hardly have done if he considered Struss only an "operator" on *Sunrise*).[40] The film opened in New York on September 23 and at the Carthay Circle in Beverly Hills on November 29. It was not until then, it would seem, that Struss saw the notorious small credit. With honors and job offers rolling in, however, the only damage done was to his ego. He later recalled: "I should have had co-credit in size on the screen, which I did not get. The individual who made the titles just made mine in smaller type, and that wasn't fair. I got the Academy Award, just the same as Charles Rosher did."[41]

UA AND THE TALKIES

Struss moved in 1927 to United Artists, where he spent the next three years working with first-class budgets and prominent stars and directors. It would be the only extended period in his entire career when he regularly enjoyed such luxuries. During this time he successfully negotiated the transition to sound, involved himself with a number of technical and mechanical innovations, and came under the influence of the great production designer William Cameron Menzies.

Joseph Schenck, then president of United Artists, had brought D. W. Griffith back to that studio after the director's unhappy interlude at Paramount. Griffith had left Hollywood just as Struss was starting there in 1919, and his return after eight years in the East was a major event. Struss was brought in to film two weeks of tests of Mary Philbin, star of the proposed Griffith picture, and he stayed to shoot all of Griffith's late Hollywood films.[42] On several of these films, Griffith's long-time cameraman G. W. Bitzer shares credit with Struss, but now it is Struss' name that appears in larger type. Struss later claimed that Bitzer wasn't even in California when these films were made, but photographic evidence does place him on the set of *The Battle*

Figure 78. D. W. Griffith with Struss and film crew on the set of *Drums of Love*. The oversized matte box on the front of Struss' Bell & Howell camera allowed the use of filters, gauzes, and other devices designed to manipulate the original camera negative. Gelatin silver print, Collection of the Grandchildren of Karl Struss

of the Sexes, at least on the day publicity shots of the crew were taken.[43]

Of his four Griffith films, Struss found the most striking visual opportunities in *Drums of Love* (fig. 78), the Francesca da Rimini story set in a mythical South American kingdom. Griffith was heavily involved and would ride on the dolly himself, enthusiastically ad-libbing instructions to cast and crew. He also asked Struss to experiment with ways to give the photography a more rounded, even stereoscopic quality, something that Struss achieved by separating the actors from the background while maintaining them in sharp focus.[44]

Struss' last silent picture, *Lady of the Pavements*, is one of his most glamorous creations, with dazzling camera effects highlighting the elegant settings and costumes of Louis Napoleon's Paris. He was especially successful with his photography of the film's two leading actresses, Lupe Velez and Jetta Goudal.[45] On this film he introduced the "Lupe Light," a funnel-shaped focusing reflector carrying a tubular, 1000-watt frosted globe and mounted on a multi-jointed arm. Placed just below the camera, it served as a softer fill light and provided just a hint of sparkle in the eyes.[46] Cameramen would previously have used a "baby spot" arc lamp in this situation, but that light was more intense and could cast a noticeable shadow. Incandescent lights had hardly ever been used in the studios before 1927, but the increasing popularity of panchromatic negative suddenly made them preferable to the conventional Cooper-Hewitt lamps, whose color temperature was better suited to orthochromatic film. Incandescents would briefly take over the industry when sound arrived, so it did not hurt Struss to have been recently associated with this little technical improvement.

In 1928 talking pictures posed formidable production problems. Entire scenes were being filmed in single takes, the performances covered by batteries of cameras closeted in soundproof booths. Arc lighting was banished, blamed for spoiling sensitive soundtracks. And powerful stars like Mary Pickford worried not just about their voices, but about how to transfer their established silent screen personas to the new medium. For Struss, who was becoming known as a photographer of women, such developments would affect many of his assignments during the first decade of the talkies.

Mary Pickford carefully prepared her first talking film, *Coquette*, with special attention to the requirements of the sound engineers, who for a few hectic months held final authority over the stages. When Charles Rosher saw what space had been allotted to his lights and cameras, he insisted that he could not photograph Pickford in his traditional style, and their relationship terminated. Pickford turned to Karl Struss, newly fashionable and with a reputation as a technical innovator. Rosher now seemed inflexible, if not out of date, and Pickford was having none of it.[47]

Struss used four cameras simultaneously on most scenes in *Coquette*, breaking up the action the way De Mille had done in 1919. He carried the technique to further lengths on *Lummox*, an epic of mother love directed by Herbert Brenon. For one sequence, sets representing two different rooms had to be constructed within earshot of one another, because piano music played in one space was to be heard in the other. This was the only way to keep the sound levels under control and allow the director to cut from one room to another in the final release print. Brenon and Struss needed to communicate by telephone while filming this apparently simple action (fig. 79).[48] Soon after, filmmakers discovered that they could record such a sound *before* filming, which would allow them almost as much flexibility as they had had during the silent era. In *1812 Overture*, a musical short that Schenck produced for United Artists release, Struss and William Cameron Menzies boldly experimented with such "playback" techniques, creating an avant-garde gem that prefigured later sound experiments by directors like Mamoulian and Lubitsch.

Struss' earliest talking films are not well known to historians, but several of them contain remarkable instances of precocious camera mobility. *The Bad One*, for example, shows exceptional technical range for a late 1929 production, with direct dialogue recorded during moving shots, excellent scene dissection in interiors and exteriors, and at least one vocal apparently done to playback. Struss' photography here is sumptuously low-key, with deep shadows and sparkling highlights enhancing a melodramatic tale of the Marseilles docks. The foggy scenes shot at the

Figure 79. Behind the scenes on the set of *Lummox*, 1930. Sound-proof booths were required to muffle camera noise during the early talkie period. This especially cumbersome installation was required on *Lummox* because there was no other way to film actress Winifred Westover (right) reacting to the piano concert in the other room. Struss and director Herbert Brenon, with Westover, wear telephone headsets. Gelatin silver print, Collection of John and Susan Edwards Harvith

harbor of San Pedro are especially notable.

From his days with the Struss Pictorial Lens, Struss had paid particular attention to the technical and mechanical aspects of his craft. In 1929, a year after he introduced the Lupe Light, he developed a new finder bracket for the Bell & Howell camera, which made focusing easier and less cumbersome. In 1930, when cameras were freed from their soundproof booths by enclosing them in extremely heavy padded shells called "blimps," he introduced a rolling tripod stand

that was strong and stable enough to carry the extra weight.[49] Such tinkering was not uncommon among Hollywood cameramen of this period; what is interesting about Struss' innovations is the fact that they involve hardware like brackets and tripods, and not just pictorial improvements like the Lupe Light. Struss was the complete cinematographer, something his peers always recognized and respected him for.

On all of his United Artists films, Struss worked with the great art director William

Figure 80. William Cameron Menzies with the first Academy Award for Art Direction, 1928. Struss photographed all the first year's Award winners. Gelatin silver print, Collection of John and Susan Edwards Harvith

Cameron Menzies (fig. 80). Menzies was one of the few designers in the industry who consciously and consistently rejected the unalloyed realism that was the hallmark of most early set designers. He felt that it was the designer's responsibility to analyze each scene and extract its essence, "the impression . . . as the mind sees it, slightly romanticized, simplified and over-textured." Even more than Rochus Gliese, he visualized each scene in exacting detail; in extreme cases, as in *Gone With the Wind*, he storyboarded large

portions of the shooting script, demanding specific lenses and camera placements.[50]

Unfortunately, Joseph Schenck's attempt to revive the fortunes of United Artists had clearly foundered by 1930. The company's release schedule was dominated by the productions of Samuel Goldwyn, who had his own technical staff, and there was not enough activity to keep Struss on the payroll. After completing *Kiki* for Mary Pickford, Struss needed to look elsewhere. He eventually signed with Paramount, which would be his home for the next fifteen years.[51]

PARAMOUNT PERIOD

At the beginning of 1931, Paramount still seemed the dominant force in the motion picture industry. The giant production-distribution-exhibition conglomerate was the successor to Struss' original Hollywood employer, the Lasky Company, and it seemed depression-proof, earning a record profit of $18 million in 1930. But the following year, the rise in ticket sales that had been fueled by the introduction of sound caught up with the movie industry. Weekly attendance, which had reached a record of 90 million in 1930, fell to 75 million the next year, then to 60 million. Paramount, which had recently expanded its theater holdings and was saddled with tremendous debts, suffered more than most. The company lost $21 million in 1932 and early the next year declared bankruptcy.[52] This terrible fiscal situation dictated how Paramount could use its resources, and Karl Struss, now one of forty-eight cameramen responsible for their one-feature-per-week release schedule, was simply another variable on the studio personnel roster.[53]

When he arrived at Paramount, Struss joined a distinguished group of cinematographers that included Lee Garmes, Harry Fischbeck, Charles B. Lang (once Struss' second cameraman at Schulberg's old studio), and Victor

Milner. George Folsey was the principal cinematographer at the company's East Coast studio,
and Bert Glennon, who had worked at Paramount in the late 1920s, would return in 1932.
All of these men had seniority at the studio and
well-established working relationships with its
most prominent stars and directors.[54] As a result,
Struss was involved with very few of the "classic"
Paramount films of the period between 1931 and
1945. He made no films with Ernst Lubitsch,
Billy Wilder, Preston Sturges, or Leo McCarey,
and he told one interviewer that he never even
saw Josef von Sternberg.[55] He made only one
film with Rouben Mamoulian. Likewise, while
at Paramount he never worked with Marlene
Dietrich, Gary Cooper, or Sylvia Sidney. He
did photograph *The Sign of the Cross*, De Mille's
first film on returning to Paramount in 1932,
and one subsequent picture, but Victor Milner
would become De Mille's regular cameraman
at Paramount.

Because he was not part of any major director's production unit, Struss felt that his assignments at Paramount were generally arbitrary.
"Struss's free—go over to stage twelve and do it,"
was the way he characterized the period in an
interview with Scott Eyman.[56] But in fact, Struss
developed connections of his own with several
major stars who arrived at the studio after he
established himself there in 1931. When Miriam
Hopkins and Claudette Colbert were sent out
from Paramount's East Coast studio that year,
Struss initially shot most of their films. Mae West
became one of his subjects in 1934 (fig. 81), after
expressing dissatisfaction with the cameramen
who had handled her earlier pictures. Struss
photographed nearly all of Bing Crosby's films
from 1934 to 1940 (see fig. 85) and made five
pictures with Dorothy Lamour between 1941 and
1944. Altogether, his work with these five stars
represents nearly 60 percent of the Paramount
films on which he received screen credit.

Figure 81. Struss with Mae West on the set of *Belle of the
Nineties*, 1934. While other cinematographers at Paramount
were teaming with the studio's great directors, Struss found
himself attached to their most important stars: Mae West,
Bing Crosby, and Dorothy Lamour. Photograph courtesy of
the Academy of Motion Picture Arts and Sciences

These were not insignificant assignments.
Two of his Mae West films, *Belle of the Nineties*
and *Goin' to Town*, were Paramount's top-grossing
films of their years, and *Rhythm on the Range*,
Mountain Music, and *Caught in the Draft* were
also blockbusters. Struss won no awards for these

pictures, and they are seldom remembered today, much less revived. But while Paramount was losing money on *Trouble in Paradise*, *The Scarlet Empress*, and even *The Crusades* (whose grosses failed to offset its large production costs), these less expensive films were keeping the studio open. Struss may have shared the opinion of Ernest Palmer, who had also worked with Murnau and had also won the Academy Award. When asked if he felt that his talents had been wasted filming Betty Grable musicals at Twentieth Century-Fox, Palmer had replied quite the contrary; Betty Grable was Fox's most important corporate asset, and the fate of the entire studio depended on the success of her films. Making Betty Grable look good was an honor and a responsibility, not something to be casually assigned to a has-been or newcomer. The same held true for the bulk of Struss' work at Paramount.[57]

In looking back at Struss' career, one should not make the mistake of valorizing only those high-profile assignments that have been canonized by textbooks or video stores—*Sunrise*, *Ben-Hur*, or *Dr. Jekyll and Mr. Hyde*, for example. Because of the necessarily limited amount of control exercised by any cinematographer, the auteur theory cannot be applied to this level of Hollywood craft worker. As a contract cameraman, Struss was delighted to be associated with films like these, but he also knew that much of his best work could be found in the many program pictures and B-movies that occupied him week in and week out. Years later, Struss was interviewed at length by a range of historians who probed all aspects of his career. While he had plenty of complaints regarding screen credits, production interference, and union difficulties, he never once complained about the overall quality of his assignments—the mark of a consummate Hollywood professional.

The first films Struss made at Paramount tended to be limp society melodramas, which

were a popular genre at that studio. But in the middle of this series Struss was assigned to *Murder by the Clock*, a tongue-in-cheek treatment of a dark house murder mystery that had no major stars and was signed by an underrated director, Edward Sloman. Struss followed the admonition of William Cameron Menzies to slightly romanticize and over-texture the imagery to suit the subject matter. There are many, many light sources and a richly textured, low-key effect that makes the highlights nearly pop off the screen. The camera moves a good deal, which when combined with the slightly stylized art direction, caused *Variety* to identify a "Murnau touch."[58] Struss was obviously out to please.

Entertaining as it was, however, *Murder by the Clock* bears no comparison to Struss' first 1932 release, *Dr. Jekyll and Mr. Hyde* (fig. 82). While other great horror films of that period, such as *King Kong* or *The Invisible Man*, made fine use of the cinema's capacity for trick and illusion, *Dr. Jekyll and Mr. Hyde* was one of the few to depend so heavily on the expressive potential of the camera. Unlike other versions of this tale, director Rouben Mamoulian's film all but ignores the debate on the nature of good and evil to focus obsessively on Jekyll's problems with lust. Mamoulian tried to do this by putting us inside Jekyll's head—literally. The film has an unprecedented number of subjective shots and opens with a virtuoso episode (nearly four minutes long) taken completely from Jekyll's point of view. The sequence begins with Jekyll in his music room as he tosses off a spirited "Toccata and Fugue," follows him out the door of his house, through the streets of London, and into a university lecture hall (where the audience is complaining about his penchant for "the spectacular"). While it does have the air of a stunt, this sequence is still a remarkable photographic tour-de-force. There had been subjective episodes in earlier films, but *Dr. Jekyll and Mr. Hyde* seemed to go out of its

Figure 82. Overhead production shot of *Dr. Jekyll and Mr. Hyde*, c. 1932. The use of large numbers of high-intensity arc lamps was a logistical problem peculiar to cinematographers of Hollywood's classic studio period. Unlike some of his peers, Struss was always fascinated by the capabilities of the many tools at his disposal. Gelatin silver print, Collection of John and Susan Edwards Harvith

slid into view from the other side, then out again in synchronization with the camera movement. The problems of lighting and reflection for this elaborate moving shot are complex and are only underscored if viewed frame by frame, when we can briefly see the reflection of a grip scurrying beneath the camera with an electrical cable.

The transformation scenes are also highly imaginative, sometimes involving subjective shots in which the camera spins on its axis, sometimes drawing close to March's face as Struss reversed his "leprosy" trick from *Ben-Hur* to begin changing Jekyll into Hyde (the full Neanderthal effect was the responsibility of make-up man Wally Westmore).[59] Indeed, there are so many superimpositions, split screen effects, gigantic close-ups (only the eyes of Jekyll and his fiancée in a romantic scene), and other attention-getting bits that one might overlook the film's lustrous photographic texture.

Working again in the low-key mode he had employed in films like *The Bad One* and *Murder by the Clock*, Struss chose to use the new Eastman Super Sensitive Panchromatic Negative. Prior to this, he had shot films like *The Bad One*, *Danger Lights*, and *Skippy* on Dupont negative, which had also been a favorite of other cameramen at Paramount; in fact, Struss had been featured in many of Dupont's trade ads.[60] Thus, transferring his allegiance to Eastman stock was a political and commercial decision as well as an aesthetic judgement. The new stock, which was two to three times faster than

way to create problems for itself. Take, for example, the extraordinary moment when the camera looks at itself in the hallway mirror and sees not an assembly of lenses and lights, but Fredric March adjusting his cravat. The "mirror" was a glass plate. As the camera approached, March

existing panchromatic stocks, had the ability to produce softer highlights than were visible in, say, *Murder by the Clock*.[61] Because of the increased speed, Struss could work with less light and still achieve a greater depth of field, increasing that suggestion of "stereoscopic" realism that he had experimented with on *Drums of Love*. It had been twenty years since he worked with Clarence White and introduced the Struss Pictorial Lens, and he was increasingly interested in crisp, well-defined images.[62]

In fact, it was the clear, "realistic" quality of *Jekyll and Hyde*'s photography that won most of the attention in the photographic trade press, not the spectacular moving shots or trick effects. The official review of the film in *American Cinematographer* praised the fact that Struss "refused to go to any of the cinematic extremes [and] had instead given the picture a restrained, yet always sympathetic treatment that will long be an example for fellow cinematographers." The following month the same writer compared *Jekyll and Hyde* with *Frankenstein*, noting that Struss' film "was photographed in a crisp, harsh manner that accentuated the realism of the setting and character." Even Mamoulian felt the need to underscore the point. He stated in one interview, "To my mind, *Dr. Jekyll and Mr. Hyde* gained force from the fact that both Karl Struss and I were early agreed that realistic, harsh photography was best suited to it. . . . Let me also pay Mr. Struss a richly-deserved tribute for this achievement, for the complete bouleversement of his usual artistic style revealed him to be an artist of the highest calibre."[63]

That is to say, Struss' abandonment of the soft focus and shallow depth of field seen in films like *Sunrise* struck some as the film's most notable breakthrough. Struss was nominated for the Academy Award for this film and his work seen as representing "the so-called school of realistic photography."[64] But in a contest with another

Paramount picture, he lost to *Shanghai Express*, photographed by Lee Garmes in a far less "realistic" manner.

Although Struss would seem to have firmly established himself at the studio with *Dr. Jekyll and Mr. Hyde*, its success did nothing to affect his future assignments. He never worked with Mamoulian again and immediately returned to a series of undistinguished melodramas (perhaps Mamoulian's thanking Struss for the "bouleversement" of his usual style indicates a certain difference of opinion on the set). Nine Struss films were released in 1932 and seven more in 1933. *Dancers in the Dark*, for example, was a moderately interesting gangster film set in a taxi-dance hall. In typical Paramount style, it was low on gangster roughhouse but very elegantly lit, designed, and costumed. One critic noted: "Using Struss' great talents for such a film as this seems as unworthy as using the Philadelphia Orchestra to play the *Peanut Vendor*."[65]

Struss worked in low key on heavy melodramas like *The Girl in 419*, *Guilty as Hell*, and *Disgraced*, livening up these program fillers with wide-angle lenses and what he referred to as "screwy" lighting effects.[66] *Guilty as Hell*, directed by fellow pictorialist Erle Kenton, is filled with peculiar transition devices: the camera will track towards a door, then back away from the opposite side after a lap dissolve. The murder that starts this film is seen as a reflection in the killer's eyeglasses. *Variety* didn't much care: "The photography is generally good, save for one or two bothersome intrusions of a camera crane," was the limit of its commentary on the film's visuals.[67]

The Story of Temple Drake (fig. 83) was the most striking of these darkly lit melodramas; a notorious adaptation of William Faulkner's *Sanctuary*, it was the last of Struss' five films with Miriam Hopkins. As Temple sinks deeper and deeper into a dissipated night world, Struss' velvety shadows conceal increasing amounts of the set. By the time of the corncrib rape scene, the action seems to be lit only by the glowing end of Jack La Rue's cigarette.

While such lighting schemes were suitable for heavy melodramas, lighter materials called for a higher key, more suitable to the soap opera or "woman's picture." Struss used plenty of shadows on *The Man from Yesterday*, his first film with Claudette Colbert, but that was still largely Clive Brooks' film. *Two Kinds of Women* is more conventionally high key, as is the lustrous *Tonight Is Ours* with Colbert and Fredric March. This was really Victor Milner territory, and until 1934 Struss got few assignments that called for such treatment.

A peculiar and almost unclassifiable work, *The Island of Lost Souls*, is part literary adaptation, part horror film, and part exploitation picture. As with *Dr. Jekyll and Mr. Hyde*, Struss refrained from conventional horror film lighting. In fact, a white-on-white fog effect dominates the picture, substituting for the traditional dark shadows. This began with real fog, which rolled in during scenes taken aboard ship en route to Catalina, and continued with the aid of fog filters for most of the action set in the studio jungle. The best of the three films Struss shot for Erle Kenton, *Island of Lost Souls* uses many of the same tricks seen in *Guilty as Hell*, such as actors suddenly looming up in close-shot, seen through a wide-angle 25mm lens. It is also one of the few Struss films at all reminiscent of his early pictorial work, at times suggesting, for example, such New York harbor views as *The Ghost Ship* (see fig. 48), *Brooklyn Bridge from Ferry Slip,* and *Lower N.Y. West Side* (see pp. 84 and 88). But now this ghostly haze was just a trick, one of the "screwy" lighting effects he might use to create an atmosphere of mystery and exoticism.

His big De Mille picture, *The Sign of the Cross*, also employed an anachronistic photo-

Figure 83. *The Story of Temple Drake*, c. 1933. It was the job of the still photographer to sum up in one shot the dramatic and visual values of an entire scene, producing a single image suitable for advertising or publicity purposes. Struss had long since stopped shooting his own stills, and this scene still of Miriam Hopkins was taken by an uncredited Paramount still man. Photograph courtesy of the International Museum of Photography, George Eastman House

graphic style, but this time for consciously nostalgic effect. "I used gauze throughout," Struss told Charles Higham, "to give a feeling of a world remembered; it wasn't much used then, as it had been in the silent period. I shot the whole black-and-white picture through bright red gauze."[68] In order to suggest the days of the ancient Romans, Struss went back to the silent movie era, all of five years earlier, when he and Rosher stretched gauzes across entire landscapes on films like *Sparrows*. *The Sign of the Cross* is not especially typical of Struss' work in this period, but instead suggests his films with Rosher, or even *Ben-Hur*. De Mille was more interested in the lighting and design of static compositions, so there are few moving shots and none of the tricky business that one sees from Mamoulian or Kenton. In a sense, it was as if De Mille were holding him back, a tension that was apparent to reviewers at the time.[69]

Although promoted as a spectacle, *The Sign of the Cross* was filmed on a relatively low budget of $700,000, a tribute to Struss' ability to suggest sequences like the burning of Rome with almost no resources. Robert Birchard suggests that the film was almost canceled in pre-production when both Jesse Lasky and B. P. Schulberg, who had brought De Mille back to Paramount, were themselves ousted.[70] Perhaps this explains not only the low budget, but Struss' presence on the film in the first place—everyone else had been assigned to some more likely project. But the film grossed four times its negative cost and reestablished De Mille in the industry. Struss was nominated for the Academy Award but again lost to another Paramount film, Charles B. Lang's *A Farewell to Arms*.

The summer of 1933 was a time of exceptional turmoil in the industry. The International Alliance of Theatrical Stage Employees (IATSE), which was battling with the International Brotherhood of Electrical Workers for the right to organize the soundmen, called a general strike in the motion picture industry.[71] While this commotion was going on, De Mille and Struss prepared to leave for Hawaii to shoot *Four Frightened People*. As Struss told one interviewer, "that was the time of the strike and De Mille had to get out of the studio. He couldn't make it there."[72] Although the strike was settled by September, when produc-

tion actually began, Struss had clearly been unwilling to walk out. De Mille was a notorious opponent of unions, but Struss, although politically conservative, had been a member of IATSE Local 659 (International Photographers) under the terms of the Studio Basic Agreement. The strike had abrogated this agreement, however, and under the circumstances Struss felt no obligation to side with the union, preferring to identify himself with the American Society of Cinematographers for purposes of collective bargaining. The IATSE lost the strike, along with much of its power within the industry, and the ASC supplanted Local 659 as the cameramen's bargaining agent.

A search through the pages of *International Photographer*, the house paper of Local 659, traces Struss' standing within the union. While his name had once been frequently mentioned in reviews, gossip columns, and photo captions, and his still photographs had been featured regularly through the July 1933 issue, he is never again mentioned in connection with cinematography. A 1934 discussion of the lighting in *Dr. Jekyll and Mr. Hyde*, for example, included an illustration but omitted any mention of Struss' name.[73] His banishment seems to have been complete: as late as July 1992, Local 659 reported that it could find no information on any Karl Struss.

He hadn't disappeared from *American Cinematographer*, however. In a review of *Four Frightened People*, which paid tribute to Struss' "versatility," the ASC journal noted that "it is incredible that even Karl Struss could bring back so successful a picture . . . the results are little short of marvelous, in view of these unphotogenic conditions" (fig. 84).[74] This curious reference to Hawaii's "unphotogenic conditions" ignores the photographs Struss made there (see pp. 164 and 165) and can only be interpreted as a veiled comment on the internecine labor difficulties raging through the industry that summer, with Struss

Figure 84. Struss and Cecil B. De Mille (between cameras) on location in "unphotogenic" Hawaii during filming of *Four Frightened People*, 1933. Photograph courtesy of the Academy of Motion Picture Arts and Sciences

and De Mille mounting an offshore "runaway" production designed to evade that season's expected labor strife. *Four Frightened People* proved to be Struss' last film with De Mille. Once the director was hot again, other camera-

men were assigned to his productions.

Although Struss had photographed Miriam Hopkins and Claudette Colbert before 1934, they were not Paramount's most important stars at that time. Colbert had been billed third, behind

Elissa Landi, in *The Sign of the Cross* and did not become an important star until her appearance in *It Happened One Night* in 1934; after that her Paramount films were usually photographed by Charles B. Lang. Hopkins, too, did her most important films with other cameramen. But Struss' fortunes changed after *Four Frightened People*, and he was assigned to Paramount's most important property, Mae West. Was this a reward for his position during the 1933 strike? Or for having had two Oscar nominations in two years? Or simply the result of an in-house production shake-up, which ousted Jesse Lasky and B. P. Schulberg and brought in Emanuel Cohen and William Le Baron? For whatever reason, the character of Struss' assignments changed dramatically from the moment he finished filming *Four Frightened People*. There were no more darkly shadowed melodramas, no more *Temple Drakes* or *Guilty as Hells*. From that point on, Struss became a specialist in musical comedies. He would almost always work in a bright, high-key style, and his films would have lots of singing and dancing. Considering that he was not associated with any particular director or production unit, this change seems very abrupt.

IDEALIZED REALISM

It is possible, of course, that Struss himself was changing, not merely his assignments. In 1934 he published "Photographic Modernism and the Cinematographer," in which he outlined an extremely passive, interpretive role for the director of photography.[75] Discussing the relationship between still photography and cinematography, he criticized "modern" photography as "a school of surrealism," devoted to "abnormally striking effects, either by unconventional composition, dynamic patterning of lines and masses, or by accentuatedly realistic rendition of textures." He felt that this movement in still photography had

been heavily influenced by "the sensational German and Russian silent films of the early part of the last decade." But when the effects of this "modern" school fed back into Hollywood cinematography, the results were simply distracting, first because the goal of motion picture photography should be "idealized realism," not an illusion-destroying focus on "facial and physical defects of the players," and second, because movement of the camera (or subject) would destroy compositions that were lit in a stylized or exaggerated manner. Struss illustrated this with two photos of the actor Lee Tracy holding a candle. While the source lighting is effective from one angle, it fails when the camera position is changed. The photo suggests some of the darker sequences of Struss' own low-key films of 1931-32, as well as the "surreal" tricks in some of the work he had done for Erle Kenton. Ultimately, he wrote, cinematography "must always remain the vehicle for the story, and as such, it may never call attention to itself at the expense of either story or players." This was quite a change from Struss' "Dramatic Cinematography" essay of 1928, where he praised a pictorially expressive camera that "seems to live with the characters and follows them around for psychologic reason."[76] In fact, Struss had definitively changed his mind about the photographic craft of Hollywood cinematography.

Soon after the release of *Belle of the Nineties*, Struss was profiled in *American Cinematographer*, not an unusual fact in itself, but significant for coming at just this moment. The author speculated that the reason Struss was so much in demand was because of his "ability to make a glowing epistle of life and beauty of all the pictures he is called to work on." Except for its jaunty tone, the piece had the air of a eulogy, an official encomium for a career of which nothing more is required, or expected. "Struss is undoubtedly a cinematographer who admits no limitations with the camera," the article continued. "The injection of a glowing quality and the effect of luxuriousness which makes Struss' pictures more than merely a replica of what is transmitted through the lens, illustrates the typical development of the art of cinematography and its students."[77]

In line with the principles that he outlined in "Photographic Modernism," Struss had developed to the point that his own style was becoming invisible. Shunning unusual camera angles, dramatic lighting schemes, or "unrealistic" diffusion effects, he now left little of himself on the screen. A fifty-yard tracking shot in *Goin' to Town*, which travels with Mae West through an audience and up on stage, was considered "some kind of a record" in the trade, but the average viewer might have overlooked it as just another element of the film's overall visual style.[78] This is exactly the way Struss now wanted to work, it seems.

Within the profession, his reputation was still very high, and Dupont was pleased to feature him once again in their advertising beginning in August 1935.[79] But after *The Sign of the Cross* he had no more Academy Award nominations for the rest of the decade; by comparison, between 1934 and 1940, Paramount's Victor Milner was nominated five times. But Struss was not likely to win much public attention for his self-effacing work on *Two for Tonight* (fig. 85), *Rhythm on the Range*, or *Waikiki Wedding*. These pleasant Bing Crosby musicals filled the studio's coffers in the late 1930s, much as Mae West's films had a few years earlier, but Struss must have known that there was no Oscar material for him here.

Within the industry, the production of musicals was considered not just a separate genre, but almost a separate craft. Singing and dancing numbers were always the focus, with comic or narrative elements secondary (at least until the ascendance of the Arthur Freed musi-

Figue 85. On *Two for Tonight*, 1935, Struss and director Frank Tuttle (center) line up a shot of one of Paramount's most important stars, Bing Crosby. Between 1934 and 1940 Struss filmed nearly all of Crosby's films. Marc Wanamaker Collection

cals at MGM in the 1940s). Since about 1930, musical numbers were prerecorded, and during filming the performers would lip-sync to a playback of this soundtrack. Struss had not been involved in the first wave of Hollywood musicals (1928-31), but Paramount pigeonholed him as a musical specialist beginning in 1934.[80] He was an excellent portraitist, extremely fastidious in technical matters, and had the stature to command large technical crews. Musicals required an almost military degree of precision in order to coordinate the work of performers, grips, and camera operators, and the director of photography had to stage manage this ensemble. Not every cinematographer had the temperament, or authority, for this, but Struss had also demonstrated on his many low-budget assignments that he could deliver high-quality results without running over schedule, a very important factor when handling costly production numbers.

Finally, his publicly stated willingness to subordinate his own style to the requirements of the project was an attitude not shared by every cinematographer of his stature. James Wong Howe and Lee Garmes, for example, had personal styles that tended to override other production considerations.[81] So it is not surprising that when Struss was asked in 1970 which cinematographers he admired, he named only three: Charles B. Lang—one of his old camera crew—and Ernest Palmer and Joseph Ruttenberg, two men of his own generation who similarly refrained from imposing their will on each assignment that came their way.[82]

Contract cameramen like Struss were occasionally loaned out to other studios, the home studio making a profit by pocketing the difference between the loan-out fee and the cameraman's weekly salary. Paramount first loaned Struss in 1939 to make *Zenobia*, a lackluster Oliver Hardy comedy, for the Hal Roach studio. Later that year Struss began working for Charlie Chaplin on *The Great Dictator*, Chaplin's first all-talking film and probably his greatest commercial gamble. A mixture of slapstick farce, heavy drama, and social commentary, this satire of Hitler and anti-Semitism went into production the week after Germany invaded Poland. Principal photography took six months, but while Struss enjoyed the work, it offered him few photographic opportunities. In fact, Struss was brought onto the picture only because Chaplin's regular cameraman, Rollie Totheroh, a camera cranker of the Mack Sennett school, lacked the ability to photograph a production of this scale. (Struss was not happy about sharing screen credit

with Totheroh, whom he claimed functioned only as an operator on the film.[83]) Chaplin's own grasp of the possibilities of photography was equally limited. Struss might have provided contrasting lighting schemes for the film's dramatic and slapstick sequences, but everything is lit in the same high-key, unshadowed style. Unfortunately, the most memorable things about the photography of *The Great Dictator* are the film's pitiful back projections and miniatures—for which, one hopes, Struss was not responsible.

He had the opposite problem with *Journey into Fear*, which he shot for Orson Welles' Mercury Theater unit at RKO in 1942. Welles needed to complete the last picture on his RKO contract before leaving to make a documentary on Brazil, so *Journey into Fear* was made in a very off-handed manner, with Welles and the bulk of his usual crew devoting most of their attention to other projects. Norman Foster was the nominal director, although Struss remembered that until Welles left for South America, he himself was clearly in charge (fig. 86). Struss was asked to work in the house style of the Mercury Theater, as established by Gregg Toland (*Citizen Kane*) and Stanley Cortez (*The Magnificent Ambersons*). Low-key lighting, unusual camera angles and transitions, and remarkable tracking shots in and around an ocean-going freighter set provided Struss with his best dramatic opportunities in years. The photography is extremely crisp, with great depth of focus and many long takes, calling for a complicated choreography of camera and actor movements within a small number of cramped sets. But the production was never properly completed or assembled, and the film falls apart dramatically. It also proved to be Struss' last dramatic feature at a major studio.

Journey into Fear must have been a refreshing break for Struss, because back at Paramount he was deep in his Dorothy Lamour period. Lamour was already an established star when

Figure 86. Karl Struss filming *Journey Into Fear*, 1943.
Collection of John and Susan Edwards Harvith

Struss began photographing her in 1941, but the
five films they made over the next three years
were important in maintaining her status as a
viable box office property. These harmless star
vehicles did provide Struss an opportunity to
work in three-color Technicolor for the first time,
and after *Aloma of the South Seas*, Paramount
never again used him on a black-and-white
picture.

While musical sequences were already
technically complex, working in Technicolor
added new levels of difficulty. The color system
demanded far greater amounts of light than
black-and-white filming, and silencing the giant
Technicolor camera (which exposed three strips
of film simultaneously) required the use of an
especially bulky blimp. Photographing a Technicolor musical was as much an engineering exercise as an artistic statement. *Aloma* won Struss
his final Academy Award nomination, as well as

another profile in *American Cinematographer.*
While spending much time on Struss' technical
experimentation (and revealing that he used
16mm film to work out some of his effects), the
article focused on one shot, which Struss called
"the most difficult single scene" in his entire
motion picture career. In a complex crane
movement, done to musical playback, the Technicolor camera closes in on a young girl's reflection in a lagoon. A falling nut disturbs the surface, and when the ripples clear the child is seen
to have grown into the adult Dorothy Lamour.
The camera then retraces its original path. To
film such a shot without casting shadows, trip-
ping over cables, or picking up reflections in
the water was a major technical accomplishment,
but making it all seem effortless was the real goal
of Struss and his crew.[84]

Aloma of the South Seas uses a restricted
color palette, as was fashionable during this
period. Jungle hues of green and blue predomi-
nate, but occasional bursts of red are used as
punctuation—flowers in the jungle, a spot of
color on a sarong, the eruption of a volcano at
the film's climax. There are few pure blacks and
whites, and with a fairly shallow depth of focus,
backgrounds are soft and indistinct. Struss' next
musical, *Happy Go Lucky* (shot after *Journey into
Fear*), has a very different quality (fig. 87). While
also set in the tropics, the characters and situations are more urban and cynical, clearly influenced by the films of Paramount's top comedy
director, Preston Sturges. Struss uses hard, bright
colors, with tremendous depth and definition.
Since the color is enough to separate the actors
from the backgrounds, there is no shallow focus
or rim lighting, although he does keep his sparkling highlights on faces. Struss' last film for
Paramount, *Bring on the Girls*, was a similar, if
less successful, experience. A lame vehicle for
Sonny Tufts and Veronica Lake, it is relieved
only by the crispness and clarity of Struss' pho-

Figure 87. Struss and director Curtis Bernhardt (facing camera at left) filming Mary Martin in *Happy Go Lucky*, 1943. The Technicolor camera (here *not* in its blimp) was designed to expose each primary color on a separate film strip. The final release print was a dye-transfer copy produced from gelatin relief printing matrixes. Richard Koszarski Collection

tography and the attractive color design of Guy Pène Du Bois.

Struss was gainfully employed at Paramount shooting such films, but the studio was not very interested in Technicolor and made relatively few

Technicolor films during the war—only four in 1943 (two of them by Struss), compared with five at MGM and seven at Fox.[85] On one of Paramount's other 1943 releases, *For Whom the Bell Tolls*, Struss spent many weeks on location prepared to advise director of photography Ray Rennahan on how to film Ingrid Bergman. Since Rennahan wanted no advice, Struss had himself assigned to the film's art director, William Cameron Menzies, and the two spent three or four additional weeks filming second unit material. Unfortunately, because he had no official position on the film, Struss was unable to supervise the printing of his footage and later claimed that it was mishandled by the lab.[86] One must ask why Struss was not assigned to this film in the first place, instead of having it done by Rennahan, an employee of the Technicolor Corporation who was rented to the studios along with the cameras. Or, for that matter, why he never had a chance at films like *Reap the Wild Wind* (1942), *Lady in the Dark* (1944), or *Frenchman's Creek* (1945), all of which would have been far better suited to his talents than *Riding High* or *Rainbow Island*.

Struss' final Paramount film was released in February 1945, and his contract was not extended. Paramount had been downsizing throughout the war years, dropping from a high of fifty-eight releases in 1939 to only twenty-three in 1945.[87] With John Seitz, Charles B. Lang, and Victor Milner all available (and attached to particular stars or directors), there were no more second-tier films for Struss to work on. At fifty-nine, he was sixteen years older than Lang and eight years older than Milner and Seitz. In fact, the only important cinematographers older than Struss who were still active in 1945 were Tony Gaudio, Ernest Palmer, and Charles Rosher, all of whom were only one year older.

It is possible that Paramount simply held Struss' age against him, but given his exceptional physical condition, a more likely reason was industry politics. Almost none of the production executives with whom he had worked were still at the studio. Emanuel Cohen, Jesse Lasky, William Le Baron, and B. P. Schulberg were long gone. Buddy DeSylva, a songwriter who had taken Le Baron's position as head of production in 1941, resigned due to ill health in September 1944; Struss left the studio soon after. Personal connections are extremely important in the motion picture industry, and were so even during the height of the studio contract system. By 1945, Struss had simply outlasted the executives he knew at Paramount, and the new crowd had their own favorites.

POST-WAR HOLLYWOOD

Now Struss found himself in the freelance market again, and building on his resumé he soon won an assignment shooting another Technicolor musical, *Wonder Man*, for Samuel Goldwyn. Unfortunately, *Wonder Man* would prove to be one of the few outright fiascos of his entire career—and certainly the most ill-timed. Goldwyn ran an independent operation, producing only one or two films a year and releasing them through RKO. In 1944 he had a substantial hit with his first Danny Kaye film, *Up in Arms*, and *Wonder Man* was to be the successor, teaming Kaye with two of Goldwyn's other recent discoveries, Virginia Mayo and Vera-Ellen. Struss was brought in to work with director H. Bruce Humberstone and shot a considerable amount of footage before being thrown off the picture. The issue revolved around a scene in which Kaye, as a spirit, was to sit on Virginia Mayo's lap while she sat on a park bench. Struss suggested that Kaye could be double-exposed to any required degree of opacity. Humberstone insisted that a steel cage be built into Mayo's dress so that Kaye could play the scene live. Struss, who was prone to characterize himself as the soul of discretion, protested vocally. Recalling

the episode for Stephen White thirty years later, he still had a very negative opinion of Humberstone's solution. However, Humberstone had as much or more experience with Techni-color musicals as Struss, having directed a number of successful Betty Grable films at Fox, and Goldwyn was not inclined to indulge his new cinematographer. Struss found himself off the picture, replaced, ironically, by Victor Milner. As it turned out, this was the last time Struss would film an "A" picture within a traditional big-studio context.

Struss' career now entered another phase, as long as the fifteen years he had spent at Paramount, but this time devoted to a string of freelance assignments for various independent producers. What one can say about the photography of these films is very limited. The most practical consideration is one of print availability: these are the scarcest and most difficult to see of any of Struss' films, including his silent pictures. Only a handful are available in 35mm prints, the color films have all faded, and the 3-D features he shot in Italy in 1953 are unavailable in stereoscopic versions. One can search the trade papers for contemporary reactions to the photography of these films, but such comments are inconsistent and seldom more than cursory. What does it mean when *Variety* writes of *The Alligator People*, "Karl Struss' photography [and the other technical credits] are decided pluses . . . particularly when the budget is taken into consideration." And this regarding a film that Struss could not even remember working on only nine years later.[88]

A second problem involves the nature and extent of Struss' contribution to these films. As director of photography, Struss was responsible for managing a great part of the technical side of production: electrical, photographic, and laboratory. This was especially the case when there was no existing studio support in these departments.

Only by arranging all aspects of production in the most professional and efficient manner could a film like *Rocketship X-M* be shot in eleven days. The producers of these films, who were in no mood to take chances on untested cinematographers, valued Struss for his managerial skills as well as his aesthetic capabilities. Looking at the list of these pictures, one can dismiss over half as low-budget westerns and horror films of no artistic consequence. But filming them was all part of making a living, and other cinematographers of Struss' standing had equally checkered postwar careers. Just as Struss filmed *Kronos* and *She Devil*, so Hal Mohr shot *Creation of the Humanoids* (1963) and Stanley Cortez made *Ghost in the Invisible Bikini* (1966).

This explains how the ASC could have chosen Struss in 1949 to take the leading role in *The Cinematographer*, a nine-minute short in a series describing the various motion picture crafts, produced by the Academy of Motion Picture Arts and Sciences. Not identified in the film by name, Struss stands in as the generic "cinematographer" in this industrial-style documentary, wielding his light meter, studying costumes, and instructing his assistants. Struss was honored, but he might have preferred a real assignment of his own. As he wrote in a thank-you letter to the Board of Directors of the ASC, "The only disappointment I had was not being permitted to photograph the picture."[89]

When John Dorr asked him in 1968 which of his films he thought may have been unfairly overlooked, Struss named two of his postwar features, *Suspense* and *Rocketship X-M*. Because they had been made for small producers on small budgets, Struss felt that they had not been seen by many in the industry, or adequately valued for the work he put into them. *Suspense* was promoted as Monogram's first "A" budget picture, but an "A" budget at Monogram did not necessarily mean the same as an "A" budget anywhere

else. Struss had never had the opportunity to shoot a true *film noir* thriller (*Journey into Fear* was unclassifiable), so he enjoyed working with the genre's oblique camera angles and visible light sources. He used many glass shots to make the settings more impressive and did his best to glamorize the stars, notably Belita, a second-string Vera Hruba Ralston (this is an ice-skating *film noir*). One would have to agree with Bob Porfirio that the film's visual style is its most interesting quality: "Struss, [director Frank] Tuttle and the art director Paul Sylos compensate for the lapses in the drama and the lengthy musical numbers by a *mise en scene* that suggests a surrealist nightmare" (fig. 88).[90]

The other film Struss mentioned, *Rocketship X-M*, was the first postwar space travel feature, rushed into production to beat the previously announced *Destination Moon* to the screen. An extremely low-budget and scientifically suspect production, *Rocketship X-M* was written, produced, and directed by Kurt Neumann, who would become Struss' main postwar collaborator. Filming took eight days in the studio and three on location at Red Rock Canyon and Death Valley, which stood in for the planet Mars (the crew takes off for the Moon, but reaches Mars by mistake). Struss was happy with his use of filters on the "Martian" landscapes, and his eerie backlighting of the Martians, seen mainly in silhouette atop high cliffs, is surprisingly effective. The interior of the crowded ship offered fewer opportunities, but Struss was obviously proud of his ability to make this low-budget quickie look competitive with George Pal's Technicolor production of *Destination Moon*.

It should not be assumed that all of Struss' postwar films were for inconsequential B-movie producers, however. He made two films for the noted German producer Seymour Nebenzal, for example, including the ill-fated Maria Montez vehicle, *Siren of Atlantis*. But Struss had few

Figure 88. Struss made the cover of *American Cinematographer* for the last time in January 1946, during the production of *Suspense*. Barry Sullivan and Belita were the stars, and Frank Tuttle again the director. Richard Koszarski Collection

his contention that director Zoltan Korda was incompetent and "rather a phoney."[91] As he had been with *The Great Dictator*, Struss was called in to help Rollie Totheroh on Charles Chaplin's *Limelight*, but this was a much faster job and less interesting for Struss. "It was very routine with [Chaplin]. You'd just set up the camera and let it go, and he and the other actors would play in front of it. He never even tried for cinematic effects."[92] Totheroh received no screen credit this time and just hung around the set with nothing to do. Still, the photography of *Limelight* seems quite an effective complement to the film's sentimental reconstruction of the lost world of the British music hall, and not at all as flat as Struss remembered it.

TWILIGHT CAREER

During the production of *Rocketship X-M*, Struss had taken a series of award-winning stereo views in Death Valley, and these brought him to the attention of the Italian producers Carlo Ponti and Dino De Laurentiis. The sensational premiere of *Bwana Devil* at the end of 1952 led to a surge of interest in 3-D motion pictures, and Struss was able to capitalize on his current celebrity as a stereo photographer by signing with the Italians to film a 3-D version of *Ulysses* starring Kirk Douglas. Early in 1953 he left for Rome with a pair of 35mm Mitchell cameras, which were assembled into a 3-D rig in Italy by Luigi Christiani (fig. 89).[93] Soon after he arrived in Italy, however, Struss learned that "through some

good things to say about the handful of higher profile films he did manage to work on in this period, including *The Macomber Affair* and *Limelight*. Remembering *The Macomber Affair*, which James Agee thought the "best movie job on Hemingway to date," Struss detailed for Charles Higham a series of anecdotes illustrating

Figure 89. Struss with his camera crew operating the Christiani stereo system during the production of one of his Italian 3-D films. Marc Wanamaker Collection

hocus-pocus" the *Ulysses* film had been assigned to another Hollywood veteran, Hal Rosson. Instead, he began production on *Il Piu Comico Spettacolo del Mondo*, a parody of De Mille's *The Greatest Show on Earth* featuring the Italian comedy star Toto. The film was shot in 3-D and Ferraniacolor, a three-color positive-negative process that Struss remembered as slower than Eastman stock and more contrasty, but with more vivid color rendition. It demanded large amounts of light, a problem compounded by the peculiarities of the Polaroid 3-D system. The film was not well received on its release later that year; the respected critic Giulio Cesare Castello noted that "the cameraman of the film was the famous Karl Struss of *Limelight*, but that did not

impeach Ferraniacolor to produce its worst results."[94]

Struss seems to have made three 3-D features in Italy, although there is some controversy about this because only one of them appears to have been released in this format. When the 3-D boom collapsed suddenly in 1953, numerous films shot in this process were released "flat," both in Hollywood and abroad. *Cavalleria Rusticana*, with Anthony Quinn and May Britt, and *Un Turco Napoletano*, another Toto picture, were both in this category. Indeed, when Struss finally saw the Quinn picture on its release in the United States, he was outraged to find that it was not only projected flat, but in an inappropriate wide-screen format that cut off the tops of the actors' heads.

Struss stayed on in Italy after the close of the 3-D boom, continuing with the same crew on *Due Notti con Cleopatra*, a broad farce with Alberto Sordi and Sophia Loren. He shot only the conclusion of *Attila*, on which Aldo Tonti was director of photography, and completed one more Toto comedy, *Miseria e Nobiltà*, which historian and critic Lorenzo Codelli recently hailed as "the highest achievement of Struss in Italy."[95] Oddly enough, Struss never discussed that film or listed it in his credits.

It should be noted that all of Struss' Italian films have shared photographic credits. Except for *Attila*, Struss insisted that he was always in complete charge and that the Italian cinematographer Riccardo Pallottini, co-credited on most of his films, was merely "my operator." Although even the American release prints of *Two Nights with Cleopatra* list "Carlo Struss" as sharing credit with Pallottini, it does seem unlikely that he would have been imported from America only to share authority with a local cameraman.

Struss was sixty-eight when he returned from Italy, well past retirement age but not very interested in retiring. Although he would never

Figure 90. Frame enlargement from *The Fly*, 1958. Whether suggesting the Martian landscape or visualizing the point of view of a large insect, Struss found ways of amusing himself on the many low-budget features he worked on in the post-war period. Photograph courtesy of Photofest

have another major project, he spent the next sixteen years filming B-movies, television series, industrial films, and commercials. Again, this was a pattern followed by other major cinematographers of his generation, including Hal Mohr and Lee Garmes. Karl Freund, another of Murnau's cameramen, was quite well known for photographing "I Love Lucy," one of the first television series filmed in Hollywood. He set a pattern of shooting these comedies with multiple cameras, a technique that had been lost since the early sound years. Struss would work on at least two filmed series, *My Friend Flicka*, which originally aired on NBC in the 1956-57 season, and another western, *Broken Arrow*, an ABC series that ran from 1956 to 1960.[96]

The bulk of Struss' final feature assignments grew out of his long working relationship with Kurt Neumann, a B-movie director with whom he had first worked in 1939. He had made five more films with Neumann after leaving Paramount, and when he returned from Italy

he found Neumann established with a producing and directing deal at Fox. Struss remembered little about the films he shot after returning from Italy. He enjoyed making *Machete* and *Counterplot*, which were filmed back-to-back in Puerto Rico using lightweight equipment, existing interiors, and local crews. But he was not impressed with *The Fly*, which he felt was "just plain ridiculous." Ironically, that film became a great success and was the last Struss picture to be widely distributed. *Variety* was pleased to note that "Karl Struss' De Luxe color, CinemaScope photography is especially notable in capturing the vivid excitement of the scientific workshop." One wonders if the famous fly's-eye-view shot, with its multiple images filling the CinemaScope screen, was a Struss touch, or the work of anonymous technicians in the special effects department (fig. 90).[97]

The Fly was clearly a breakthrough picture for Kurt Neumann, and according to Struss its success allowed him to negotiate a much better deal at Fox, with increased budgets and better properties. Struss certainly would have been involved in these projects, but one month after *The Fly* was released, Kurt Neumann died at the age of fifty. With Neumann gone, Struss had few contacts left at the studios, and his career in features came to an end. But he continued to work at Fox's Western Avenue studio (where *Sunrise* had been shot more than thirty years earlier) on innumerable television commercials.

The advertising agencies in New York controlled this aspect of the business and carefully storyboarded each detail of their commercials back on Madison Avenue. Producers would bid on these storyboards, and while there were many New York firms specializing in such work, an increasing number of Hollywood producers were also entering the field. Struss found it easy to get such work, which fit conveniently into his "retirement" schedule. He would work three or four days, pocket the fees, and collect unemployment insurance the rest of the month. "I'd make about 250 bucks a month unemployed, and the pension was only about $210," he told an interviewer.[98]

Commercials were ideal for someone of Struss' age, talent, and temperament. They did not take too much time, the exact effect was specified by the agency, and considerable sums could be spent on the photography for thirty seconds' worth of film. There were no temperamental stars to deal with, and no studio politics. Best of all, the assignments were pure photography, and Struss could indulge his penchant for losing himself in the technical details. For example, one of the greatest challenges he remembered was calculating the exposure required for a high-speed camera to film a drop of Foremost Milk falling into a glass. Another time he spent hours preparing to film hidden camera interviews in a department store, arranging the lighting not only for multiple cameras but for unknown and unpredictable subjects.

His first job was for Toni shampoo—no problem for a man who had spent years photographing Colbert, Lamour, and Mae West. But he had no specialty, and before retiring in 1970 he had filmed beer, cigarettes, toothpaste, colas, vitamins, automobiles, telephones, suntan lotion, breakfast food, razors, margarine, and "that's only the half of it." There were awards, too, including a 1959 citation at the Cannes Film Festival for a two-minute Chevrolet commercial that, like so many of Struss' commercials, was a miniature narrative designed to "glorify" the agency's product. In his lengthy 1968 oral history interview with John Dorr, Struss described at length the difficulties of arranging bottles of beer into efficient and dynamic compositions. He was concerned with filling the cramped television frame with a proper balance of mass and tone, and he worried about the poor quality of television reception and how that would affect the viewer's ability to read the product label.

Dorr, a young film lecturer at the University of California at Los Angeles, never asked Struss very much about the work he did before entering the motion picture business. He never asked why Struss seemed so interested in photographing toothpaste and beer bottles in 1968, when he had hated photographing kitchen stoves and furniture fifty years earlier. The explanation, however, is implicit in the five-hundred-page transcript of their interviews and lies somewhere between Cecil B. De Mille and Kurt Neumann. Struss had arrived in Hollywood as an artist photographer, a newcomer from the East whose contempt for film industry standards was deep-rooted. But it did not take long for Hollywood's cult of professionalism to change Struss, probably without his even being aware of it. He learned that motion pictures were created by teams of artists, and that the writer, director, designer, and cameraman all had specific roles to play on each individual project. More importantly, he learned that the art of motion pictures was not a zero-sum game, and that his own contribution was not diminished by the successes of Griffith, or Menzies, or Mae West. Every cinematographer will say, "I served the director," or "I served the script." What Struss could do was to accommodate the professional requirements of the project without compromising the integrity of his personal vision. Achieving this simple harmony was, in Hollywood, the ultimate goal of the studio professional. In retrospect, his associates in the ASC had made the right decision in 1949. Karl Struss was not just one of the finest cinematographers in the industry: he was *the* cinematographer.

NOTES

1. George Jean Nathan, *The Popular Theatre* (New York: Alfred Knopf, 1918), p. 122.

2. See Hartmann's essay on "The Esthetic Significance of the Motion Picture," reprinted in Sadakichi Hartmann, *The Valiant Knights of Daguerre* (Berkeley: University of California Press, 1978), p. 154. Because the original had appeared in *Camera Work* 38, the same April 1912 issue in which eight of Struss' photogravures were prominently featured, we may assume that Struss was familiar with this position.

3. Patricia King Hanson, ed., *The American Film Institute Catalogue . . . Feature Films 1911-1920* (Berkeley: University of California Press, 1988), p. 590, cites the sources that credit Carl Strauss; proper credit to Karl Struss came later in *American Cinematographer* (February 1, 1922), p. 12, and "Who Did It First?", *International Photographer* (November 1933), p. 29.

4. Karl Struss to Mother [Marie Struss], August 14, 1918, Struss Family Papers.

5. Karl Struss to Mother [Marie Struss], August 4, 1918, Struss Family Papers.

6. Richard and Diane Koszarski, interview with Karl Struss, August 1976 (hereafter Koszarski interview).

7. Antony E. Anderson, "The Next Genius—A Cameraman?", *Photoplay* (April 1919), p. 45; Karl Struss to Mother [Marie Struss], March 5, 1919, Struss Family Papers.

8. Koszarski interview.

9. Karl Struss to Mother [Marie Struss], March 3, 1919, Struss Family Papers.

10. Koszarski interview.

11. Struss to Mother, March 3, 1919.

12. Cecil B. De Mille, "Motion Picture Directing," *Transactions of the Society of Motion Picture Engineers*, no. 34 (1928): 295.

13. Cecil B. De Mille, "Photodrama a New Art," *Moving Picture World* (July 21, 1917), p. 374. Karl Struss was not the only photographer of note to be employed by De Mille on his films in this period. For example, Edward S. Curtis was a still photographer and part-time extra cameraman on *The Ten Commandments*, and William Mortenson shot stills on *King of Kings*.

14. Karl Struss to Mother [Marie Struss], March 22, 1919, Struss Family Papers; Koszarski interview. Sometimes two cameras would be employed to provide a duplicate "original" negative for export, but that is not what De Mille was doing here.

15. Karl Struss to Mother [Marie Struss], May 3, 1920, Struss Family Papers.

16. Karl Struss to Mother [Marie Struss], March 15, 1919, and March 17, 1919, Struss Family Papers.

17. Karl Struss to Mother [Marie Struss], May 25, 1919, Struss Family Papers. This version of *Peg o' My Heart* was never released, apparently because of legal problems.

18. Karl Struss to Mother [Marie Struss], February 4, 1920, Struss Family Papers.

19. Karl Struss to Mother [Marie Struss], October 5, 1919, Struss Family Papers.

20. Karl Struss to Will Hays, July 28, 1922, Stephen White Collection.

21. Struss still had this letter at the time of his death. See letter of reference from L. L. Baxtera, Marshall Neilan Productions, April 17, 1922, Stephen White Collection.

22. Scott Eyman, "An Interview with Karl Struss," *Journal of Popular Film* 4, no. 4 (1975): 311.

23. Doris Kenyon to Karl Struss, November 23, 1924, Stephen White Collection, refers to Struss' failed expectations after Ince's death.

24. Eyman, "Interview," p. 312; Charles Higham, *Hollywood Cameramen* (Bloomington: Indiana University Press, 1970), p. 123; Koszarski interview. See also Kevin Brownlow, *The Parade's Gone By* (New York: Knopf, 1968), pp. 385-414, for background on *Ben-Hur*.

25. Susan and John Harvith, *Karl Struss: Man with a Camera* (Ann Arbor: Cranbrook Academy, 1976), p. 13.

26. Koszarski interview.

27. Koszarski interview; Eyman, "Interview," p. 312.

28. Koszarski interview; Leonard Maltin, *The Art of the Cinematographer* (New York: Dover, 1978), p. 81 (Mohr).

29. Brownlow, *The Parade's Gone By*, p. 232.

30. Karl Struss, "Dramatic Cinematography," *Transactions of the Society of Motion Picture Engineers*, no. 34 (1928): 317.

31. Lotte Eisner, *Murnau* (Berkeley: University of California Press, 1973), pp. 167-185.

32. Eyman, "Interview," p. 314; Brownlow, *The Parade's Gone By*, p. 232 (Rosher).

33. For either "one week" (Higham, *Hollywood Cameramen*, p. 126) or "ten days" (Koszarski interview).

34. Higham, *Hollywood Cameramen*, p. 126.

35. Koszarski interview.

36. Struss, "Dramatic Cinematography."

37. John Dorr, interview with Karl Struss, July-October 1968, UCLA Oral History Project.

38. Koszarski interview.

39. Academy of Motion Picture Arts and Sciences, Organization Banquet, May 11, 1927, seating plan, in Stephen White Collection. Other cameramen attending were George Barnes, J. A. Ball, Fred Jackman, Harry Perry, Charles Rosher, Henrik Sartov, Arthur Edeson, Tony Gaudio, Bert Glennon, Al Gilks, Victor Milner, Hal Mohr, Arthur Miller, and Oliver Marsh.

40. Karl Struss, American Society of Cinematographers membership nomination certificate, August 12, 1927, American Society of Cinematographers Archives.

41. Harviths, *Man with a Camera*, p. 12.

42. The lengthy tests proved beneficial: "She had a different wig every day. It was tedious, but it paid off with a natural-looking wig, unlike that phony thing Janet Gaynor wore in *Sunrise*, where we didn't do any tests like that." Eyman, "Interview," p. 315.

43. Koszarski interview.

44. Edward Wagenknecht and Anthony Slide, *The Films of D. W. Griffith* (New York: Crown, 1975), p. 231.

45. One spectacular scene, where Lupe Velez sees William Boyd's image in the face of all the men attending her cabaret, has been attributed to trick expert Ned Mann; Iris Barry and Eileen Bowser, *D. W. Griffith, American Film Master* (New York: Museum of Modern Art, 1965), p. 82.

46. Walter Blanchard, "Aces of the Camera VI: Karl Struss, ASC," *American Cinematographer* (June 1941), p. 268.

47. Brownlow, *The Parade's Gone By*, p. 234; Koszarski interview.

48. For more detail on Struss' early talkie technique, see Karl Struss, "Photographing with Multiple Cameras," *Transactions of the Society of Motion Picture Engineers*, no. 38 (May 1929), reprinted as "The Camera Battery," *International Photographer* (July 1929), p. 17, and "Generalship on a Sound Stage," *International Photographer* (August 1929), p. 16. In addition to all this trouble, many early talking films were also partially reshot as silent pictures to service those theaters that had not installed talkie equipment. The *International Photographer* reported in March 1929 that Struss was about to begin filming the silent version of *Coquette* now that the talking version had been completed, but it appears that such a version was never released; "Pans and Tilts," p. 12.

49. "Pans and Tilts," *International Photographer* (March 1929), p. 12; "Out of Focus," *American Cinematographer* (July 1929), p. 36; "Karl Struss, ASC, Invents New Device for Finders," *American Cinematographer* (May 1929), p. 30; *American Cinematographer* (March 1930), p. 41; "Tilt Heads and Rolling Tripods for Camera Blimps," *American Cinematographer* (August 1930), p. 11.

50. W. Howe Cameron Menzies [*sic*], "Cinema Design," *Theatre Arts Monthly* (September 1929), p. 676; Alan David Vertrees, "Reconstructing the 'Script in Sketch Form'," *Film History* 3, no. 2 (1989): 87-104 (*GWTW*).

51. It is possible that Struss was brought to Paramount by B. P. Schulberg, who had been general manager of their West Coast studio since 1928.

52. Robert Stanley, *Celluloid Empire* (New York: Hastings House, 1978), pp. 84-88.

53. "Studio Personnel Roster," *Motion Picture Almanac* (New York: Quigley Publishing Co., 1931), p. 72.

54. For a detailed exposition of Paramount's house lighting style at the time Struss arrived there, see Victor Milner, "Painting With Light," *Cinematographic Annual*, vol. 1 (Hollywood: ASC, 1930), p. 91.

55. Koszarski interview.

56. Eyman, "Interview," p. 318.

57. Ernest Palmer interviewed by Richard Koszarski, January 22, 1972.

58. "Murder by the Clock," *Variety*, July 21, 1931.

59. Frank Westmore and Muriel Davidson, *The Westmores of Hollywood* (Philadelphia: J.B. Lippincott, 1976), pp. 18-20.

60. Dupont Film Manufacturing Company ad, *Motion Picture Almanac* (1932), p. iv. See also Dupont ads on inside front covers of *International Photographer* for April, May, and July 1930, and *American Cinematographer* for June 1930. Eastman's Hollywood agent sent Struss a personal thank-you note, acknowledging the commercial ramifications of this change, which Struss also kept in his files until his death. See Jules Brulatour, Inc., to Karl Struss, February 9, 1932, Stephen White Collection.

61. Emery Huse and Gordon Chambers, "Eastman Supersensitive Panchromatic Type Two Motion Picture Film," *Cinematographic Annual*, vol. 2 (Hollywood: American Society of Cinematographers, 1931), p. 103.

62. This approach is of course not visible in every one of his films, and Struss always boasted that he varied his lighting schemes according to mood and genre. "No two pictures were photographed the same," he told the Harviths (*Man with a Camera*, p. 16).

63. William Stull, "Concerning Cinematography: Critical Comments on Current Pictures," *American Cinematographer* (January 1932), p. 22; "Concerning Cinematography," *American Cinematographer* (February 1932), pp. 24, 26 (Mamoulian).

64. "Nominees for Academy Awards," *American Cinematographer* (November 1932), p. 38.

65. "Concerning Cinematography," *American Cinematographer* (April 1932), p. 24.

66. Harviths, *Man with a Camera*, p. 16.

67. "Guilty as Hell," *Variety*, August 9, 1932.

68. Higham, *Hollywood Cameramen*, p. 128.

69. "Photography of the Month," *American Cinematographer* (March 1933), p. 16.

70. Robert Birchard, *Cecil B. De Mille: Notes for a Three-Part Film Retrospective* (New York: American Museum of the Moving Image, 1989), n.p.

71. Murray Ross, *Stars and Strikes* (New York: Columbia University Press, 1941), pp. 142-148.

72. Koszarski interview.

73. Walter Bluemell, "Composition in Practice, Part II," *International Photographer* (September 1934), p. 19. In a search of *International Photographer* through December 1936, Struss is mentioned twice in connection with still photography: once as a supplier of the Struss Pictorial Lens to John Leezer (November 1933) and once as an exhibitor in a San Diego photography salon (July 1935). Dupont began featuring him in their advertising once more in August 1935.

74. "Photography of the Month," *American Cinematographer* (February 1934), p. 405.

75. Karl Struss, "Photographic Modernism and the Cinematographer," *American Cinematographer* (November 1934), p. 296.

76. Struss, "Dramatic Cinematography."

77. James L. Fritz, "Struss' Photography Luxurious," *American Cinematographer* (February 1935), p. 52.

78. "Telephoto Shots—Playing With Dollies," *American Cinematographer* (April 1935), p. 153.

79. See August 1935 issues of both *American Cinematographer* and *International Photographer*, inside front covers.

80. There were a handful of exceptions: *The Preview Murder Mystery* and *Hollywood Boulevard*, a pair of Robert Florey melodramas, and *Thunder Trail*, a western. All of these were B-budget assignments to which Struss was probably referring when he remembered Paramount as scheduling him to work on whatever was shooting that day.

81. Higham, *Hollywood Cameramen*, pp. 35, 75.

82. Eyman, "Interview," p. 324.

83. Eyman, "Interview," pp. 320-32; Koszarski interview.

84. Blanchard, "Aces of the Camera."

85. Fred Basten, *Glorious Technicolor: The Movies' Magic Rainbow* (Cranbury, N.J.: A. S. Barnes, 1980), p. 172.

86. Eyman, "Interview," pp. 322-323.

87. "Distribution," *Film Daily Yearbook of Motion Pictures* (New York: The Film Daily, 1953), p. 123.

88. "The Alligator People," *Variety*, July 15, 1959; Dorr interview.

89. Karl Struss to American Society of Cinematographers, August 17, 1949, American Society of Cinematographers Archives.

90. Alain Silver and Elizabeth Ward, eds., *Film Noir: An Encyclopedic Reference* (Woodstock: Overlook Press, 1979), p. 277.

91. *Nation*, August 30, 1947, quoted in *Agee on Film* (New York: Beacon, 1964), p. 273. See also Higham, *Hollywood Cameramen*, p. 131.

92. Higham, *Hollywood Cameramen*, p. 131.

93. The most complete account of Struss' Italian films is found in John Dorr's interview.

94. *Cinema* (Milan), December 30, 1953, courtesy of Lorenzo Codelli.

95. Lorenzo Codelli to Richard Koszarski, April 25, 1992.

96. Again, the most detailed information on Struss' late features and television commercials is contained in the Dorr interview.

97. Higham, *Hollywood Cameramen*, p. 133; "The Fly," *Variety*, July 16, 1958. In fact, Struss was one of the first cinematographers to work in a wide-screen format, having photographed *Danger Lights* in the short-lived Spoor-Berggren Natural Vision 65mm process in 1930. During a symposium on proper screen ratios hosted at that time by the Academy of Motion Picture Arts and Sciences, Struss proposed a compromise wide-screen ratio of 1.66:1. That proportion would be unofficially adopted by the industry in the 1950s as a means of giving a "wide screen look" to films shot in the old 1.33:1 standard. Fred Westerberg, "The Academy's Symposium," *International Photographer* (October 1930), p. 14.

98. Koszarski interview.

Figure 91. David Margolick photographed Karl Struss going through one of his custom-made albums at home, 1975, gelatin silver print, Collection of John and Susan Edwards Harvith

THE MAN BEHIND THE CAMERA

John and Susan Edwards Harvith

The two of us first met Karl Struss in California in late 1974. We were conducting interviews for a book and exhibition on the history of recorded music and while in Los Angeles decided to pursue another of our primary research interests: the interrelationship between still and motion picture photography. Skeptical of Andrew Sarris' then-popular "auteur" theory[1]—which led critics to credit all aspects of a film's production to the director—we hoped to discover a celebrated cinematographer equally gifted as a still art photographer, whose filmic style was a natural outgrowth of his photographic vision and not one imposed by a director.

In addition, we wished to bridge the scholarly worlds of film and photography, because the more we spoke to historians and curators of film and photography, the more amazed we became at how little people in one field knew about the most basic historical facts in the other. Individuals in still photography had never heard of *Sunrise* or of its director, F. W. Murnau. Those in film did not seem to be cognizant of the Photo-Secession or Alfred Stieglitz. But the Photo-Secession, we were to discover in the course of our later research on Struss, was a primary force in molding his artistry and that of cinematographer Joseph Walker (director of photography for all but one of director Frank Capra's 1930s films), according to their own testimony.[2] Yet in the mid-1970s, film scholars did not realize that studying the work of the Photo-Secessionists could provide an understanding of the visual styles that Struss and Walker employed in their classic Hollywood films.[3]

We had read about Struss in Charles Higham's book of interviews with cinematographers.[4] In introductory passages of his interview with Higham, Struss spoke of doing portraiture and magazine and advertising illustration during his pre-Hollywood years but gave no hint of the depth of his involvement with pictorial photography in the 1910s and never mentioned Clarence White, Alfred Stieglitz, or the Photo-Secession. In December 1974, while combing the photography shelves of a used-book store in Hollywood, we discovered a hardbound 1931 compilation of photographs by the Camera Pictorialists of Los Angeles (titled *The Pictorialist*), which included a pictorial photograph (*Tugs*, a harbor scene) by Karl Struss. We resolved on the spot to phone Struss who, to our astonishment and delight, was listed in the Los Angeles phone directory. Our intention was to meet him, view whatever photographs were in his possession, and, if they were of sufficient quality, interest him in exhibiting them together with a festival of his films.

Our first meeting with Karl and Ethel Struss took place at their modest bungalow on Orange Grove Avenue near Sunset Boulevard. The soft-spoken Struss, whose telephone conversation with Susan had been carefully measured, with unmistakable remnants of a New York accent, turned out to be an imposing, magisterial (even awe-inspiring) presence: tall (about six-feet-two), distinguished-looking, trim and erect, with a shock of silvery-white, unruly hair and wire-rim glasses. He had an expansive air about him that immediately put us at ease. His wife Ethel exuded good-natured charm and a gentle, self-effacing sense of humor; she was never afraid to poke fun, with a Shirley Temple-like puckishness, at Karl's human foibles, despite his best attempts to appear perfect and in control at all times. He would call her "Etch" or "Etchie" (she was an accomplished printmaker), and she would address him as "Angie" (as in angel).

Struss had brought out of storage a selection of his vintage work—matted platinum and silver bromide prints from enlarged negatives dating from the early decades of the century—and had them strewn about on a cardtable, on chairs, and leaning against furniture. We were struck immediately by their beauty, technical finish, and, in a few cases—*Balcony, Sorrento* (see p. 65), *Metropolitan Life Insurance Tower* (see fig. 40), *Brooklyn Bridge, Nocturne* (see fig. 32)— by their unique and compelling vision. After a preliminary interview, we told Struss of our interest in doing an exhibition and catalogue of his early work and soon had his permission to interest museums in a major Struss retrospective. We had a self-imposed deadline of one year for creating both the exhibition (*Karl Struss: Man with a Camera*) and an accompanying book, because we wanted to be sure Struss could witness the rediscovery of his early still photography.

Late in the summer of 1975 we returned to Hollywood to spend a solid month with the Strusses and to interview a number of Karl's fellow cinematographers.[5] Through the UCLA Film and Television Archive, we were able to arrange frequent private screenings for Karl and ourselves of his 1930s Paramount films, all in nitrate prints.[6] On screening days we would pick Karl up at about 8 a.m., drive over to UCLA, see three films, return to the bungalow for a light lunch, then go through photographs and documentary materials, make detailed notes on all of the photographs considered for inclusion in the exhibition, discuss everything from Karl's career to politics, have a snack, conduct formal taped interviews, socialize, and have another of Ethel's meatless repasts. Somehow, we would always manage to break away, totally exhausted, by about midnight, despite Karl's willingness to forge ahead, as fresh and full of energy at the end of the day as he was in the morning.

In the course of this month-long research sojourn, several things became quite clear to us. First and most important, we discovered, after going through Struss' numerous custom-made 1910s photo albums (fig. 91), that he was a far greater photographer than we had ever dared imagine from our limited exposure to his platinum and silver bromide enlargements. Some of the small, contact-size vintage platinum prints in those albums (mounted on the same stock paper that Stieglitz had used in *Camera Work*) astounded us. They were so remarkably modern for their time, so far in advance of what other photographers were then doing, that they anticipated the work of Walker Evans, Andre Kertesz, Berenice Abbott, and E. O. Hoppé years later. They also were richly profound and satisfying images in themselves, some of them laced with humorous incongruity, others mysterious, surreal, abstract, or haunting commentaries on urban life. And Struss' Hollywood portrait studies of Gloria Swanson, Bebe Daniels, and others from 1919 and 1920 predated the glamour work of Edward Steichen and other photographers.[7] These landmark Struss photographs were unknown to the art world—a body of work that had been ignored for some sixty years and could have ended up being lost forever.

Our second discovery—which made the organization and selection of the exhibition an ongoing challenge—was that although Karl realized he was a skilled photographer, he never fully appreciated his own significance in the history of pictorial photography. He placed the greatest value on what he saw as his innovative contributions to photographic technique. He retained among his papers a 1915 article in *American Photography* in which John Wallace Gillies wrote, "I am inclined to think that his [Struss'] heart is in the technical side of photography," and as Struss himself put it during one of our 1975 interviews: "I believe in progress. I don't believe in being tied to the past; I think of the future."[8] Karl felt that the pinnacle of his achievement as a photographer was a 1909-10 experiment, in which he printed his 1907 negative of an unexceptional New Hampshire landscape seven different ways, from straight platinum to an "expressionist" stippled multiple gum print

(see figs. 12 and 13). At each installation of the *Man with a Camera* exhibition he visited (University of Michigan, George Eastman House, Los Angeles County Museum of Art, and the Phillips Collection), he asked that a photo be taken of himself in front of the New Hampshire landscape grouping: "This is what makes the whole exhibition," he said on more than one occasion. When asked why, he stated, "Because that's never been done before in the history of photography." He was similarly proud of *Sunset, Simplon Pass* (see p. 70), another traditionally pictorial image from 1909, because it incorporated his unique method of multiple platinum printing, in which the hand-coated paper was repeatedly resensitized and exposed both on the front and, by reverse registration, on the back of the print.[9]

During one of our 1975 interviews, Karl even went so far as to say that he didn't think of what he did in photography "as being artistic": "I seemed to think of pictures with my eye, and then it was how to record the image." He said that he was interested in "mostly landscapes and scenes around the big city, the buildings and the river and the bridges. Lots of mechanical things . . . anything of that nature. A combination of science and art, you might say. . . . I have a scientific background . . . and I utilize that when it comes to making pictures." He was always interested in "the mechanics of the situation"—lenses, lighting, the balance of lights and darks that he equated with "space-filling" in a composition. His definition of "pure photography," he told us, was using original negatives to make platinum prints; "impure photography," he said, was the production of literal, wide-angle glossy bromide prints without any diffusion.

We became convinced that his inventive 1910s photographs were the result of an ingeniously intuitive eye rather than any conscious attempt at modernism. By 1975, Karl was so focused on his technical achievements that he simply could not, for instance, appreciate the significance of his modernistic and sardonic *The Wheel* (c. 1912, reproduced in *Man with a Camera*), in which the front end of a gleaming, elegant automobile appears to push two plain, parasol-wielding women out of the frame. Karl preferred enlarged prints of jewel-like images such as *Low Tide* (1911, reproduced in *Man with a Camera*) and *Metropolitan Life Insurance Tower* (see fig. 40), whose messages, we felt, were best served in their small, original contact-size formats.

In selecting images for the *Man with a Camera* exhibition, we therefore had to struggle with Karl to keep in all of his path-breaking, forward-looking contact-size platinum prints while excluding less interesting enlarged European views from 1909, nondistinctive 1950s European color photographs derived from his stereo slides, and other conventionally pictorial work from the 1910s and 1920s. For all the dynamic imagery of the Brooklyn Bridge, New York City, and Long Island beaches, there was also a body of technically proficient pictorial imagery that was either derivative (of Coburn, Stieglitz, White, and others) or typical of what one saw in camera annuals of the time—bucolic landscapes, travel scenes, soft-focus outlines of trees, graceful nymphs—of which Karl was inordinately fond. A prime complicating factor was Karl's ignorance of photographic history beyond the mid-1920s.[10] His personal library of photography books, periodicals, and catalogues dated almost totally from before the 1930s.[11] When we first laid eyes on *The Open Window* (see p. 75) and *Street Scene* (see fig. 53)—both taken from his father's factory around 1910—we blurted out in amazed delight, "These remind us of Evans," meaning that the keen sense for city life was like that in Walker Evans' photographs of the 1930s. Karl's immediate response was, "Ah, Frederick Evans, I knew him well." When we explained that we had

meant Walker Evans, both Karl and Ethel looked at us blankly; they had never heard of him.

He was also endlessly fascinated by the possibilities of color photography and was quite proud, for instance, of his accomplished but unadventurous Hess-Ives images, perhaps because Hess-Ives was a technically demanding process (one he had described in detail in the August 1917 issue of *American Photography*). In truth, the only Struss color images we saw that could compete in visual interest with his best black-and-white work were his autochromes, which we did not see for some time. Karl was likewise proud of his color work in the film *Aloma of the South Seas* (1941), and he kept a copy of the June 1941 issue of *American Cinematographer* that praised him as "one of the very few 'production' cinematographers qualified, in the opinion of Technicolor's extremely conservative executives, to take complete and unaided charge of filming a Technicolor production." He carried a Kodak Instamatic with him during his travels to the *Man with a Camera* exhibition sites and never tired of taking color snapshots. He told us that he had been taking and exhibiting stereo color slides since 1950, had thousands upon thousands of them and still took them occasionally, and that he always had film in his stereo camera.[12] The slide images Karl showed us were technically accomplished but bland, with one exception: a quirky, askew composition of the rear of a Volkswagen Beetle that had a bit of the idiosyncratic flavor of some of his best early photography.

A third noteworthy characteristic of Karl that quickly became evident to us was his extreme political conservatism. He was an ardent Reagan supporter long before that was fashionable. He was forever spouting anti-liberal and anti-Democratic Party bon mots. He railed against Communists infiltrating the government and against Democrats always wanting to raise taxes ("Soak the rich, soak the rich, that's all they understand"). He would never compromise on what he felt were sacred political principles; according to Joseph Walker, some meetings at the American Society of Cinematographers went past midnight, to the exasperation of fellow members, because Karl insisted on taking certain stands and wouldn't give an inch.[13] In the midst of World War II, Karl also authored and published his own "peace plan," whose central tenet obligated the United States to bomb off the face of the earth any nation that "ever dares start another" war. When we knew him, Karl was still exceedingly proud of this document as well as a novel time zone plan he had devised in 1934 that would have reduced America's time zones to three.

Nevertheless, in looking back on our experiences with Karl, we must say that one of the most refreshing things about him was his tolerance of people who held views opposite his own. He worked with Chaplin on *Limelight* at a time when Chaplin had been accused of being a Communist. He maintained a lifelong friendship with Imogen Cunningham, whose outspoken ultra-liberal views must certainly have been anathema to him, and she, in turn, was well aware of his conservative political leanings: for her 1976 photograph of Karl in her book *After Ninety* (published posthumously by the University of Washington Press in 1977), Cunningham added the line, "I couldn't understand how such a creative filmmaker could be right wing." Karl worked on five films with Frank Tuttle between 1934 and 1946 and highly regarded Tuttle as a director, yet he chuckled as he told us of being invited to accompany Tuttle to a big Hollywood rally, where Karl was having a wonderful time until it had finally dawned on him that he, of all people, was attending a Communist gathering! He had nothing negative to say about Tuttle because of this; he simply found the whole inci-

dent quite humorous and supremely incongruous.

Our fourth revelation about Karl was that he seemed to have been a modernist in his early years almost in spite of himself. He spoke disdainfully of Coburn's pioneering vortographs; he dismissed the 1913 Armory Show, which he had seen; and he made disparaging comments about Marcel Duchamp's *Nude Descending a Staircase*. He said that the only worthwhile Paul Strand image was the photograph of a white picket fence illustrated in the final issue of *Camera Work*, and he dismissed a 1976 Strand show as "just very ordinary snapshots—if you saw one print of Strand's, you saw the whole works."[14] The only Steichen images worth mentioning, according to Karl, were that master photographer's studies of Rodin sculptures.

Of course, in the last two instances, personal bitterness may have played a significant role. After featuring Struss' work in both the 1910 Albright Art Gallery exhibition and in *Camera Work*, Stieglitz had dropped Struss in favor of Strand, who, launched and backed by Stieglitz, had a celebrated career as an art photographer. Not only that, but Stieglitz did Struss a grave disservice by selecting for *Camera Work* some of Struss' least interesting and most conventional work: only *Over the Housetops, Meissen [Meissen Rooftops]* (see p. 66) hinted at the forward-looking bent of his best photographs.[15] That Stieglitz did not, for instance, reproduce one of Karl's finest images, *Balcony, Sorrento* (see p. 65), after it had appeared in the 1910 Albright Show is a mystery and, in light of Struss' subsequent obscurity, a frustrating act of omission.[16] In fairness to Stieglitz, however, it must be noted that his selection of twelve Struss images for the 1910 Albright Art Gallery show was also limited by Karl's own biases. In a 1975 interview, Karl told us that in advance of the exhibition he only showed Stieglitz twenty-four "special" enlarged hand-coated multiple platinum, gum, gum-platinum, and two-tone bromide prints, the latter prints' sepia and black-and-white toning effects "done with a brush dipped in chemicals after the enlargements had been made." In other words, Karl sought to impress Stieglitz with what he himself considered most significant about his work—his technical prowess—rather than the freshness of his vision.

Interestingly, Karl had nothing but positive things to say about Stieglitz in our conversations.[17] His bitterness about Steichen, by contrast, was palpable. In January 1976 Struss sent us a 1959 news clipping about Steichen purchasing another photographer's prints for the Museum of Modern Art, circled Steichen's name, and wrote, "This is the individual who has been responsible for my photographs never have [*sic*] been shown in the New York art museums."[18] Yet it was obvious that Strand's and Steichen's work had made a powerful impression on him back in the 1910s. He had detached numerous gravure pages from the final Strand issue of *Camera Work* (49-50) in order to display them on the walls of his New York studio. Similarly he had removed Steichen's portrait of George Bernard Shaw, *Nocturne—Orangerie Staircase*, and *Late Afternoon-Venice* from issue 42-43 and Stieglitz's *The Steerage* from issue 36.[19]

Karl's bitterness was not limited to the photographers in Stieglitz's circle. He voiced genuine hurt at receiving subsidiary camera credit—on a lower line and in smaller lettering than Charles Rosher—for *Sunrise*. He stated in one of our interviews that Rosher himself had been responsible for making and shooting the credits; cinematographer George Folsey told us he wasn't surprised, because "Rosher was a flamboyant guy that would get all the credit" while Karl was "a more modest, less aggressive kind of fellow than Rosher." In addition, *Sunrise* co-star George O'Brien, whom we interviewed following the

January 1977 Los Angeles opening of the *Man with a Camera* exhibition, stated flatly that he always considered Karl an equal participant in the camera work, since he usually saw him conferring with Murnau and because Karl was the one he remembers experimenting and coming up with novel solutions to problems posed by Carl Mayer's script. O'Brien, for instance, credited Struss with a brief but psychologically telling sequence: while O'Brien's character sleeps fitfully, with unsettling dreams of drowning his wife, bundles of bulrushes he has stashed away (to save himself after the planned drowning) zoom into view—an image that awakens the character with a start. Before the age of zoom lenses, Karl constructed a skateboard-like contraption, attached the camera to it, placed the assemblage on a sloping floor, set the focus, and put ropes on the side to control the speed of the assemblage as the camera raced toward the bulrushes.

Karl related with undisguised satisfaction that at the premiere of *Sunrise*, Murnau, in his address to the opening-night audience, said, "I especially want to commend Karl Struss" for the film's photography, and the applause drowned out Murnau's subsequent mention of Rosher. For his part, Rosher, in a full-page advertisement in the 1928 *Film Daily Year Book*, proclaimed himself "Chief Cinematographer with F. W. Murnau's First American Production, *Sunrise*," and in his interview with Kevin Brownlow, Rosher made it sound as if Struss' only role in the film was as a camera operator in the marsh scene.[20] According to O'Brien, however, Karl's involvement in this key scene—one of the most taxing of the film to make—was far greater than Rosher would admit: Struss not only photographed the scene's lengthy moving camera sequence from an aerial track but lit the scene and achieved the remarkable effects of light on water, in a scene that required fifty-four takes. Karl himself told us of his photographing other

Figure 92. David Margolick, *Karl Struss*, 1975, gelatin silver print, Collection of John and Susan Edwards Harvith

that he had shot over 52 percent of the footage. He was indignant that veteran D. W. Griffith cameraman Billy Bitzer was given co-camera credit on Karl's three silent films with Griffith when, Karl said, Bitzer never even appeared on the set.[22] He couldn't believe that when Fredric March received his Oscar for *Dr. Jekyll and Mr. Hyde*, "he [March] gave all the credit to Wally [Westmore], his makeup man. He never mentioned me, and I was nominated for the picture. The makeup man just did what I told him."

Struss felt that many of the Hollywood cinematographers he encountered in the early 1920s lacked his technical abilities: "The majority of what we called then cameramen were not photographers: They knew nothing of lighting, they knew nothing of photography, and it was all guesswork. They came from all kinds of fields and they got in. They tinkered around the camera and they were cameramen." According to George Clemens—who was the camera operator for some of Struss' finest films and also worked as an operator for legendary cameramen Rosher, Charles Lang, Victor Milner, and John Arnold before becoming a cinematographer himself— Karl was "one of the ten great cameramen in the business": "He had a style that was all his own when he came out here from his still work in New York. It was completely different than lots of the other cameramen." Clemens also called Karl "a great teacher," because he would allow him to try his hand at lighting and then correct him and tell him where he had

Sunrise scenes solo, among them the complex and dazzling split-screen jazz dance fantasy sequence and an overhead nighttime scene of Margaret Livingston watching as George O'Brien is brought in from the lake after the storm.[21]

Karl was also upset that he did not get first camera credit for *Ben-Hur*, since he estimated

gone wrong. L. William O'Connell, who had photographed the nativity scene in *Ben-Hur*, was also grateful to Karl for teaching him in the 1920s the technique of altering an actor's appearance through the use of filters and panchromatic film. O'Connell told us that he put this knowledge to work in photographing Alla Nazimova's pockmarked face; he was the cinematographer for two 1925 Nazimova films, *My Son* and *The Redeeming Sin*. (Nazimova, incidentally, was one of Karl's favorite silent actresses.)

According to Clemens, "Karl was more of a cross-light cameraman," whereas "Rosher was more of a flat cameraman. He shot things flat, and sometimes it was complimentary to women, and sometimes it wasn't." Because of this distinction, Clemens felt he could pick out the scenes in *Sunrise* that Struss had shot solo. During one of our 1975 interviews, Karl actually took Rosher to task for his method of filming Mary Pickford in the silent period, stating that "Charlie really put her in a rut in how she had to look" by setting only one angle for her to be photographed from and saying "Monkey Face!" on the set if she changed that prearranged angle. Karl said that he would tell actresses who insisted upon being photographed in a particular way, "Don't worry about it, that's my responsibility."[23]

Struss considered C. B. De Mille a man of the theater rather than a filmmaker with a photographic sense, but in his clipping file Karl kept at the ready a photocopy from De Mille's *Autobiography*, where the director called Struss "a cameraman whose brilliant mastery of black-and-white cinematography was, I have always believed, one of the factors in keeping the place that black-and-white still holds in American motion pictures."[24] De Mille obviously thought just as highly of Struss' work for him as a still photographer: in our 1975 interview, George Clemens told us that when Steichen was photographing glamour stills in Hollywood in 1932,

De Mille said to Clemens, "Well, I'll take Struss anytime." Despite Karl's aversion to Rouben Mamoulian's simian conception of Mr. Hyde, Clemens told us that working for Mamoulian on Dr. Jekyll and Mr. Hyde was "a very delightful experience" because "Mamoulian had a wild idea that he wanted to make a completely different picture than anybody else had done. So he put it in Karl's and my hand to see what we could do. . . . Once he saw what we were trying to do for him and could do for him, he was more than cooperative, and he said, 'You just take your time. Anything you want to do, we'll do it'."[25]

Karl had kind words for a number of the directors he worked with, among them Louis Gasnier ("He had a pictorial mind, and we got along just great"); fellow Los Angeles pictorialist Erle Kenton, for his command of English and understanding of photography[26]; Murnau, for his mastery of the moving camera; and D. W. Griffith, for his handling of large groups of people and for his ability, even when shooting a complex crowd scene, to succumb to sudden inspiration and change his conception on the spot. Karl had "great respect" for Frank Tuttle, whom he had known since the 1910s, when Tuttle was an assistant editor of *Vanity Fair* in New York. And he considered Marshall Neilan "a genius" who never had a script: "It was all up here," Karl said admiringly, pointing to his head.

After our intensive exposure to Karl's still and motion picture photography in 1975, we were able to see the unmistakable relationship between them, regardless of the film director with whom he worked. The same tightly framed compositions and the same subtle gradations in tone from deep, rich blacks, through finely differentiated grays, to glistening highlights could be seen in his finest platinum prints and in vintage nitrate prints of some of his best-photographed 1930s films, among them *Dr. Jekyll and Mr. Hyde*, *Guilty as Hell*, *The Island of Lost Souls*,

The Preview Murder Mystery, and *The Story of Temple Drake*. Even in *Journey into Fear* (1942), with the extreme angles and claustrophobic feeling one associates with Orson Welles' films, the camera work is still unequivocally that of Struss, as distinct from Gregg Toland (in *Citizen Kane*) or Stanley Cortez (in *The Magnificent Ambersons*). One sees the same framing devices and full range of tonality that characterizes Karl's finest work, together with a shallower depth of field than that favored by either Toland or Cortez.

Because he was so proud of his individual artistic contribution to films, Karl had acted during the 1920s to protect the sanctity of his cinematographic compositions. He equipped his motion picture camera with an inside adapter that matched the frame lines of the finished film with the frame lines on projectors, so that projectionists could not alter his compositions during screenings: "I said to the projectionists, 'You're not going to have the liberty of playing with my pictures, cutting heads or cutting feet just to suit you'." He said that he thought of his compositions as being the same, whether in still or motion picture photography, and that, during rehearsals in sound films, he would have his camera operator look through the finder (set for parallax view) at the same time he, Karl, looked through the lens itself to establish compositions. He felt that the "luminous quality" of his still photography carried over into his motion pictures, and that the same principles applied. "The sharp image is too literal, it's just a map for us to see," he said, and spoke of the Struss Pictorial Lens putting in "atmosphere" that "you can control . . . by the iris diaphragm that you use" to make the image "sharp but still have a degree of softness in the details. . . . You get away from the literal, you get a poetic effect. With women especially you try to soften all the physical defects." One distinction that he drew between

still photography and film was that "in motion pictures, the chief thing is recording the action of the actors and you're interpreting with the photography the mood of the picture. . . . you want to interpret what the director is trying to put over."

Because we discovered that some of Karl's greatest still photographic images existed as only one or two vintage prints, we decided in 1976 to produce, under his supervision, a limited-edition, platinum-print portfolio of those images from surviving glass plates and film negatives; in this way, we hoped to disseminate some of his best images to museums and private collections.[27] We enlisted Philip Davis, an authority on early photographic printing processes, and lent him the vintage prints, so that he could match them as closely as possible with modern materials and papers.

After all that Karl had told us about previsualizing his compositions and "trimming in the camera" on his groundglass ("There was no trimming of any of my compositions," he said to us in one interview, "because I believed in filling the space"), it was fascinating to learn in the course of the portfolio project that Karl had, indeed, trimmed and cropped some of his prints in order to get the compositions he wanted. *Consolidated Edison* (see fig. 54), for instance, had to be trimmed around the edges in order to match the image in the vintage print, and a winter-time variant of *East Side Promenade* (fig. 61) that Karl was considering for inclusion in the portfolio had to be cropped severely in order to yield the composition that he had in mind. We also discovered from studying portfolio test prints and vintage silver prints that some of Karl's images taken with an anastigmat lens appeared soft in platinum, yet had surprising clarity and definition when printed in silver—among them *Balcony, Sorrento* (see p. 65); *Brooklyn Bridge from Ferry Slip, Evening*; *Brooklyn Bridge, Nocturne* (see fig. 32); *Shadows* (1909, reproduced in *Man with a Camera*); and

Lower New York: Water Street and the Brooklyn Bridge Tower (1910, reproduced in *Man with a Camera*). In the case of *Brooklyn Bridge, Nocturne*, the clarity of the image in silver radically altered its meaning. The softened contours of platinum printing created the unencumbered aura of a monumental, idealized sweep of bridge and skyline. In silver, the image is yet another Struss exercise in incongruity: in the foreground, beneath the bridge's soaring span and city skyline, is a clearly delineated array of urban litter, an ugly planked wooden wall topped with a double row of barbed wire, and a ramshackle barge.

One challenge in dealing with Karl and Ethel was their sometimes forgetting or withholding materials and information. After our rediscovery exhibition had been on the road for nearly a year, in January 1977, Karl remembered that he had a large steamer trunk stored above the rafters of his garage, and he asked us to climb up there and retrieve the contents. It had been there since the 1920s and, as it turned out, contained a remarkable cache of photographs, magazines, clippings, and documents that would have added immeasurably to the exhibition, including some gelatin-silver "Illustration" prints that Karl had shown to prospective clients in the 1910s to interest them in his work. Among them was a nighttime, high-angle study of New York City light patterns (see p. 89) that predated by many years Berenice Abbott's *New York at Night*. Also in the trunk, in the original "291" envelope and in pristine condition, was Stieglitz's 1912 letter to Struss, in which he admitted that his selection of Karl's images for illustration in *Camera Work* was less than ideal, but held out the prospect of including more of Karl's work in a forthcoming issue. Unfortunately, Stieglitz never represented Struss in *Camera Work* again, despite the fact that between 1912 and 1916 Karl was producing some of the most forward-looking pictorial photography anywhere.

During this same January 1977 visit, Karl and Ethel started pulling out of cabinets and drawers more contact-size platinum prints that were, in some cases, even more striking and forward-looking than the images they had shown us in 1975, when we had asked to see absolutely everything in the house. Among these landmark images were *The Flatiron* (c. 1911; see fig. 47)—with its abstract overhead patterning of long shadows, pedestrians, traffic, trolley-car tracks, and smeared street pavement—that anticipates 1920s photographs by Moholy-Nagy and others; a geometrically constructed overhead view, c. 1911, in which lower Broadway skyscrapers and a park form triangles and upward-thrusting trapezoids (see fig. 46); and a 1911 study of two steelworkers suspended in midair on a cable and steel beam (see p. 8), which looks forward to Lewis Hine's 1929 series of skyscraper construction photographs. In our excitement upon seeing the latter photograph for the first time, we marveled aloud at the image's prefiguring of Hine, and the Strusses looked at us quizzically: just as they had never heard of Walker Evans, so they knew nothing of Hine.

Karl had told us during our preparations for *Man with a Camera* that he had done autochromes, but since they had never surfaced, despite our repeated and insistent requests that he unearth them, we made no mention of them in either the exhibition or book. Finally, for our January 1977 visit, Karl retrieved the autochromes (dating from 1907 to 1916) from a local camera shop to which he had lent them. We had asked to see all of them, and on the spot we decided to bring three, dating from 1916, to the attention of the art world. They were truly extraordinary, unlike any autochromes we had ever seen. The first was a view taken head-on, many stories up, of steelworkers on the girdered framework of a skyscraper under construction (see p. 7). The others were two scenes of the boardwalk and beach at

Long Beach, Long Island. The first of the Long Beach pair was a sensuous panorama whose composition is remarkably similar to Matisse's 1921 painting, *Fêtes des Fleurs*, of the seaside at Nice. The second of the pair was a vigorous exercise in compositional solidity offset by riotous blurs and swirls of color in the foreground—all that was left of clusters of boardwalk promenaders who failed to appear in corporeal form via the slow autochrome process; the image turned one of the weaknesses of the process, the slow speed of the film plate, into a strength (see p. 2). Our intention was to make modern dye-transfer prints from the originals, but unfortunately, only a small number of prints of two of the images were made before Karl's death. We would discover later that, although we had asked to see all of the autochromes in 1977, the Strusses had shown us only some of them: a few remarkable images that they did not share with us are now among the Struss autochromes in the collection of the Amon Carter Museum.

When Karl spoke with us about his involvement in World War I, he steadfastly adhered to the story of his doing secret work in infrared photography—so secret, he said, that he was still sworn to secrecy nearly sixty years later.[28] The only reasons he gave for his move to California and cinematography were the warmer climate—he was always ill during the New York winters, he told us—and the artistry and expertise he felt he could bring to motion picture photography. He had spent a lot of time looking at movies, he said, and had found the camera work in films inferior: "They just didn't know anything about photography."[29]

Karl had a selective memory concerning his dual career in film and photography. He could remember incredibly minute details about cameras, lenses, dates, papers, chemicals, f-stops, exposure times, filters, and more. But he had little or nothing whatever to say about personal details: no memories of his conversations with Stieglitz or of his encounters with Coburn, Gertrude Käsebier, or White; no revealing anecdotes about Murnau, Mary Pickford, or Louis Gasnier. When we weren't talking to him, Karl always seemed to be totally preoccupied with some personal project related to his coins, stamps, or photographs. It may be that it was always thus: he was so wrapped up in his own work and thoughts that he simply paid little heed to what was going on around him and put a low priority on his personal interactions with others.[30] Karl's attitude about human interactions came through clearly in 1975 when we were trying, unsuccessfully, to get him to give us more information on fellow Photo-Secessionists. After repeated questioning concerning Coburn, about all Karl could proffer was that "he wasn't aggressive at all—he was soft-spoken." But then came the most telling comment of all: "I don't analyze people too much. I take them as they come."

Karl and Ethel finally decided in late 1976 that they were going to sell their collection of Karl's work piecemeal instead of transferring it complete to a museum. After years of neglect, Karl was measuring his artistic success in terms of financial reward, and he appeared to take immense satisfaction from it. Having made the decision to scatter his collection, Karl at the same time showed great generosity by giving work to institutions and individuals connected with the *Man with a Camera* exhibition tour.

He remained a person of amazing physical vigor into his nineties and adhered strictly to a lifestyle of exercise and restricted diet. He won a Senior Olympics Octogenarian tennis doubles tournament in 105-degree heat at age eighty-six and continued to play golf after he finally had to give up tennis at age eighty-eight, when his ankles could no longer support his weight in the game. When Susan and Ethel were out of earshot one evening during his February 1976

University of Michigan artist-in-residency, Karl turned to John and said gleefully, "You know, all of my original equipment still works perfectly, and I mean ALL of it," as he poked John in the ribs with his elbow and gave him a sly wink.

A mere nine months later, at the time of his ninetieth birthday, Karl was stricken with spinal meningitis and double pneumonia, and his prognosis was guarded at best. Because of this—a supremely bitter irony—he was unable to return to New York City in triumph for a December 1976 tribute by the Museum of Modern Art and recognition by the International Center for Photography (ICP), where the *Man with a Camera* exhibition had been shown to critical acclaim that fall. He had been particularly anxious to have the show appear in New York ("As a native New Yorker, they owe it to me," he told us during a September 1975 interview), and later hinted at problems he had had in New York years earlier, but refused to elaborate: "There were some people in New York who didn't like me," he said. "I won't ever divulge what went on there. Well, these people have all passed on."

Even though Ethel was a devout Christian Scientist and later refused to discuss the precise nature of Karl's near-fatal illness in 1976, she never stood in the way of his receiving the best available medical treatment. Karl fought back and made a miraculous recovery in a month's time, so that he could savor the gala opening of the *Man with a Camera* exhibition and film festival at the Los Angeles County Museum of Art on January 5, 1977. At that opening, he was besieged by autograph-seekers at a standing-room-only screening of *Sunrise* that had Hollywood stars and fellow cinematographers and photographers in the audience. He was interviewed by Jim Brown for the Los Angeles NBC-TV affiliate station and was lionized in local press coverage. His doctor said that it was as if Karl had gone to Lourdes and had been cured; he could not

believe that such a thing was medically possible.

Karl was back to his former ebullient self for the final opening of the *Man with a Camera* tour in July 1977 at the Phillips Collection in Washington, D.C., accompanied by an American Film Institute tribute at the Kennedy Center. As in Michigan, Rochester, and Los Angeles, the Washington opening was a jam-packed affair with local celebrities in attendance—notably Joseph Hirshhorn, Phillips Collection director Laughlin Phillips, and Maynard P. White—and a glittering reception by the press, including a National Public Radio interview by Susan Stamberg.

During the final few years of his life, Karl had the satisfaction of seeing his still photography receive the recognition he knew it had deserved. He lived to see glowing reviews in the *New York Times*, *Art News*, the *Los Angeles Times*, the *Washington Post*, and elsewhere. He lived to see his work enter the permanent collections of museums throughout the United States, including the Museum of Modern Art and the Metropolitan Museum of Art in his former hometown of New York. And he lived to celebrate his ninety-fifth birthday. When he died on December 15, 1981, he had seen his hero Ronald Reagan elected president a year earlier and had seen his beloved daughter Barbara die of cancer.

When we look back now on our experiences with Karl, the overriding impression is of an irrepressible joie de vivre. Despite the bitterness over his setbacks, he derived such enjoyment from life's simple pleasures, had such an ability to have fun and convey a sense of his joy in living to others, and had such an indomitable spirit, that he was an inspiration. We will always treasure our memories of his hilariously angular gesturings with his arms and legs as he caricatured Nijinsky's dancing in *The Afternoon of a Faun* for our amusement one evening; his merriment at pointing to a large diamond ring on his finger and telling us how Mae West had ordered it for him and had to have it replaced when she realized her jeweler had given Karl a fake diamond; or his childlike delight in Michigan at being able to order and eat a bucket of mussels for the first time in many years. That same openness, that innate and infectious ability to drop his guard, laugh at life's absurdities and be himself, may have been behind the intuitive freshness and bracing originality of vision in his finest photographs. For just as he said, "I take people as they come," Karl was always himself. Although this revealed personal flaws and caused him no small amount of trouble over his lifetime, we now think, with the passage of years, that it was also his greatest source of strength.

NOTES

1. Sarris' theory is set forth in his book *The American Cinema: Directors and Directions, 1929-68* (New York: E. P. Dutton, 1968).

2. In our interviews with him on September 14, 1975, and January 1, 1977, Joseph Walker told us that he had subscribed to *Camera Work*, had studied photographs by Stieglitz, White, Käsebier, and Steichen, and tried to emulate in his cinematography what he had seen in still pictorial photographs. "[A]rtistically I wanted to be like Stieglitz, I wanted to try and do what I saw in still pictures. I wanted to get those wonderful effects onto this little film, which was practically then like taking it up to the corner drugstore." He also told us that he was inspired by Struss and the effects he was able to achieve in his still photographs with the Struss Pictorial Lens.

3. This has now begun to change: *The Classical Hollywood Cinema* by David Bordwell, Janet Staiger, and Kristin Thompson (New York: Columbia University Press, 1985), for instance, considers still art photography to explain the evolution of Hollywood's visual style in the 1920s and 1930s, giving Struss and the Struss Pictorial Lens a share of the credit.

4. Charles Higham, *Hollywood Cameramen: Sources of Light* (Bloomington: Indiana University Press, 1970).

5. Unless otherwise noted, all Struss quotations are from interviews we conducted with Struss between December 3, 1974, and September 16, 1976. We also spoke with a number of Struss' colleagues, among them George Folsey (September 13, 1975), L. William O'Connell (January 7 and 21, 1977), and George Clemens (September 17, 1975). All of the cinematographers to whom we spoke were generous in their praise of Karl, and a number of them—including Joseph Ruttenberg, George Folsey, Ernest Laszlo, Paul Ivano, and Milton Krasner—attended the January 5, 1977, gala opening of the *Man with a Camera* exhibition at the Los Angeles County Museum of Art. These good feelings toward Karl appear to have been long-lived: in the first *Cinematographic Annual*, published in 1930 by the American Society of Cinematographers (ASC), Karl was given the honor of leading the book's "Pictorial Section" with halftone reproductions of four of his photographs, among them *Sails* (see p. 163) and *City of Dreams* (see fig. 35). His ASC colleagues chose him to portray the unnamed

director of photography in the 1949 industry short *The Cinematographer*. When we talked to him about this film, Karl grumbled about receiving a common actor's salary instead of the cinematographer's payment to which he was accustomed.

6. Unfortunately, Karl could remember little or nothing about the making of some of the best of these films, including *The Story of Temple Drake*, *Guilty as Hell*, and *Belle of the Nineties*. He made an apt comment to us when we asked him in August 1975 about the circumstances surrounding his photographs of Gloria Swanson holding a ball: after stating that he had no recollection of the sitting, Karl said, "Once it's shot, it's forgotten."

7. We also discovered that a number of widely published, uncredited photographs of Gloria Swanson in *Male and Female*, including the famous shot of her in a lion's den, were Struss images. Given all of this, it was fascinating to learn years later that "[p]erhaps the greatest influence" on Clarence Sinclair Bull, MGM's celebrated portrait photographer and the preeminent portraitist of Greta Garbo, "in the early 1920s was his friendship with Karl Struss," according to Terence Pepper in *The Man Who Shot Garbo* (New York: Simon and Schuster, 1989), p. 17. Pepper also notes that Bull "avidly studied the work of the major photographers" in *Camera Work*.

8. Thus Karl was already thinking, in a 1940 radio interview, about the need for cameramen to prepare themselves for television photography.

9. Struss' endless fascination with photographic technique extended to his creation of unique photographic title cards for De Mille features shortly after his arrival in Los Angeles. Cinematographer L. William O'Connell—who had shared lodgings with Karl during his earliest days in Hollywood and had been an assistant director for De Mille—told us during a January 1977 interview that in making the cards, Karl would take a positive still photograph, superimpose the negative of the same photograph over the positive still image, but slightly out of registration, and then rephotograph the two. Through this novel method, "he made it look like the Roman block figures in stone . . . a bas relief," O'Connell said. "Simple," he added, "but who thinks of those things?"

10. Because he was largely unaware of the contemporary trends swirling around him, we find two art photographs Karl took in 1930 on the set of *Danger Lights* especially

fascinating. One, a sharp-focus, overhead view of bridge girders and their textured shadows, is a complex and powerful abstract study in triangles, and looks like pure Moholy-Nagy, whose work Karl would not have known. The other is an abstract pattern of the top of a telephone pole and wires against a cloudy sky, the sort of photograph one would expect to see in *Fortune* magazine in the 1930s. These photographs, taken in Chicago, give one pause, because they are unlike anything else Karl did before or after; might they be an indication of the direction his still work would have taken had he stayed in the East? To the best of our knowledge, he never made any prints from the negatives, and we only know them from study prints made by the Amon Carter Museum. Indeed, now that the Amon Carter Museum has made study prints of all Struss' negatives, one can see that he also made remarkable and forward-looking images from the 1910s that, alas, he apparently never printed.

11. Among the publications in his library were *Camera Work*, Pictorial Photographers of America annuals, selected numbers of the *American Annual of Photography* from 1909 to 1930, the *Pictorial Annual* of the Royal Photographic Society of Great Britain from 1926 and 1928, Paul Anderson's early books on pictorial photography, Alvin Langdon Coburn's *London*, and catalogues from 1910s and 1920s exhibitions. He had a smattering of catalogues from later pictorial salons (well into the 1960s) in which he was represented, often by photographs from the 1910s and 1920s.

12. Karl's interest in stereoscopic photography, by the way, was hardly a passing one: in some of his most interesting early photographs of New York—including *Consolidated Edison from the Second Avenue Elevated*, *Water Street & the Brooklyn Bridge Tower*, *Shadows*, *On the Pier*, *Vanishing Point II: Brooklyn Bridge from New York Side*, and *Brooklyn Bridge from Ferry Slip, Evening*—he was able to create the illusion of depth by having objects in the foreground appear deep, rich, and black as structures in the background recede into separate planes of increasing brightness. George Clemens spoke to us about the "stereoscopic" quality of Karl's cinematography, using "light in the background to project the character or face forward." According to publicity material for *Drums of Love* (1928), D. W. Griffith experimented with Karl for weeks on achieving three-dimensional effects in that film. Karl photographed *Danger Lights* (1930), the pioneering RKO "wide (65mm) stereoscopic" film using the Spoor-Berggren process of wide-film cameras. In a 1940 radio interview (whose transcript Karl kept among his papers) he predicted the film industry's adoption of a 3-D

process achieved through color, and, of course, he eventually went to Italy to work on a series of 3-D color films in 1953-54. In a speech text from about 1950, Struss wrote: "In all our photography, working in a two-dimensional medium, we try as much as we possibly can to light for a third dimensional result having roundness or stereoscopic effect."

13. Back in the 1930s, Struss's sympathies were anti-union, and he gladly went off to Hawaii with De Mille in 1933 to photograph *Four Frightened People* during the Hollywood strike that year; before they left, Ethel told us, they were getting threatening phone calls at home. In our interview of January 21, 1977, L. William O'Connell said that in 1933, "If you didn't feel like going on the strike, you were a no-good nothing." He remembered one large gathering of the International Photographers union at the time, when Karl and his Paramount crew attended: "Alvin Wyckoff was president of our union (International Alliance of Theatrical Stage Employees Local No. 659) . . . and [business representative Howard E.] Hurd got up and talked for a whole hour and a half trying to convince the gathering of the union members to go on a strike, and I smelled a rat. I said, 'If any man can talk for an hour and a half on a subject, there's something wrong with it.' So, in the meantime, Karl Struss got up with his group from Paramount and walked out of the meeting. . . . After that, Karl Struss went into the books of the union of this fellow Hurd and found out that he'd gone South with $90,000 out of the account." A founding member of the Academy of Motion Picture Arts and Sciences, Karl in 1933 had been a member of the Academy's Board of Directors when it proposed an eight-week industry-wide salary cut that spurred immediate union opposition, according to Gary Carey in *All the Stars in Heaven* (New York: E. P. Dutton, 1981), pp. 168-70. Among his papers, Karl had a handwritten text dating from about 1940 (probably for a speech) that spoke of "the closed shop" tending "to prevent new brains and intelligence from crashing the gates." Because of unions, he said, "it is becoming increasingly . . . difficult to get the first start on the road to becoming, say, a Director of Photography."

14. When scholar Naomi Rosenblum asked Strand about Struss, all he would comment on was his early use of the Struss Pictorial Lens.

15. Photographer, cinematographer, and documentary filmmaker Willard Van Dyke told us during our May 10, 1976, interview that *Over the Housetops, Meissen* was one of the photographs reproduced in *Camera Work* that his men-

tor John Paul Edwards brought to his attention when Van Dyke was a young photographer in the 1920s. Edwards "thought that he [Struss] was one of the good photographers," Van Dyke said, but "deplored the fact that he had gone into movies" because "he just thought that that wasn't an art, and that photography was." Van Dyke added that Edward Weston, showing Van Dyke his famous image of Karl with his motion picture camera, referred disparagingly to "Karl Struss, that Hollywood cameraman" and "didn't think much of his (Struss') photography." The additional photographs Weston took of Karl were unknown to Van Dyke or Cole Weston until they were exhibited as part of the *Man with a Camera* show. Ethel Struss, incidentally, told us that she was not fond of the photograph Weston took of her and Karl, because Weston would not let her be herself in front of the camera—he insisted that she nestle on Karl's shoulder "like a leaf blown in by the wind."

16. This unique view of five standing figures in animated conversation, caught leaning over a balustrade and crowded to one side of the frame, is both a decisive moment and an image of sublime tension. The rock-solid composition is anchored by the balustrade and by the hat of the man at the extreme right, yet the frame is nevertheless rife with movement, from the restless geometric patterns on the floor, stripes on trousers and parasol, and finely etched decorative detailing on the women's hats and dresses, to the leftward tilt of the men's bodies, which leads our eyes over the edge of the balcony into an abyss. In hindsight, this photograph epitomizes the end of the Edwardian Age, as elegantly dressed ladies and gentlemen chat amiably, blissfully unaware that within five years their seemingly secure vantage point would topple into World War I.

17. In 1975, Struss still had two polemical pamphlets that Stieglitz had published in 1910 ("Photo-Secessionism and Its Opponents: Five Recent Letters" and "Another Letter: The Sixth") and over half of the issues of *Camera Work*, including all of those published from July 1910 to the final issue of June 1917, which featured some of Strand's most striking work. We found it intriguing that Karl subscribed to *Camera Work* to the end, when it was featuring reproductions of avant-garde paintings by Picasso, Matisse, John Marin, and others and at a time when subscriptions were declining steeply; by 1912, there were only about 200 subscribers in the U.S. (according to Weston Naef in *The Collection of Alfred Stieglitz* [New York: Viking, 1978], p. 208), and by the time of the final issue there were only 37 subscribers in all, according to Stieglitz himself (in a 1938

letter quoted by Dorothy Norman in *Alfred Stieglitz: An American Seer* [New York: Random House, 1973], p. 134.) In fact, Karl was still such a devoted Stieglitz partisan that he ordered us to remove passages critical of Stieglitz from the draft of our essay to accompany the Struss platinum print portfolio we produced in 1978. The offending passages questioned Steiglitz's withholding of *Balcony, Sorrento* from *Camera Work* 38 and his failure to include such forward-looking Struss images as *East Side Promenade* in later *Camera Work* issues that offered masterpieces by Steichen, Strand, and De Meyer next to mediocre work by Frederick H. Pratt, Arthur Allen Lewis, and others. Through negotiation, we were able to restore the substance of the offending passages, though we were forced to omit mention of Paul Haviland's representation in three issues of *Camera Work* and Stieglitz's inclusion of lesser work by other photographers in subsequent issues.

18. For years Struss had been trying on his own to interest museums in doing exhibitions of his work. During our initial phone conversation with Struss, he had indicated that the Los Angeles County Museum was going to do an exhibition, but LACMA had never heard of Struss; instead, the science and technology branch of the County Museum, which used to house the annual Los Angeles pictorial salons, had been getting insistent calls from Struss, whom they had written off as a crackpot. Struss told us later that he was "a patron member" of LACMA "with access to museums," and he was attempting, without success, to use the clout to which he felt that membership entitled him. Princeton University photography historian and curator Peter Bunnell wrote to us in June 1976 that he had pursued the idea of a Struss exhibition at Eastman House in the mid-1960s, but Struss had shown him only the early images that had been published in *Camera Work* and had "placed much too much emphasis on his recent work with amateur color, &c."

We suspect that, just as he had been pestering the Los Angeles County Museum to show his work, Karl had been petitioning Steichen to do the same—perhaps by sending slides of his conventional 1950s color work—and was met with a curt rebuff. In fact, according to MOMA's photography department, Steichen had included one Struss image (*The Outlook, Villa Carlotta*, and not, unfortunately, *Over the Housetops, Meissen*) in his 1948 exhibition of *Camera Work* and *Camera Notes* gravures at the Museum of Modern Art. Among Struss' papers was a September 30, 1948, *New York Times* review of the exhibition, billed as the first Photo-Secession show since the 1910 Albright Art Gallery exhibition; since it made no mention of Struss, Karl

probably assumed he was not included in that show. Steichen's selection of gravures, as might be expected, was idiosyncratic: he had accorded the largest number of works (17) to himself, followed closely by Stieglitz (16), White (16), Frank Eugene (15), and Coburn (12), but had entirely omitted Baron De Meyer, Frederick Evans, J. Craig Annan, and Strand (because he considered Strand part of a "new period" in photography).

19. In *Camera Work* 42-43, the young Struss had highlighted a short passage from Arthur Hoeber's *New York Globe* review of Stieglitz's one-man photography retrospective at "291." Part of the highlighted material read: "Of course these are the visualized things of nature, as the man in the street is likely to observe them, just good old nature, with some reasonable construction, drawing, form, and all that sort of thing. There has been no deep research after inner consciousness and the significance of life. . . ." Struss wrote next to the passage, "See page 14," where Marius De Zayas, in his essay "Photography and Artistic-Photography," contrasts the "two sides of Photography," with "Steichen as an artist" "expressing the perfect fusion of the subject and the object," and with "Stieglitz as an experimentalist" "trying to do synthetically, with the means of a mechanical process, what some of the most advanced artists of the modern movement are trying to do analytically with the means of Art." Given Karl's statements to us that he had no philosophy in mind in his photography, merely the art of "space filling," we suspect that he was very much in sympathy with Hoeber's description of Stieglitz's photography.

20. The advertisement is on p. 28 of *Film Daily 1928 Year Book* (New York and Los Angeles: The Film Daily, 1928), and the interview in Kevin Brownlow, *The Parade's Gone By . . .* (New York: Alfred A. Knopf, 1968), p. 232.

21. Karl must have felt somewhat vindicated by two clippings he had kept with his papers. The first, a 1931 *Hollywood Filmograph* obituary for F. W. Murnau, contains a photograph of Murnau and Struss on the barbershop set of *Sunrise*; the author of the obituary, Harry Burns, writes in the article, "Karl Struss was the late director's cameraman on this epic (Sunrise)." The second is a full-page advertisement for National Photographic Carbons in the September 1929 *American Cinematographer* showing a large production still with the cutline, "F. W. Murnau and Karl Struss directing a scene with Janet Gaynor and George O'Brien for *Sunrise*."

22.   To bolster his claim, Karl retained the program from a gala D. W. Griffith "Testimonial" screening of *Drums of Love* in 1928, which credits him as the film's sole photographer. The 1929 *Film Daily Year Book* gives co-credit to Billy Bitzer and Harry Jackson (who, Karl said, was only a second cameraman); it is noteworthy that Struss received an Academy Award nomination for his work on *Drums of Love*, but Bitzer and Jackson did not.

23.   For his part, Karl went on to great success photographing Pickford in the initial three of her four sound films, the first of which (*Coquette*, 1929) won her the Academy Award for Best Actress.

24.   Cecil B. De Mille, *Autobiography* (Englewood Cliffs, N.J.: Prentice-Hall, 1959), p. 230.

25.   In an interview published in *The Celluloid Muse: Hollywood Directors Speak*, by Charles Higham and Joel Greenberg (New York: New American Library, 1969), Mamoulian explains and then takes credit for Karl's photographic means of transforming Jekyll into Hyde. Although Higham and Greenberg claim in their introduction that Mamoulian had disclosed "for the first time the secret of the cinematic transformation," Karl in fact had revealed his "secret" in detail many years before, in the July 22, 1933, *Saturday Evening Post* article "Aces of the Camera." When both were present for a screening of the film at the University of Southern California in the fall of 1975, however, Mamoulian forbade Karl from revealing to a student audience his technical method for achieving the transformation! Perhaps Mamoulian realized that news travels slowly at times: Joseph Ruttenberg, who photographed MGM's 1941 remake of *Dr. Jekyll and Mr. Hyde* with Spencer Tracy and Ingrid Bergman, was amazed to learn during a September 1975 interview how Karl had managed Fredric March's transformation scenes; MGM, he said, spent weeks running unsuccessful tests and finally placed Tracy in a head brace, applied one piece of makeup at a time, and ground one frame of film at a time—"Everything was stop motion." When we told Karl of our conversation with Ruttenberg, he said, "I wish he had asked me then; I would have been happy to tell him!"

26.   Although we had wanted to interview Erle Kenton as part of the *Man with a Camera* exhibition and book, Karl was very protective of his friend and colleague, who had been suffering for years from Parkinson's disease, and told us point-blank that Erle was too ill to be disturbed. When we met Kenton's wife Claire at the Los Angeles opening of the *Man with a Camera* exhibition and asked about the possibility of our interviewing her husband, she said that he'd be delighted to see us, as, indeed, he was. Even though Kenton spoke extremely slowly and with great difficulty because of his illness, his mind and memory were unimpaired. Kenton told us in one of our January 1977 interviews with him that "Karl Struss and I were both pictorialists . . . I was very happy to have him because we could speak a different language. And he was very happy to work with me because his suggestions could be carefully analyzed by another photographer." According to Kenton, he and Karl made joint decisions on the use of some of the lenses in *The Island of Lost Souls* ("We used a one-inch lens, which was a mystery to a lot of people, but not to Karl and not to me. . . . We also used a converter lens and the one-inch lens that [together] gave twice as much distortion"), while Karl used the Struss Pictorial Lens to photograph part of the film. Kenton also spoke about Karl having to create special lighting for distorted close-ups of actors who were only eighteen inches from the camera: Karl, Kenton said, rigged up neon lighting around a frame that he attached to the lens box. In one scene, Kenton said he wanted the eyes of two ape men in the darkness of a cave to show up as cat eyes; Karl had a pair of glasses frames made with small lights inserted instead of lenses, and the duo, Kenton said, appeared to have animal eyes, just as he had requested. In another scene, Kenton wanted Karl to make the shadows of actors running from Dr. Moreau's house loom ever larger on a wall, just as, in *Dr. Jekyll and Mr. Hyde*, Karl had made Fredric March's shadow balloon in size as he was fleeing the police, whose shadows also expanded. But, Kenton said, Karl had forgotten how he had achieved this effect a year earlier, "and he had a hell of a time doing it."

27.   While going through Karl's negatives to select images for the portfolio, we also came across his 1916 contact silver prints of Nijinsky performing *The Afternoon of a Faun*. These images, which had been stored with the negatives for over sixty years and thus had been all but unknown to the dance world, reveal more about the mechanics of Nijinsky's performance than the atmospheric but hazy De Meyer images.

28.   In 1977, Clarence White's grandson, historian Maynard P. White, told us that in the course of research on his grandfather, he had come across information indicating that Karl was interned during World War I—White thought it had something to do with Karl's father being overheard voicing pro-German sentiments—but added that he was sure Karl would not talk about it. The full story has not been revealed

until the publication of Barbara McCandless' essay in this volume.

29.   Of course, Struss had already made one contribution to cinematography before 1919. He used his Struss Pictorial Lens not only for still work in New York but also, in a three-inch focal length version, to film legendary dancer Adolph Bolm in 1916. According to the *American Cinematographer* of February 1, 1922, John Leezer (a cameraman with D. W. Griffith) employed the first soft-focus lens, a custom-made three-inch focal length Struss Pictorial Lens, in motion pictures in the 1916 film *The Marriage of Molly O.* Joseph Walker told us that the Struss Pictorial Lens, which he had used in still work, inspired him to come up with his own soft-focus lenses for use in cinematography. Among other noted owners of the Struss Pictorial Lens were Paul Anderson, Arnold Genthe, Clara Sipprell, Mabel Watson, Clarence White, cinematographers Charles G. Clarke and James Wong Howe, and the young Paul Strand. Although Karl never said that he had used the lens in making films once he was in Hollywood, his papers included publicity material for *Rose of Cimarron* (1952) stating that he used the Struss Pictorial Lens in making that film, and Erle Kenton told us that Karl had used it in filming *The Island of Lost Souls.*

An April 1919 *Photoplay* article ("The Next Genius—A Cameraman?" by *Los Angeles Times* art critic Antony E. Anderson), which Karl mentioned to his mother in his letter of March 5, 1919, probably strengthened his resolve to make additional contributions to cinematography; see Richard Koszarski's essay. The one surprise is Karl's overnight development as a glamour photographer of stars, since this had been a weakness in his New York work. According to Nicholas Haz in "From Salons to Screens" (*The American Annual of Photography*, 1938): "At first [in 1914], Struss set himself up as a portrait photographer. Then, as now, portraiture built its success on effective flattery, and Struss was no great shakes at this, as he modestly admits. He switched over to magazine illustration and advertising photography."

30.   This is corroborated by Tom Weaver and Michael Brunas' interview with Rose Hobart, who played opposite Fredric March in *Dr. Jekyll and Mr. Hyde* (1931). When asked about Struss, all Hobart could report was, "He concentrated only on what he was doing; he was always absolutely absorbed" (*Filmfax* [October/ November 1991]). Of course, Karl also said tartly to us on one occasion, "I never talked to the actors. Period. Because I don't give a hoot what they think I think."

APPENDIX

Lifetime Exhibition Record

November 3-December 1, 1910 - International Exhibition of Pictorial Photography, Albright Art Gallery, Buffalo, New York, Buffalo Fine Arts Academy with the Photo-Secession; Open Section. Exhibited: *Over the Housetops, Meisseo [sic]; The Balcony, Sorrento; In the Outskirts of Rome; Near Amalfi; Villa Carlotta, Lake Como; A Bridge, Venice; Ducks, Lake Como; Along the Elbe, Dresden; Columbia University, Night; Across the Hudson, Riverside Drive; On the East River, New York; Interior, Villa Carlotta, Lake Como.*

April 6-May 4, 1911 - *What the Camera Does in the Hands of the Artist*, Free Public Library, Newark, New Jersey, Newark Museum Association group pictorial exhibition of professionals and students at Columbia University and Brooklyn Institute. Exhibited: *The White Girl; Sunset, Simplon Pass; A By-way, Bellagio; Portrait, Mrs. F.; The Cigarette; Under the Boardwalk; Lake Como; Over the Housetops, Meissen; Twilight Across the Hudson; Near Amalfi; A Bridge, Venice; Across the Hudson; Columbia University, Night.*

January 17-27, 1912 - *Photographs of New York* (solo exhibition), Teachers College, Columbia University, New York. Exhibited: *Chatham Square; State Street, Northward; New York, from Montague Street; The Financial Center; West Street; The Sky-Line, Wall Street Ferry; New York, Past and Present; The Robert Fulton; The Queensboro Bridge; 110th Street "L" Station, Evening; Park Avenue, Southward; Fifth Avenue; St. Johns Cathedral, Twilight; Sunlight, Snow, Steam and Shadow; The Watering Trough; The Waldorf-Astoria; The White Ferryboat; The Library, Columbia University; First Avenue; Earl Hall, Columbia University, Night; Along the Rockaway Coast; Unloading, East 36th Street; The Pennsylvania Station; High Bridge; Twilight, Across the Hudson; The Village Across the River; On the East River; Hotel Plaza, Night; The Grave Yard, Trinity Church; The Lafayette Boulevard; The Poplars, Riverside Park; St. Nicholas Avenue, Morning; Altman's Delivery, 6 p.m.; Broadway and 33rd Street, Twilight; Morningside Park; The Tunnel, East 42nd Street; Madison Square; Metropolitan Tower, Dusk; Monday, First Avenue; The Front Stoop.*

October 10-31, 1912 - *An Exhibition Illustrating the Progress of the Art of Photography in America*, Montross Art Galleries, New York. Exhibited: *Columbia University, Night; Arverne, Moonlight; Lower New York; Hamilton, Bermuda, Moonlight; Landscape, Chester, Nova Scotia; Fifth Avenue, New York; The East River; The East Side, New York.*

January 19-February 4, 1914 - *An International Exhibition of Pictorial Photography*, Ehrich Art Galleries, New York. Exhibited: *Interpretation—Venice; Meissen; Lake Como.*

August 24-October 3, 1914 - *Fifty-ninth Annual Exhibition of the Royal Photographic Society of Great Britain*, Gallery of the Royal Society of British Artists, London. Exhibited: *Near Amalfi; Balcony, Sorrento; Landscape, Nova Scotia; East Side Promenade; Columbia University, Night.*

October 5-8, 1914 - *Mergenthaler Linotype Company Exhibit* at United Typothetae Convention, Waldorf-Astoria, New York. Exhibited: *Boston Library; Carnegie Library, Pittsburgh; Congressional Library at Washington, D.C.; Newspaper Row, N.Y.*

January 18-30, 1915 - *An Exhibition Illustrating the Progress of the Art of Photography in America*, Photographic Society of Philadelphia, Rosenbach Galleries, Philadelphia. Exhibited: *Lower New York; The Boardwalk; Nova Scotia Landscape; Meissen Housetops; Near Bellagio; Columbia University—Night.*

March 1-15, 1915 - *Tenth Annual Exhibition - Photographs*, John Wanamaker, Philadelphia. Exhibited: *The Front Stoop; Decorative Arrangement; A Byway; On the Hillside; A Window; Sunlight on the Water; Early Morning; Reflections* ($5 prize); *The Anchorage; Sunday Morning, Landscape; Moonlight Silhouettes; Lucerne; The Landing Place, Capri; Landscape [Windswept]* (third prize, $25); *High Bridge* ($5 prize); *Chatham Square* (honorable mention).

March 1-31, 1915 - *Second Annual Pittsburgh Salon of National Photographic Art*, presented by the Photo-

graphic Section of the Academy of Science and Art of Pittsburgh, The Carnegie Institute. Exhibited under the "Platinum Print" Collection, New York: *The Boardwalk; Interior (Carnegie Institute); Nova Scotia Landscape; Columbia University (Night); Lower New York (From Brooklyn Bridge).*

March 1915 - *Sixteenth Annual Exhibition*, Portland Society of Art, Photographic Section, Portland, Maine. Two prints: *Near Bellegio [sic]; Dresden.* [Paul Anderson exhibited *Portrait of Karl Struss*].

May 17-31, 1915 - *An Exhibition of American Pictorial Photography*, College of Fine Arts, Syracuse University, Syracuse, New York. Exhibited: *Sunday Morning, Chester, Nova Scotia; Over the House Tops, Meissen; Ducks, Lake Como; Columbia University, Night; Fifth Avenue, New York; The Outlook, Villa Carlotta.*

June 1-12, 1915 - *Third Annual Exhibition*, Fine Arts Gallery, Public Library, presented by Fotocraft of Bangor, Maine. Exhibited: *Sunlight on the Water; Lake Como; The Harbor, Chester, Nova Scotia; Hamilton, Bermuda, By Moonlight.*

August 23-October 2, 1915 - *Sixtieth Annual Exhibition of the Royal Photographic Society of Great Britain*, Gallery of the Royal Society of British Artists, London. Exhibited: *Morning on East River; The Ferry, Bermuda; Hamilton, Moonlight; Marjorie; First Avenue, New York.*

September 1915 - *Exhibition of Pictorial Photography*, Toledo Museum of Art, Professional Photographers section. Exhibited: *Meissen; Bellagio; Landscape, Nova Scotia; Lower New York; Columbia University, Night; The Balcony, Sorrento; Near Amalfi; Sunset, Simplon Pass; Sailboats, Venice; The Beach; Interior, Villa Carlotta; The Palisades.*

December 1915 - *An Exhibition of Pictorial Photography*, Print Gallery, New York. Exhibited: *Near Amalfi.*

1915 - *Panama/Pacific International Exposition Exhibit of Pictorial Photography*, San Francisco. Exhibited: *Columbia University, Night*; *Summer on the Pincion Hills*; *Nova Scotia*.

February 22-26, 1916 - *Fifteenth Annual Exhibit of the Wilkes-Barre Camera Club.* Exhibited: *Pennsylvania Station*; *Across the River-Late Afternoon*; *On the Hillside—Chester, Nova Scotia*; *Spring*; *Italian Landscape—A Byway, Bellagio*; *Lower New York—Under Brooklyn Bridge*; *Hamilton, Bermuda—Moonlight*; *Decorative Landscape*.

March 1-17, 1916 - *Eleventh Annual Exhibition, Photographs*, John Wanamaker, Philadelphia. Exhibited: *A Street, Meissen* (honorable mention); *Portrait of a Young Girl*; *Pennsylvania Station* (honorable mention); *Florentine Pines* ($5 prize); *Fifth Avenue Twilight*; *Fast Asleep*; *Late Afternoon*; *Soap Bubbles* (honorable mention); *Lower New York*; *The Sun Dance*; *Charlotte of the Hippodrome*; *Katie Schmidt*; *The National Capitol* (honorable mention); *Into the Sunlight* (honorable mention); *The Porterfield Poplar* ($10 prize); *Hamilton Harbor, Twilight*; *The Cliffs, Sorrento* (honorable mention); *Grand Central Station* (honorable mention).

March 1-31, 1916 - *Third Annual Pittsburgh Salon of National Photographic Art*, presented by the Photographic Section of the Academy of Science and Art of Pittsburgh, Carnegie Institute, Pittsburgh. Exhibited: *Pennsylvania Station*; *Venice*; *Fifth Avenue*; *Connecticut Landscape*.

April 27-May 21, 1916 - *The Twenty-sixth Annual Exhibition by the Department of Photography, Brooklyn Institute of Arts and Sciences*, Brooklyn Museum, New York. By Invitation section. Exhibited: *Porterfield Poplar*; *Pennsylvania Station*; *New York, Twilight*.

August 21-September 30, 1916 - *Sixty-first Annual Exhibition of the Royal Photographic Society of Great Britain*, Gallery of the Royal Society of British Artists, London. Exhibited: *Under Brooklyn Bridge*; *Connect-icut Landscape*; *Lower New York—Twilight*; *Niagara*; *Florentine Pines*; *National Capitol*.

September 16-October 14, 1916 - *International Exhibition of the London Salon of Photography* at the Galleries of the Royal Society of Painters in Water-Colours, London. Exhibited: *Sun Dance*; *Pennsylvania Station*; *Fifth Avenue—Twilight*.

March 1-17, 1917 - Twelfth Annual Exhibition of Photography, John Wanamaker, Philadelphia. Prizewinners: *East Side [Promenade]* (fifth prize, $10); *Lower New York-Water Street and Brooklyn Bridge Tower* ($5 prize); *Arverne* (honorable mention); *The Library* (honorable mention).

March 1917 - *Fourth Annual Pittsburgh Salon of National Photographic Art*, presented by the Photographic Section of the Academy of Science and Art of Pittsburgh, Carnegie Institute, Pittsburgh. Exhibited: *The Woodland Dance*; *Clermont [sic] Inn*; *Niagara*.

May 17-27, 1917 - *First Annual Photographic Salon*, Southern California Camera Club, Los Angeles. Six prints: *The Landing Place*; *The South American*; *Capri*; *Fifth Avenue—Twilight*; *Metropolitan Tower—Twilight*; *Florentine Pines*.

June-July 1, 1917 - *Chelsea Neighborhood Art Gallery*, New York. Exhibited: Title(s) unknown.

September 1917 - *An Exhibition of Pictorial Photography by American Artists, Collected by the Pictorial Photographers of America*, Minneapolis Institute of Arts. Exhibited: *Pennsylvania Station*; *The Capitol, Washington*; *Capri*.

1917 - *Exhibition of Photographs by the Alumni Association of the Clarence H. White School of Photography*, New York. Exhibited: *East Side, New York City*; *Roof Tops, New York City*; *The East River*.

1917 - *International Exhibition of the London Salon of Photography* at Galleries of the Royal Society of Painters in Water-Colours, London. Exhibited:

Hoboken; *Brooklyn Bridge*.

October 4-November 10, 1917? (or earlier) - *An Exhibition of Photography*, American Institute of Graphic Arts, National Arts Club, New York. Exhibit-ed: *Columbia University—Night*; *Sail Boats—Venice*; *Pennsylvania Station*; *Fifth Avenue—New York*.

February 28-April 1921 - *First Annual Competition*, organized by *American Photography*, toured to Boston, New York Camera Club, Pennsylvania State College. Prize Winners: *Laguna* (fifth prize, $10); *The Release of the Hamadryad* (honorable mention).

March 7-26, 1921 - *Fifteenth Annual Exhibition of Photographs*, John Wanamaker, Philadelphia. Exhibited: *The Canyon [Detail]* (third prize, $25); *Design for a Poster*; *The Dance to the Morn*.

September 10-October 8, 1921 - *International Exhibition of the London Salon of Photography* at the Galleries of the Royal Society of Painters in Water-Colours, London. Exhibited: *Rhythm*; *Nocturne*; *On the Pier*; *Cables*.

October 30-November 26, 1921 - *The Annual Salon of Photography*, Municipal Art Gallery, Oakland, California. Exhibited: *The Span at Twilight*; *Grand Canyon—Detail*; *Man's Construction*.

November 1-12, 1921 - *The Frederick & Nelson Second Annual Exhibition of Pictorial Photography*, Frederick and Nelson Auditorium, Seattle. Exhibited: *Snow Peaks*; *Eucalyptus*; *Drifting Clouds*; *Moonlight—Samarkand*; *Storm Clouds*; *Grand Canyon—Arizona*; *Miss Betty Compson*; *Spring*; *At Home*; *Avalon*; *Wave Patterns*; *Iris*.

March-October 1922 - *Second Annual Competition*, organized by *American Photography*, toured to New York Camera Club, Pennsylvania State College, Wilkes-Barre Camera Club, Worcester Art Museum, Boston Y.M.C.U. Camera Club. Prize winners (honorable mention): *Spring*; *Moonlight, Samarkand*.

April 15-May 15, 1922? - *First Annual Salon of Pictorial Photography*, San Diego Museum Art Galleries, California. Exhibited: *Phantom Ferry*; *On the Terrace, Night*; *Brooklyn Bridge*; *A Byway, Bellagio*; *The Anchorage*.

May 20-June 18, 1922 - *First Annual International Exhibition of Pictorial Photography*, Pictorial Photographic Society of San Francisco, Palace of Fine Arts, San Francisco. Exhibited: *Metropolitan Tower*; *Traffic*; *Lake Como*.

September 9-October 7, 1922 - *International Exhibition of the London Salon of Photography*, Galleries of the Royal Society of Painters in Water-colours, London. Exhibited: *Above the Pacific—Twilight*; *Ann Forrest*.

November 6-18, 1922 - *The Frederick & Nelson Third Annual Exhibition of Pictorial Photography*, Frederick & Nelson Auditorium, Seattle. Exhibited: *Samarkand*; *The Storm*; *La Danseuse*; *Landscape* (honorable mention); *Faith Healer* (second prize, $75; also honorable mention).

January 3-31, 1923 - *Southern California Camera Club Exhibit of Pictorial Photography*, Southwest Museum, Los Angeles. Exhibited: *Japanesque*; *Shadows*; *Waves*; *Across the Hudson—Twilight*; *Early Morning*; *Housetops—Winter*; *Cables*; *Nocturne*; *Monterey Coast*.

August-November 1923 - *Second Annual International Exhibition of Pictorial Photography*, Pictorial Photographic Society of San Francisco and the Photographic Section of the Oakland Art Association. Exhibited: *Storm Clouds*; *Sun Dance*; *The Avenue—Dusk*.

September 8-October 6, 1923 - *International Exhibition of the London Salon of Photography*, Galleries of the Royal Society of Painters in Water-Colours, London. Exhibited: *Samarkand*; *White Ferryboat*.

September 28-October 6, 1923 - *Third Annual Pictorial Photographic Exhibition*, The Emporium, San Francisco. Exhibited: *Catalina* (seventh prize, $5); *Hollywood Hillside*; *Samarkand—Moonlight*; *Laguna*; *Balboa*.

October 15-November 5, 1923 - *Seventh International Salon of Photography*, Los Angeles. Exhibited: *Ann Forrest*; *Lake Como*; *Near Amalfi*.

November 5-17, 1923 - *The Frederick & Nelson Fourth Annual Salon of Pictorial Photography*, Frederick & Nelson Auditorium, Seattle. Exhibited: *Between Scenes—Ruth Miller*; *Out of the West—Clarence Burton, La Danseuse*; *In the Harbor—Chester, Nova Scotia*.

1923 - *Prize Winning Prints in the Third Annual Competition*, organized by *American Photography*, toured to Maine, Massachusetts, New York, Pennsylvania, Colorado, California. Exhibited: *Traffic* (fifth prize); *Metropolitan Tower—Twilight*.

February 3-29, 1924 - *Second Exhibit of Pictorial Photography*, Southern California Camera Club and the Southwest Museum, Los Angeles. Exhibited: *Storm Clouds*; *Release of the Hamadryad*; *Rhythm*; *Lake Como*.

March 2-31, 1924 - *Fourth National Salon of Pictorial Photography*, *Buffalo Camera Club*, Albright Art Gallery, Buffalo, New York. Exhibited: *Samarkand*; *Morning, Santa Barbara*; *Moonlight, Samarkand*; *Grand Canyon*; *Grand Canyon, Detail*; *Grand Canyon, The Inferno*.

September 6-October 4, 1924 - *International Exhibition of the London Salon of Photography*, Galleries of the Royal Society of Painters in Water-Colours, London. Exhibited: *Still Life*; *The Old Story*.

October-November 1924 - *Eighth International Salon of Photography, Camera Pictorialists of Los Angeles*, Los Angeles Museum. Exhibited: *Phantom Ferry*; *On the East River*; *The Schooner*.

October 20-November 1, 1924 - The Frederick & Nelson Fifth Annual Salon of Pictorial Photography, Frederick and Nelson Auditorium, Seattle. Exhibited: *Silhouette Dance*; *Release of the Hamadryad*; *Approaching Storm*.

October-December 1924 - *Third Annual International Exhibit of Pictorial Photography*, Pictorial Photographic Society of San Francisco. Exhibited: *Pismo*; *Across the Hudson (Twilight)*; *Grand Canyon—The Inferno*.

1924 - *Thirty-Third Annual Salon of Pictorial Photography, Canadian National Exhibition*, sponsored by the Toronto Camera Club. Exhibited: *The White Ferry Boat*.

September 12-October 10, 1925 - *International Exhibition of the London Salon of Photography*, Galleries of the Royal Society of Painters in Water-Colours, London. Exhibited: *At Anchor*; *The Sierra Madres*.

December 1-31, 1925 - *Fourth Annual Exhibition of Pictorial Photography, Southern California Camera Club*, Southwest Museum, Los Angeles. Exhibited: *The Ferry, Bermuda*; *Earl Hall, Night*; *Capri*; *On Lake Como*; *Still Life*; *The Attic Window*.

January 1926 - *Ninth International Salon of Photography, Camera Pictorialists of Los Angeles*, Los Angeles Museum. Exhibited: *The Madelon, Paris*; *City of Dreams*; *Chicago River*.

September 11-October 9, 1926 - *International Exhibition of the London Salon of Photography*, Galleries of the Royal Society of Painters in Water-Colours, London. Exhibited: *City of Dreams*; *Chicago River*.

October 1926 - *Fourth International Exhibition of Pictorial Photography, Pictorial Photographic Society of San Francisco*. Exhibited: *Pleasant Valley*; *Man's Construction*.

November 15-December 13 and December 15-30, 1926 - *Fifth Annual Western Salon of Pictorial Photography*, Southern California Camera Club, Los Angeles Public Library and Southwest Museum. Exhibited: *Poems; The Sierra Madres; Along Shore, Catalina.*

January 1927 - *Tenth International Salon of Photography, Camera Pictorialists of Los Angeles*, Los Angeles Museum. Exhibited: *Capri.*

October 30-November 20, 1927 - *All American Photographic Salon, Los Angeles Camera Club*, Los Angeles Public Library. Exhibited: *The Madelon, Paris; Wave Patterns.*

October 1-16, 1927 - *XXII Salon International d'Art Photographique*, Photo-Club de Paris et la Société Francaise de Photographie, Paris. Exhibited: *Reflections, Venice; A Byway, Bellagio.*

December 3-31, 1927 - *Royal Photographic Society of Great Britain, London, Exhibition of Prints by Camera Pictorialists of Los Angeles*. Exhibited: *Grand Canyon, Detail; On the River; The Passing Throng; Storm Clouds; In the Southland, California; Metropolitan Tower.*

January 1928 - *Eleventh International Salon of Photography, Camera Pictorialists of Los Angeles*, Los Angeles Museum. Exhibited: *Detail—Grand Canyon.*

September 16-October 7, 1928 - *Fifth International Exhibition of Pictorial Photography, Pictorial Photographic Society of San Francisco*, Palace of the Legion of Honor, San Francisco. Exhibited: *Bavarian Village* [from the set of *Sunrise*]; *Sunlight; On the River.*

January 1929 - *Twelfth International Salon of Photography, Camera Pictorialists of Los Angeles*, Los Angeles Museum. Exhibited: *Brittany Gables; Sails; Hollywood.*

April 15-27, 1929 - *Third International Salon of the Pictorial Photographers of America*, Art Center, New York. Exhibited: *Sails; On the Campagna—Rome.*

June 1-30, 1929 - *California Camera Club, San Francisco.* Exhibited: Title(s) unknown.

September 18-28, October 5-15, 1929 - *Pacific International Salon of Photographic Art*, Portland Art Museum, Portland, Oregon and University of Oregon, Eugene, Oregon. Exhibited: *The City of Dreams; The Chicago River; Sails; On the Campagna.*

January 1930 - *Thirteenth International Salon of Photography, Camera Pictorialists of Los Angeles*, Los Angeles Museum. Exhibited: *Chimneys; Brooklyn Bridge.*

February 2-22, 1930 - *Eleventh Annual Salon of Pictorial Photography, Buffalo Camera Club*, Albright Art Gallery, Buffalo, New York. Exhibited: *Sails.*

March-April 1930 - *Seventeenth Annual Pittsburgh Salon of Photographic Art*, The Academy of Science and Art, Carnegie Institute. Exhibited: *Poems.*

December 1930 - *Second Rochester International Salon of Photography*, The Memorial Art Gallery of Rochester. Exhibited: Title(s) unknown.

1930 - *Invitation Salon of Photography at Tokyo*, sponsored by the Japan Photographic Society. Exhibited: *Hilltops—San Luis Obispo.*

January 1931 - *Fourteenth International Salon of Photography, Camera Pictorialists of Los Angeles*, Los Angeles Museum. Exhibited: *Tugs.*

March 20-April 19, 1931 - *Eighteenth Annual Pittsburgh Salon of Photographic Art*, The Academy of Science and Art, Carnegie Institute. Exhibited: *On the Pier.*

May 1-31, 1931 - *First Annual International Salon of Photography*, Fine Arts Gallery, Balboa Park, San Diego. Exhibited: *The City of Dreams; Sails; The Anchorage.*

June 13-30, 1931 - *All-American Photographic Salon*, Los Angeles Museum, Exposition Park, Los Angeles. Exhibited: *Flight Formation*; *Outward Bound*.

January 1932 - *Fifteenth Annual International Salon of Photography, Camera Pictorialists of Los Angeles*, Los Angeles Museum. Exhibited: *William Cameron Menzies*.

1933 - *Royal Photographic Society of Great Britain*, London, prints by Camera Pictorialists of Los Angeles. Exhibited: *Outward Bound*; *Sails*; *Hollywood*; *The Anchorage*.

December 31, 1933-March 4, 1934 - *Seventeenth Annual International Salon of Pictorial Photography, Camera Pictorialists of Los Angeles*, Los Angeles Museum and M. H. de Young Memorial Museum, San Francisco. Exhibited: *Along the Shore, Hilo*; *Papaia*; *Shoreline, Hilo*.

November 9-23, 1936 - *Views of New York—Old and New, Members' Exhibition of Photographs of New York Organized by the Pictorial Photographers of America (Celebrating the Twentieth Anniversary of Pictorial Photographers of America)*, Museum of the City of New York. Exhibited: *On the East River, New York [The White Ferry Boat]*; *291*; *New York Housetops—Winter*; *Metropolitan Life Insurance Tower*; *Street Scene—First Avenue & 36th Street*; *Lower New York: Water Street & the Brooklyn Bridge Tower*; *Shadows—42nd Ave. & Madison Ave.*; *Fifth Avenue, Twilight*; *New York Harbor, Brooklyn Bridge*; *Arrival of the Imperator*; *The Ghost Ship [Waterfront, East Side]*; *Brooklyn Bridge from Ferry Slip, Evening*; *Poplar Street—Brooklyn Bridge, Main Tower*; *Cables—Singer Building, Late Afternoon*.

March 29-April 17, 1937 - *Fourth International Salon, Pictorial Photographers of America (Celebrating the Twentieth Anniversary of Pictorial Photographers of America)*, American Museum of Natural History, New York. Exhibited: *Primeval Forest—Fog*; *Papaia*; *On the River, 1909*; *In the Harbor, 1937*.

March 12-26, 1939 - *Fourth San Antonio Salon of Pictorial Photography International, San Antonio Pictorial Camera Club*, Witte Memorial Museum, San Antonio, Texas. Exhibited: *Reflections—Venice*; *Sunset, Simplon Pass*; *Earl Hall, Night*.

January 1948 - *Thirty-first International Los Angeles Salon of Photography*, Los Angeles County Museum, Exposition Park, Los Angeles. Exhibited: Title(s) unknown.

September 30-November 28, 1948 - *An Exhibition of Gravures from Camera Work and Camera Notes Organized by Edward Steichen*, Museum of Modern Art, New York. Exhibited: *The Outlook, Villa Carlotta*.

April-May 1950 - *Third El Camino Real International Color Slide Exhibition*, Los Angeles. Exhibited: *Roller Coaster*.

March 10-17, 1951 - *Seventh San Francisco International Color Slide Exhibition*, San Francisco Museum of Art, sponsored by the Photochrome Club of San Francisco. Exhibited: *Zion National Park*.

May 4-7, 1951 - *Third N.Y. International Color Slide Exhibition*, Central High School of Needle Trades, sponsored by the N.Y. Color Slide Club, Inc. Exhibited: *Storm Clouds—Bryce Canyon*; *Zion National Park*; *Sunset—Utah*.

June 29-July 8, 1951 - *Southwest International Exhibition of Photography, Southern California Association of Camera Clubs*, San Diego County Fair, Del Mar. Exhibited: [transparencies] *Storm Clouds—Bryce Canyon*; *Sunset—Utah*.

August 3- October 23, 1966 - *Photographic Exhibition '66*, Los Angeles County Museum of Natural History. Exhibited: *Sails*.

1976-77 - *Karl Struss: Man With a Camera*, Cranbrook Academy of Art/Museum, Bloomfield Hills, Michigan (January 13-February 15, 1976), The University of Michigan Museum of Art, Ann Arbor,

Michigan (February 25-March 28, 1976), International Museum of Photography at George Eastman House, Rochester, New York (June 15-August 1, 1976), International Center of Photography, New York (September 24-November 7, 1976), Stamford Museum, Stamford, Connecticut (November 15-De-cember 26, 1976), Los Angeles County Museum of Art, Los Angeles (January 5-February 23, 1977), Phillips Collection, Washington, D.C. (July 9-31, 1977). Exhibited ninety-six vintage prints in the artist's collection; for a complete listing, see exhibition catalogue.

January 11-February 26, 1977 - *Karl Struss*, The Photo Album Gallery, Los Angeles. Exhibited: 126 prints, 1909-1954, offered for sale.

1977 - *California Pictorialism*, San Francisco Museum of Modern Art, San Francisco (January 7-February 27), Minneapolis Institute of Arts, Minneapolis (May 16-June 26), Los Angeles County Museum of Art, Los Angeles (August 1-September 11), University Art Museum, The University of Texas, Austin (October 17-November 27). Exhibited: *Along the Elbe, Dresden*; *Metropolitan Tower at Twilight*; *On Lake Como*; *Sunset, Simplon Pass*; *Cables*; *Fifth Avenue—Twilight*; *Windswept, Nova Scotia*; *Brooklyn Bridge, Nocturne*; *Sand Dunes, Arverne*; *Sparkling Waters, Arverne*; *Lafayette Boulevard*; *The Passing Throng*; *Storm Clouds*; *Sundown, Hudson River*.

1977 - *The Modern Spirit: American Painting 1908-35*, organized by the Arts Council of Great Britain in association with the Edinburgh Festival Society and the Royal Scottish Academy, Edinburgh (August 20-September 11), Hayward Gallery, London (September 28-November 20). Exhibited: *Lower New York—Water Street & the Brooklyn Bridge Tower*.

January 14-March 26, 1978 - *Stieglitz and the Photo-Secession: Pictorialism to Modernism, 1902-1917*, New Jersey State Museum, Trenton. Exhibited: *Low Tide, Arverne*; *Fifth Avenue, Twilight, New York*; *Cables*.

May 4-June 11, 1978 - *Pictorial Photography in Britain, 1900-1920*, Hayward Gallery, London, sponsored by the Arts Council of Great Britain in association with The Royal Photographic Society; traveled throughout Great Britain to nine other venues from July 26, 1978-June 10, 1979. Exhibited: *The Balcony, Sorrento*; *Metropolitan Life Insurance Tower, New York*; *Brooklyn Bridge, Nocturne*; *Lower Broadway*; *The Claremont Inn, Riverside Drive, New York*.

October 2-November 2, 1978 - *Photo-Secessionist Karl Struss & Erle C. Kenton*, The Arcade Gallery, Ann Arbor, Michigan. Exhibited: modern platinum prints *[Karl Struss: A Portfolio]*.

January 4-February 4, 1979 - *Karl Struss: A Portfolio*, The Blixt Gallery, Ann Arbor, Michigan.

September 19-November 25, 1979 - *Photography Rediscovered: American Photographs, 1900-1930*, Whitney Museum of American Art, New York; traveled to The Art Institute of Chicago (December 22, 1979-February 4, 1980). Exhibited: *1st Avenue*; *Brooklyn Bridge*; *Fifth Avenue, Night, New York*; *Low Tide, Arverne, New York*; *Maine*; *Arverne, L.I.*; *Cables, Brooklyn Bridge*; *Bermuda*; *Moonlight on the Water*; *Near San Luis Obispo*.

May 20-September 7, 1981 - *Karl Struss: A Retrospective View of His Photography*, The Fine Arts Center, Cheekwood, Nashville, Tennessee. Exhibited: smaller version of *Karl Struss: Man with a Camera*, with additional photographs.

October 31-December 6, 1981 - *Cubism and American Photography, 1910-1930*, organized by Sterling and Francine Clark Art Institute, Williamstown, Massachusetts. Exhibited: *Overhead View, New York City [Madison Square]*; *The Flatiron*; *West Shore—Ferry Slip on West Shore of New York*.

Filmography

Richard Koszarski

Except where noted, all films were photographed by Karl Struss. This list does not include films for which Struss contracted for a day or two of work making only stills. Unless otherwise noted, films are black and white.

Silent Films

For Better, For Worse (Famous Players-Lasky, April 27, 1919, 6939 ft.) Photographed by Alvin Wyckoff; uncredited stills and second camera by Karl Struss. Directed by Cecil B. De Mille. With Gloria Swanson. [In production January 27-March 24, 1919; Struss joined the company on March 17]

Male and Female (Famous Players-Lasky, November 16, 1919, 8952 ft.) Photographed by Alvin Wyckoff; uncredited stills and second camera by Karl Struss. Directed by Cecil B. De Mille. With Gloria Swanson, Thomas Meighan, Lila Lee. [In production June 15-July 30, 1919]

Why Change Your Wife? (Famous Players-Lasky, May 2, 1920, 7613 ft.) Photographed by Alvin Wyckoff; uncredited stills and second camera by Karl Struss. Directed by Cecil B. De Mille. With Thomas Meighan, Gloria Swanson, Bebe Daniels. [In production September 2-October 22, 1919]

Something to Think About (Famous Players-Lasky, October 3, 1920, 7140 ft.) Co-photographed with Alvin Wyckoff. Directed by Cecil B. De Mille. With Elliott Dexter, Gloria Swanson, Theodore Roberts. [In production January 20-March 30, 1920; Struss' first screen credit]

Forbidden Fruit (Famous Players-Lasky, January 23, 1921, 7804 ft.) Co-photographed with Alvin Wyckoff (also stills) Directed by Cecil B. De Mille. With Agnes Ayres, Clarence Burton, Theodore Roberts. [In production July 13-October 2, 1920]

Not Guilty (Whitman Bennett Productions, January 1921, 6170 ft.) No cinematographer credited; still photographs by Karl Struss. Directed by Sidney Franklin. With Sylvia Breamer, Richard Dix, Molly Malone.

The Faith Healer (Famous Players-Lasky, April 3, 1921, 6346 ft.) Photographed by Harry Perry; uncredited second camera by Karl Struss. Directed by George Medford. With Milton Sills, Ann Forrest, Adolphe Menjou.

The Affairs of Anatole (Famous Players-Lasky, September 25, 1921, 8806 ft.) Co-photographed with Alvin Wyckoff. Directed by Cecil B. De Mille. With Wallace Reid, Gloria Swanson, Elliott Dexter, Bebe Daniels. [In production December 2, 1920-January 25, 1921]

Fool's Paradise (Famous Players-Lasky, December 9, 1921, 8681 ft.) Co-photographed with Alvin Wyckoff. Directed by Cecil B. De Mille. With Dorothy Dalton, Mildred Harris, Conrad Nagel. [In production April 4-June 2, 1921]

Saturday Night (Famous Players-Lasky, January 22, 1922, 8443 ft.) Co-photographed with Alvin Wyckoff. Directed by Cecil B. De Mille. With Leatrice Joy, Conrad Nagel. [In production September 26, 1921-January 2, 1922]

The Law and the Woman (Famous Players-Lasky, January 15, 1922, 6461 ft.) Directed by Penrhyn Stanlaws. With Betty Compson, William P. Carleton, Cleo Ridgely.

Fools First (Marshall Neilan Productions, May 27, 1922, 5773 ft.) Co-photographed with David Kesson; also stills. Directed by Marshall Neilan. With Richard Dix, Claire Windsor, Claude Gillingwater, Raymond Griffith.

Rich Men's Wives (Preferred Pictures, August 19, 1922, c. 6500-7040 ft.) Directed by Louis Gasnier. With House Peters, Claire Windsor, Rosemary Theby.

Thorns and Orange Blossoms (Preferred Pictures, December 19, 1922, 6971 ft.) Directed by Louis Gasnier. With Estelle Taylor, Kenneth Harlan.

Minnie (Marshall Neilan Productions, December

1922, 6696 ft.) Co-photographed with David Kesson; also stills. Directed by Marshall Neilan. With Leatrice Joy, Matt Moore.

The Hero (Preferred Pictures, January 1, 1923, 6800 ft.) Directed by Louis Gasnier. With Gaston Glass, Barbara La Marr.

Poor Men's Wives (Preferred Pictures, January 28, 1923, c. 6900 ft.) Directed by Louis Gasnier. With Barbara La Marr, David Butler.

Daughters of the Rich (B. P. Schulberg Productions, June 15, 1923, 6073 ft.) Directed by Louis Gasnier. With Miriam Cooper, Gaston Glass.

Mothers-in-Law (B. P. Schulberg Productions, September 9, 1923, 6725 ft.) Directed by Louis Gasnier. With Ruth Clifford, Gaston Glass.

Maytime (B. P. Schulberg Productions, November 16, 1923, 7500 ft.) Also stills. Directed by Louis Gasnier. With Ethel Shannon, Harrison Ford, Clara Bow.

Poisoned Paradise: The Forbidden Story of Monte Carlo (Preferred Pictures, February 29, 1924, 6800 ft.) Also stills. Directed by Louis Gasnier. With Kenneth Harlan, Clara Bow, Barbara Tennant.

The Legend of Hollywood (Charles R. Rogers Productions, August 3, 1924, 5414 ft.) Directed by Renaud Hoffman. With Percy Marmont, Zasu Pitts.

White Man (B. P. Schulberg Productions, November 1, 1924, 6337 ft.) Directed by Louis Gasnier. With Kenneth Harlan, Alice Joyce.

Idle Tongues (Thomas H. Ince Corp., December 21, 1924, 5300 or 5447 ft.) Directed by Lambert Hillyer. With Percy Marmont, Doris Kenyon, Claude Gillingwater.

Barbara Frietchie (Regal Pictures [Thomas Ince], September 26, 1924, 7179 ft.) Photographed by

Henry Sharp; still photographs only by Struss. Directed by Lambert Hillyer. With Florence Vidor, Edmund Lowe.

Ben-Hur (MGM, December 30, 1925, 11,693 ft.) Co-photographed with Rene Guissart, Percy Hilburn, and Clyde De Vinna. Directed by Fred Niblo. With Ramon Novarro, Francis X. Bushman. [Film contains Technicolor sequences]

The Winding Stair (Fox Film Corp., October 25, 1925, c. 6100 ft.) Directed by John Griffith Wray. With Alma Rubens, Edmund Lowe, Warner Oland.

Forever After (First National Pictures, October 24, 1926, 6330 ft.) Directed by F. Harmon Weight. With Lloyd Hughes, Mary Astor.

Hell's 400 (Fox Film Corp., March 14, 1926, 5582 ft.) Directed by John Griffith Wray. With Margaret Livingston, Harrison Ford. [Film contains dream sequence in Technicolor].

Meet the Prince (Metropolitan Pictures Corp. of California, August 9, 1926, 5929 ft.) Directed by Joseph Henaberry. With Joseph Schildkraut, Marguerite De La Motte.

Sparrows (Pickford Corporation, September 19, 1926, 7763 ft.) Co-photographed with Hal Mohr, Charles Rosher. Directed by William Beaudine. With Mary Pickford, Gustav von Seyffertitz.

Babe Comes Home (First National Pictures, May 22, 1927, 5761 ft.) Directed by Ted Wilde. With George Herman "Babe" Ruth, Anna Q. Nilsson.

Sunrise—A Song of Two Humans (Fox Film Corp., September 23, 1927, 8729 ft.) Co-photographed with Charles Rosher. Directed by F. W. Murnau. With George O'Brien, Janet Gaynor.

The Battle of the Sexes (Art Cinema Corp., October 12, 1928, 8180 ft.) Co-photographed with G. W. Bitzer. Directed by D. W. Griffith. With Jean

Hersholt, Phyllis Haver.

Drums of Love (United Artists, January 24, 1928, 8350 ft.) Directed by D. W. Griffith. With Mary Philbin, Lionel Barrymore.

The Night Watch (First National Pictures, September 9, 1928, 6676 ft.) Directed by Alexander Korda. With Billie Dove, Paul Lukas.

Talking Pictures

Lady of the Pavements (Art Cinema Corp., January 22, 1929, 8329 ft.) Directed by D. W. Griffith. With Lupe Velez, William Boyd, Jetta Goudal. [Only portions of this film included talking and singing sequences; also released in all silent version]

Coquette (Pickford Corporation, April 12, 1929, 6993 ft.) Directed by Sam Taylor. With Mary Pickford, John Mack Brown, Matt Moore.

The Taming of the Shrew (Pickford Corporation/Elton Corporation, October 26, 1929, 6116 ft.) Directed by Sam Taylor. With Mary Pickford, Douglas Fairbanks.

1812 Overture (United Artists, 1930, 1 reel) Produced by William Cameron Menzies and Hugo Reisenfeld.

Abraham Lincoln (Feature Productions, August 25, 1930, 8704 ft.) Directed by D. W. Griffith. With Walter Huston, Una Merkel.

The Bad One (United Artists, May 3, 1930, 6673 ft.) Directed by George Fitzmaurice. With Dolores Del Rio, Edmund Lowe.

Be Yourself! (United Artists, February 8, 1930, 6900 ft.) Co-photographed with Robert Planck. Directed by Thornton Freeland. With Fanny Brice, Robert Armstrong.

Danger Lights (RKO, August 21, 1930, 6550 ft.) Co-photographed with John Boyle. Directed by George B. Seitz. With Louis Wolheim, Robert Armstrong, Jean Arthur. [Also photographed in 65mm Spoor-Berggren Natural Vision; 65mm version released November 15, 1930]

Lummox (Feature Productions, January 18, 1930, 7533 ft.) Directed by Herbert Brenon. With Winifred Westover, Dorothy Janis.

One Romantic Night (United Artists, May 3, 1930, 6592 ft.) Directed by Paul Stein. With Lillian Gish, Rod La Rocque, Conrad Nagel.

Kiki (Feature Productions, March 14, 1931, 8000 ft.) Directed by Sam Taylor. With Mary Pickford, Reginald Denny.

Skippy (Paramount, April 25, 1931, 88 mins.) Directed by Norman Taurog. With Jackie Cooper.

Up Pops the Devil (Paramount, May 30, 1931, 85 mins.) Directed by A. Edward Sutherland. With Norman Foster, Carole Lombard.

Women Love Once (Paramount, July 4, 1931, 74 mins.) Directed by Edward Goodman. With Paul Lukas, Eleanor Boardman.

Murder by the Clock (Paramount, August 8, 1931, 75 mins.) Directed by Edward Sloman. With William Boyd, Lilyan Tashman.

The Road to Reno (Paramount, September 26, 1931, 74 mins.) Directed by Richard Wallace. With Charles "Buddy" Rogers, Lilyan Tashman.

Dr. Jekyll and Mr. Hyde (Paramount, January 2, 1932, 98 mins.) Directed by Rouben Mamoulian. With Fredric March, Miriam Hopkins.

Two Kinds of Women (Paramount, January 6, 1932, 73 mins.) Directed by William deMille. With Miriam Hopkins, Phillips Holmes, Irving Pichel.

Dangers in the Dark (Paramount, March 14, 1932, 74 mins.) Directed by David Burton. With Miriam Hopkins, Jack Oakie, George Raft.

The World and the Flesh (Paramount, April 22, 1932, 75 mins.) Directed by John Cromwell. With George Bancroft, Miriam Hopkins.

Forgotten Commandments (Paramount, May 27, 1932, 65 mins.) Direction credited to Louis Gasnier and William Schorr; Struss rejects Schorr credit. With Sari Maritza, Gene Raymond.

The Man from Yesterday (Paramount, July 1, 1932, 70 mins.) Directed by Berthold Viertel. With Claudette Colbert, Clive Brook, Charles Boyer.

Guilty as Hell (Paramount, August 5, 1932, 81 mins.) Directed by Erle C. Kenton. With Edmund Lowe, Victor MacLaglen.

The Sign of the Cross (Paramount, November 30, 1932, 11,262 ft.) Directed by Cecil B. De Mille. With Fredric March, Elissa Landi, Claudette Colbert. [In production July 25-September 29, 1932]

Island of Lost Souls (Paramount, December 1932, 70 mins.) Directed by Erle C. Kenton. With Charles Laughton, Richard Arlen, Kathleen Burke.

Tonight Is Ours (Paramount, January 13, 1933, 76 mins.) Directed by Stuart Walker. With Fredric March, Claudette Colbert.

The Woman Accused (Paramount, February 17, 1933, 73 mins.) Directed by Paul Sloane. With Nancy Carroll, John Halliday, Cary Grant.

The Story of Temple Drake (Paramount, May 12, 1933, 72 mins.) Directed by Stephen Roberts. With Miriam Hopkins, William Gargan, Jack La Rue.

The Girl in 419 (Paramount, May 26, 1933, 76 mins.) Directed by Alexander Hall. With James Dunn, Gloria Stuart.

Disgraced (Paramount, July 7, 1933, 65 mins.) Directed by Erle C. Kenton. With Helen Twelvetrees, Bruce Cabot.

One Sunday Afternoon (Paramount, September 1, 1933, 85 mins.) Photography credited to Victor Milner; Karl Struss uncredited. Directed by Stephen Roberts. With Gary Cooper, Fay Wray.

Torch Singer (Paramount, September 8, 1933, 72 mins.) Directed by Alexander Hall. With Claudette Colbert, Ricardo Cortez.

Four Frightened People (Paramount, January 26, 1934, 7028 ft.) Directed by Cecil B. De Mille. With Claudette Colbert, Herbert Marshall, Mary Boland. [In production September 16-November 3, 1933]

Belle of the Nineties (Paramount, September 21, 1934, 75 mins.) Directed by Leo McCarey. With Mae West. [In production March 13-July 9, 1934]

The Pursuit of Happiness (Paramount, September 28, 1934, 85 mins.) Directed by Alexander Hall. With Francis Lederer, Joan Bennett.

Here Is My Heart (Paramount, December 28, 1934, 80 mins.) Directed by Frank Tuttle. With Bing Crosby, Kitty Carlisle.

Goin' To Town (Paramount, May 17, 1935, 75 mins.) Directed by Alexander Hall. With Mae West.

Two for Tonight (Paramount, September 13, 1935, 61 mins.) Directed by Frank Tuttle. With Bing Crosby, Joan Bennett.

Anything Goes (Paramount, January 24, 1936, 92 mins.) Directed by Lewis Milestone. With Bing Crosby, Ethel Merman.

The Preview Murder Mystery (Paramount, February 28, 1936, 65 mins.) Directed by Robert Florey. With Frances Drake, Reginald Denny.

Too Many Parents (Paramount, March 20, 1936, 73 mins.) Directed by Robert MacGowan. With Frances Farmer.

Rhythm on the Range (Paramount, July 31, 1936, 85 mins.) Directed by Norman Taurog. With Bing Crosby, Frances Farmer.

Hollywood Boulevard (Paramount, August 21, 1936, 75 mins.) Directed by Robert Florey. With John Halliday, Marsha Hunt.

Go West, Young Man (Paramount, November 13, 1936, 82 mins.) Directed by Henry Hathaway. With Mae West, Randolph Scott, Warren William.

Let's Make a Million (Paramount, December 13, 1936, 61 mins.) Directed by Raymond McCarey. With Edward Everett Horton.

Waikiki Wedding (Paramount, March 26, 1937, 89 mins.) Directed by Frank Tuttle. With Bing Crosby, Martha Raye.

Mountain Music (Paramount, June 18, 1937, 76 mins.) Directed by Robert Florey. With Bob Burns, Martha Raye.

Double or Nothing (Paramount, September 17, 1937, 95 mins.) Directed by Jay Theodore Reed. With Bing Crosby, Martha Raye.

Thunder Trail (Paramount, October 22, 1937, 56 mins.) Directed by Charles Barton. Gilbert Roland, Charles Bickford.

Every Day's a Holiday (Major Pictures Corp., January 14, 1938, 80 mins.) Directed by Eddie Sutherland. With Mae West, Edmund Lowe. [In production September 8—mid-November 1937]

Dangerous to Know (Paramount, March 11, 1938, 70 mins.) Photography credited to Theodor Sparkhul; Karl Struss and Charles Schoenbaum uncredited. Directed by Robert Florey. With Akim Tamiroff, Anna May Wong, Gail Patrick.

Thanks for the Memory (Paramount, November 18, 1938, 77 mins.) Directed by George Archainbaud. With Bob Hope, Shirley Ross.

Sing, You Sinners (Paramount, September 2, 1938, 88 mins.) Directed by Wesley Ruggles. With Bing Crosby, Fred MacMurray, Donald O'Connor.

Paris Honeymoon (Paramount, January 27, 1939, 92 mins.) Directed by Frank Tuttle. With Bing Crosby, Shirley Ross, Edward Everett Horton.

Zenobia (Hal Roach Studios, April 21, 1939, 71 mins.) Some sources credit Norbert Brodine as photographer. Directed by Gordon Douglas. With Oliver Hardy, Harry Langdon.

Some Like It Hot (Paramount, May 19, 1939, 64 mins.) Directed by George Archainbaud. With Bob Hope, Shirley Ross.

Island of Lost Men (Paramount, July 28, 1939, 63 mins.) Directed by Kurt Neumann. With Anna May Wong, J. Carrol Naish.

The Star Maker (Paramount, August 25, 1939, 94 mins.) Directed by Roy Del Ruth. With Bing Crosby, Louise Campbell.

Rhythm on the River (Paramount, September 6, 1940, 92 mins.) Photography credited to Ted Tetzlaff; Karl Struss uncredited fill-in photography. Directed by Victor Schertzinger. With Bing Crosby, Mary Martin, Basil Rathbone.

The Great Dictator (Charles Chaplin Film Corp./UA, 1940, 126 mins.) Co-photographed with Rollie Totheroh. Directed by Charles Chaplin. With Charles Chaplin, Paulette Goddard, Jack Oakie.

Caught in the Draft (Paramount, July 4, 1941, 80 mins.) Directed by David Butler. With Bob Hope, Dorothy Lamour.

Aloma of the South Seas (Paramount, August 15, 1941, 77 mins.) Ben Kline and William Snyder credited as Associate Photographers. (Technicolor) Directed by Alfred Santell. With Dorothy Lamour, Jon Hall.

Journey into Fear (RKO, February 12, 1943, 71 mins.) Directed by Norman Foster. With Joseph Cotten, Dolores Del Rio.

For Whom the Bell Tolls (Paramount, July 1943, 166 mins.) Photographed by Ray Rennahan (Technicolor); uncredited second unit photography by Karl Struss. Directed by Sam Wood. With Gary Cooper, Ingrid Bergman.

Happy Go Lucky (Paramount, 1943, 81 mins.) Co-photographed with Ben Kline. (Technicolor) Directed by Curtis Bernhardt. With Mary Martin, Dick Powell, Rudy Vallee.

Riding High (Paramount, 1943, 88 mins.) Co-photographed with Harry Hallenberger. (Technicolor) Directed by George Marshall. With Dorothy Lamour, Dick Powell, Victor Moore.

And the Angels Sing (Paramount, 1944, 96 mins.) Directed by Claude Binyon. With Dorothy Lamour, Fred MacMurray, Betty Hutton.

Rainbow Island (Paramount, 1944, 97 mins.) (Technicolor) Directed by Ralph Murphy. With Dorothy Lamour, Eddie Bracken, Barry Sullivan.

Bring on the Girls (Paramount, 1945, 92 mins.) (Technicolor) Directed by Sidney Lanfield. With Veronica Lake, Sonny Tufts, Eddie Bracken.

Wonder Man (Goldwyn, April 1945, 95 mins.) Karl Struss was replaced in mid-production; photography credited to Victor Milner and William Snyder. (Technicolor) Directed by H. Bruce Humberstone. With Danny Kaye.

Tarzan and the Leopard Woman (RKO, February 1946, 72 mins.) Directed by Kurt Neumann. With Johnny Weissmuller, Brenda Joyce.

Suspense (Monogram, June 15, 1946, 101 mins.) Directed by Frank Tuttle. With Belita, Barry Sullivan, Bonita Granville.

Mr. Ace (Benedict Bogeus/UA, August 2, 1946, 84 mins.) Directed by Edwin Marin. With George Raft, Sylvia Sidney.

The Macomber Affair (Award/UA, March 21, 1947, 90 mins.) African photography by Freddie Francis, John Wilcox and O. H. Borradaile. Directed by Zoltan Korda. With Gregory Peck, Joan Bennett. [63 days in production]

Heaven Only Knows (Nero/UA, 1947, 97 mins.) Directed by Al Rogell. With Bob Cummings, Brian Donlevy. [71 days in production]

The Dude Goes West (King Bros./Allied Artists, May 30, 1948, 86 mins.) Directed by Kurt Neumann. With Eddie Albert, Gale Storm, James Gleason. [22 days in production]

Siren of Atlantis (Nebenzal/UA, 1948, 75 mins.) Direction credited to Gregg Tallas, but Struss claims Arthur Ripley directed; retakes directed by John Brahm and Douglas Sirk. With Maria Montez, Dennis O'Keefe, Jean Pierre Aumont. [50 days in production]

Tarzan's Magic Fountain (Lesser/RKO, 1948, 73 mins.) Directed by Lee Sholem. With Lex Barker, Brenda Joyce, Albert Dekker.

Bad Boy (Paul Short/UA, 1949, 87 mins.) Directed by Kurt Neumann. With Lloyd Nolan, Jane Wyatt, Audie Murphy. [23 days in production]

Rocketship X-M (Lippert, June 3, 1950, 77 mins.) Directed by Kurt Neumann. With Lloyd Bridges, Osa Massen, John Emery. [11 days in production]

It's a Small World (Eagle-Lion, June 1950, 74 mins.) Directed by William Castle. With Paul Dale, Lorraine Miller.

The Return of Jesse James (Lippert, Sept. 8, 1950, 75 mins.) Directed by Arthur Hilton. With John Ireland, Ann Dvorak, Henry Hull.

The Texan Meets Calamity Jane (Columbia, November 1950, 71 mins.) (Cinecolor) Directed by Ande Lamb. With Evelyn Ankers, James Ellison.

Father's Wild Game (Monogram, 1950, 60 mins.) Directed by Herbert Leeds. With Raymond Walburn.

Tarzan's Peril (Sol Lesser/RKO, 1951, 79 mins.) Directed by Byron Haskin. With Lex Barker, Virginia Huston.

Lady Possessed (Portland Pictures/Republic, February 1952, 87 mins.) Directed by William Spier and Roy Kellino. With James Mason, June Havoc.

Rose of Cimarron (Alco Pictures Corp., 1952, 74 mins.) (Natural Color) Directed by Harry Keller.

Tarzan's Savage Fury (Sol Lesser/RKO, 1952, 80 mins.) Directed by Cy Endfield. With Lex Barker, Dorothy Hart.

Limelight (Charles Chaplin Productions/UA, 1952, 135 mins.) Directed by Charles Chaplin. With Chaplin, Claire Bloom.

Face to Face (Huntington Hartford/RKO, November 1952, 89 mins.) "The Secret Sharer" episode, directed by John Brahm. With James Mason, Gene Lockhart.

Tarzan and the She Devil (Sol Lesser/RKO, 1953, 76 mins.) Directed by Kurt Neumann.

Il Piu Comico Spettacolo del Mondo (1953) Co-photographed with Fernando Riri and Riccardo Pallottini. (3-D [Poldelvision] Ferraniacolor) Directed by Mario Mattoli. With Toto.

Il Turco Napoletano (September 1953, 90 mins.) Co-photographed with Riccardo Pallottini. (3-D Ferraniacolor) Directed by Mario Mattoli. With Toto. [Not released in 3-D]

Cavalleria Rusticana (January 1954, 80 mins.) Co-photographed with Riccardo Pallottini. (3-D Ferrania-color) Directed by Carmine Gallone. With Anthony Quinn, May Britt. [Not released in 3-D]

Attila (Lux Films, 1954 [reviewed by *Variety* March 6, 1955, 87 mins. opened in New York, May 17, 1958, 73 mins.]) Co-photographed with Aldo Tonti and Luciano Trasatti. (Technicolor) Directed by Pietro Francisci. With Anthony Quinn, Sophia Loren.

Due Notti con Cleopatra (February 1954, 72 mins.) Co-photographed with Riccardo Pallottini. (Ferrania-color) Directed by Mario Mattoli. With Alberto Sordi, Sophia Loren.

Miseria e Nobiltà (April 1954) Co-photographed with Luciano Trasatti. (Ferraniacolor) Directed by Mario Mattoli. With Toto.

Mohawk (1955, 79 mins.) (Wide Vision and East-mancolor [Pathecolor?]) Directed by Kurt Neumann. With Scott Brady, Rita Gam.

She Devil (Regal Films, 1957, 77 mins.) (Regal-scope) Directed by Kurt Neumann. With Mari Blanchard.

Kronos (Regal Films, 1957, 78 mins.) (Regalscope) Directed by Kurt Neumann. With Jeff Morrow, Barbara Lawrence.

The Deerslayer (Twentieth Century-Fox, 1957, 78 mins.) (CinemaScope and DeLuxe Color) Directed by Kurt Neumann. With Lex Barker, Rita Moreno.

The Rawhide Trail (Allied Artists, 1958, 68 mins.) Directed by Robert Gordon. With Rex Reason.

The Fly (Twentieth Century-Fox, 1958, 94 mins.) (CinemaScope and DeLuxe Color) Directed by Kurt Neumann. With Al Hedison, Patricia Owens, Vincent Price.

Machete (Odell/United Artists, 1958, 75 mins.) Directed by Kurt Neumann.

The Hot Angel (Paragon Productions, 1958, 73 mins.) Directed by Joe Parker.

Here Come the Jets (Associated Producers, 1959, 70 mins.) (Regalscope) Directed by Gene Fowler, Jr.

The Sad Horse (Richard E. Lyons Production, 1959, 78 mins. (CinemaScope and Deluxe Color) Directed by James Clark. With David Ladd, Chill Wills.

The Rebel Set (E & L Productions, 1959, 72 mins.) Directed by Gene Fowler, Jr. With Gregg Palmer.

The Alligator People (Jack Leewood Production, 1959, 73 mins.) (CinemaScope) Directed by Roy Del Ruth. With Beverly Garland, George Macready.

Counterplot (Kurt Neumann Production, 1959, 76 mins.) Directed by Kurt Neumann. With Forrest Tucker, Allison Hayes.

INDEX

Numbers in bold face indicate
illustration as well as text

New York to Hollywood:
The Photography of Karl Struss

was designed, composed, and set in Electra 11 point,
with initial caps in Electra Bold Display, and
heads in Electra Display,
on Macintosh IIci, in QuarkXPress 3.3.

Design and composition by James A. Ledbetter, Dallas, Texas
Type output by Typography Plus, Dallas, Texas
Separations by Colortek, Inc., Dallas, Texas
Printed by Friesen Printers, Altona, Manitoba, Canada